D0216045

SAVING LIVES

SAVING LIVES

The S.A.F.E. Model for Resolving Hostage and Crisis Incidents

Mitchell R. Hammer

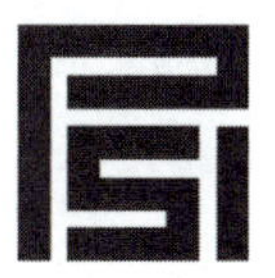

PRAEGER SECURITY INTERNATIONAL
Westport, Connecticut • London

Library of Congress Cataloging-in-Publication Data

Hammer, Mitchell R., 1951–
Saving lives : the S.A.F.E. model for resolving hostage and crisis incidents /
Mitchell R. Hammer.
p. cm.
Includes bibliographical references and index.
ISBN 978–0–275–99295–8 (alk. paper)
1. Hostage negotiations. 2. Hostage negotiations—Case studies. 3. Crisis management.
I. Title.
HV8058.H66 2007
363.2′3—dc22 2007020618

British Library Cataloguing in Publication Data is available.

Library of Congress Catalog Card Number: 2007020618
ISBN-13: 978–0–275–99295–8
ISBN-10: 0–275–99295–0

First published in 2007

Praeger Security International, 88 Post Road West, Westport, CT 06881
An imprint of Greenwood Publishing Group, Inc.
www.praeger.com

Printed in the United States of America

The paper used in this book complies with the
Permanent Paper Standard issued by the National
Information Standards Organization (Z39.48–1984).

10 9 8 7 6 5 4 3 2 1

This book is dedicated to hostage/crisis negotiators who each and every day put their lives at risk in order to save lives.

CONTENTS

ACKNOWLEDGMENTS

I would first like to thank Dr. Randall Rogan, professor from Wake Forest University. He has been a steady friend and colleague for many years. I owe a debt of gratitude to Randy for sharing his insightful observations concerning communicative dynamics involved in critical incidents and in the initial formulation of the S.A.F.E. framework. I would also like to thank Major Robert Beach, Tony Hare, William Hogewood, William Kidd, Fred Lanceley, and Chuck Paris for their steadfast encouragement over the years to make the S.A.F.E. model useful to crisis/hostage negotiators. With the training we are now conducting to teach negotiators the S.A.F.E. model and with the publication of this book, I can finally say that your encouragement has been realized.

I have analyzed over 50 audiotapes and transcripts of critical incidents from which four are presented in *Saving Lives*. This review and then in-depth analysis of these four events took hundreds and hundreds of hours over a number of years. I would like to thank the following students at American University who graciously volunteered their time and expertise in transcribing audiotapes and then assisting in the various coding protocols of the discourse that greatly informed my overall analysis of the S.A.F.E. frames: Jennifer Addington, Lisa Amore, Jynks Burton, Anne Champlin, Rebecca Clothey, Jennifer Cord, Justin Connealy, Steven Dorsey, Laura Dillon, Cynthia Dowdell, Sergio Farre, Brian Fisher, Susan Finnigan, Lynn Foley, Jurene Fremstad, Jane Galvin, Bill Hart, Michael Jaffe, Samuel Jones, Lori Knisely, Bryan Larson, Alla Lipetsker, Jody Manning, Heather McBride, Susan McCaslin, Elizabeth Morgan, Sharon Perlin, Keri Schoenborn, Kerry Schwed, Edward Steiner, Janet Wagner, and L. Kirk Wolcott.

In addition, kudos go to Haleigh LaChance for her dogged determination in editing and preparing this manuscript for submission to the publisher. Suzanne Staszak-Silva, my editor at Greenwood/Praeger Press, deserves the "patience of the years" award. Without her willingness to support this book, it likely would not have been completed.

Finally, and most importantly, I would like to most gratefully express my appreciation to Diann Hammer. Diann, with her unwavering belief that I should "write a book on the S.A.F.E. model," has made mountains move in order for me to finally complete this manuscript.

PART I

The Emerging Field of Hostage/ Crisis Negotiation

CHAPTER 1

The Devastation of Crisis and Violence

THE REALITY OF CRISIS/HOSTAGE EVENTS

Critical incidents (Adler, Rosen, & Silverstein, 1998), kidnappings, hostage taking, and other crisis situations cut a wide swath of devastation and violence across the global and domestic landscape.[1] These types of events include natural disasters such as the recent destructive force of Hurricane Katrina in 2005 on New Orleans, Louisiana, as well as human-made carnage, including terrorist attacks, international kidnappings of political and business leaders, and armed confrontations with survivalist groups, cults, and barricaded and suicidal individuals.

While these crisis events oftentimes affect large numbers of people, the reality of the havoc created as these critical incidents unfold are experienced at very personal levels. I just finished listening to a heart-wrenching audiotape of a crisis situation that involved "Stan," a suicidal individual.

A Suicide

One autumn day, Stan climbs into his car and drives to an off-the-beaten path in a rural area outside the city in which he lived with his wife and children.[2] He brings along an audiotape cassette player/recorder and a handgun. Sitting alone in his car, he turns on the cassette player and immediately begins recording a "final" message to his wife.

> Hi, Lilly! Uh, I'm sorry. Um... It's Friday at, uh, five o'clock, I guess. And, uh, I love you just like I've done for so many years. I'll probably never get my answer back. I'll probably never get that letter back that I sent you. I'll never know how you feel. And uh...You don't care, I guess. You just don't care how I feel. I love you and the kids. I love you a lot. And it just don't mean nothing to you.

Shortly thereafter, Stan begins verbalizing his own suicide. If he was convinced of the need to kill himself and end his pain, he would have already completed the act. No, he is not so certain. In reality, he is using the tape player as a means to either talk himself into completing suicide or to talk himself out of it.

> Uh, Lilly, uhm...I always loved you. I don't know what's on the other side of this tape or the rest of this tape. It was just one I found. But my tape player and all my tapes I leave to my children. I would like Lilly to keep the car. Whatever money that is found on me I'd like for my wife to have. I ask that no one be allowed to view me. I don't want nobody to be at my funeral. The city can take and do what they want with me. The insurance money, whatever, will go to my wife. Um...whatever.

As I listen to the tape, I realize that Stan has made the choice to commit suicide, and he begins saying his "goodbyes."

> I love all my kids and my wife. But I can't take it no more. I just can't take not knowing which way to go. I have ran out of people to talk to. I have ran out of people. Nobody will help. Right now I am just too tired. Too tired to care. Too tired to see my wife talkin' to someone else again and having a good time like we always did in the summer. It won't take five minutes to send me pictures of my kids. That's all I asked for, pictures of my kids. For weeks! But my wife—which I will not get upset about—won't send me my pictures.
>
> What am I supposed to do, Lilly? Please, please remember that I loved you. That I always did, that I always cared. Please. Oh, God, I loved you; you should've answered me. We coulda tried.

As the tape continues, Stan reveals that he has had a number of problems in his life, including substance abuse issues and issues that involved social workers and his children. Further, his relationship with his wife was not stable and in his descriptions of some situations, not positive or healthy for either of them.

The tape is nearing the end and by now Stan has convinced himself that suicide is the best solution for himself, his wife, and his children.

> I am so tired.
>
> Tape's coming to end. Gee, how time flies when you're having fun.
>
> I love you. I do love you. But I can't go on without you. I can't go on without looking at pictures of my children. I don't know, did somebody tell you that if I had pictures of my children it would make me more depressed? Why? I look at my children, I write my letters, and I feel better. So tell these sh-, tell these shrinks that reverse psychology sometime does work. But then again, it don't. Everybody's different.
>
> Well, I guess I'm supposed to tell them where to pick me up. Well, won't be long. Won't be long. I do love you. Always did, always will.

At this point, he calls the authorities and tells them his location. Shortly thereafter, a gunshot is heard. Stan is dead. For Stan, there was nobody present to intervene and try to convince him that living is a better solution than ending his internal pain through suicide.

This book is written most broadly for anyone who may be called upon to intervene, de-escalate the crisis, and, hopefully, help save lives—whether in potential suicide situations, terrorist events, or hostage-taking situations. To this goal, the S.A.F.E. (*S*ubstantive demands, *A*ttunement, *F*ace, and *E*motional distress) crisis negotiation model I developed (with initial collaboration from Dr. Randall Rogan) is presented, and the research I conducted that supports this model is discussed.

A PRACTITIONER

I am a hostage/crisis negotiator. My own practice for the past 20 years has focused on the application of theory and research to the life and death struggles involved in crises and critical incidents. I have attended the two-week hostage negotiation school conducted by the Federal Bureau of Investigation (FBI), I have provided advisement to international hostage-taking incidents, and I have been a "S.A.F.E. advisor" and have gone out "on call" with hostage negotiation units in the Washington, D.C., area. Further, I actively conduct advanced hostage/crisis negotiation training for law enforcement and private security critical incident response teams.

As a practitioner, I know all too well that inappropriate negotiation practices with violent subjects can lead to unanticipated and unwanted life-threatening outcomes for bystanders, hostages, police officers, and the hostage taker or barricaded subject. The insights presented in this book are developed with a conscious focus on the applied arena of critical incident management and hostage/crisis negotiation. That is, the S.A.F.E. model and its associated research findings are designed to improve the practice of hostage/crisis negotiators. In this respect, the final arbiter of the value of this work is the simple but true observation, "if it works, use it."

AN ACADEMIC SCHOLAR

I am also an academic scholar. For the past 25 years, I have been a professor at American University in Washington, D.C., specializing in intercultural communication and conflict and crisis resolution. In 2006, I took an early retirement as "Professor Emeritus." As an academic scholar, my work is devoted to a maxim coined by Kurt Lewin, one of the most influential scholars in the twentieth century. He stated, "there is nothing so practical as a good theory" (Hunt, 1987). This maxim captures two essential qualities that ground the work of both practitioners and academic scholars in their pursuit of the improvement of the human condition. In my own case, it speaks directly to my efforts to save lives when violence or the threat of violence is present.

A "Good" Theory

First, Lewin's observation suggests that a good theory is able to identify and articulate those core aspects of human experience that pattern or order our interactions with others. That is, our thoughts, feelings, beliefs, values, intentions, and behavior often reflect an orderliness and a relationship to one another that provide individuals with a coherent view of the world and a logical set of behaviors to act in the world. The purpose of theory construction, then, is to shine a light on this structure or order of human experience. This idea of a theoretical framework that is coherent and grounded in experience can have very practical applications in improving human responses to various situations—including those in which violence is threatening our very existence.

Second, the converse is also true, "there is nothing so theoretical as good practice" (Hunt, 1987). This highlights the idea that without rich practice (experience), theory development is seriously curtailed. In fact, theory that is developed devoid of sensitivity to real-life, human experiences often has detrimental effects insofar as attention is directed away from the more important and compelling issues and concerns of social interaction toward intellectual "flights of fancy." In short, "experience-poor" theory typically has little lasting power.

The work I present in this book represents a conscious effort to develop "good" theory. That is, a conceptual framework that richly explains negotiation dynamics involved in critical incidents and directly speaks to improving the "practice" of hostage/crisis negotiation through the articulation of specific negotiation strategies for de-escalating violent events.

FOCUS OF THE BOOK

The purpose of this book is to summarize the S.A.F.E. theoretical framework for de-escalating hostage/crisis events and the supporting research findings upon which it is based. My goal is to discuss a communication-based approach that is grounded in "real-life" crisis interactions so that the actual practice of negotiators may be enhanced. The S.A.F.E. framework focuses on the communicative dynamics of crisis negotiation and is developed through a systematic analysis of authentic crisis negotiation incidents.

The overarching theoretical question that guides my work in developing the S.A.F.E. framework is, *What are the communicative dynamics in crisis negotiation situations that escalate and de-escalate critical incidents?* The core "applied" focus of the research study is, *What communication-based strategies can negotiators employ to help de-escalate potential violence in crisis situations?*

In pursuing these questions, it is critical that the development of the S.A.F.E. model be grounded in real-life experiences—actual hostage-taking and barricade situations. To meet these criteria, four crisis incidents are systematically examined using discourse analytic protocols. These incidents were carefully selected to reflect a range of different incident types [e.g., domestic (emotionally upsetting) events, suicide situations, and criminal incidents], whether hostages were held, and how the incident was resolved (e.g., peaceful surrender and suicide).

WHY STUDY CRISIS NEGOTIATION?

As I mentioned earlier, I have been working with international governments, law enforcement agencies, mediators, and other conflict resolution professionals in the area of critical incident management and hostage/crisis negotiation for many years. As both a field of practice and an emerging area of scholarly inquiry, the current status of hostage/crisis negotiation primarily consists of anecdotal information that is limited in its reliability and generalizability to a broad spectrum of critical incident events. As Dr. Rogan and I suggested in 1997, "hostage negotiation is rapidly emerging as a field of behavioral science application, poised to move beyond largely anecdotal accounts of effective and ineffective negotiation strategies toward increasing efforts at systematically incorporating alternative disciplinary perspectives and employing more rigorous methodological approaches for analyzing the dynamics of crisis negotiation" (Rogan, Hammer, & Van Zandt, 1997, p. 2). This book represents one effort at furthering the social scientific basis of crisis negotiation theory and practice.

The S.A.F.E. model and the insights presented in this book are not limited, however, to critical incident situations. Rather, the model and the accompanying analysis are useful for the investigation of other forms of conflictual interaction. The S.A.F.E. model is applicable more generally to a variety of difficult conversations and more specifically relevant to communication dynamics enacted under three core conditions: (1) a condition of perceived threat (e.g., when violence or the threat of violence exists), (2) a condition of interdependence (when the contending parties cannot accomplish their goals without the cooperation of one another), and (3) a condition of high stress/emotion (when intense, largely negative emotional realities such as anxiety, fear, anger, and shame are present).

The S.A.F.E. framework and the findings from this research are salient, therefore, to those individuals who examine communication and negotiation dynamics involved in international peace talks, domestic family violence, community and ethnic tensions, gang-on-gang violence, interreligious conflicts, violence in schools and the workplace, and suicide prevention both globally and within the U.S. setting.

Theory and practice in crisis negotiation is often unknown and consequently underutilized by individuals who must negotiate emotionally intense, high-stress, violent situations. In this regard, insights concerning crisis negotiation are important for government diplomats who often inappropriately apply more formalized, diplomatic negotiation practices when confronted with crisis or terrorist situations. Similarly, crisis negotiation insights are important for organizational and community conflict resolution practitioners who may, at times, inappropriately apply various "team-building" or "dialogue" practices for resolving emotionally intense conflicts. In short, effective crisis negotiation is different from other conflict resolution approaches. It is, therefore, my hope that the information offered in the chapters that follow will be incorporated by scholars and practitioners when they work with conflict under conditions of violence, interdependence, and high stress.

VIOLENCE AND THE CRISIS INCIDENT

Three Critical Events

Let us take a brief look at three violent critical incidents. The first event took place over the course of 51 days in 1993. David Koresh and the 129 members of the Branch Davidian religious sect were locked in a life-and-death struggle with agents from the FBI and the Bureau of Alcohol, Tobacco, Firearms and Explosives in Waco, Texas. During the siege, FBI negotiators repeatedly communicated with Koresh in an effort to end the situation peacefully. After using numerous tactics to convince Koresh and his followers to surrender, federal agents in armored personnel carriers injected tear gas into the buildings of the Mount Carmel compound. Rather than producing the anticipated, nonviolent resolution to the standoff, several cult members, according to FBI reports, set fires within the compound, resulting in the death of 81 individuals, including 17 children.

On December 14, 1997, Tupac Amaru rebels seized the Japanese Embassy residence and took 500 people hostage in Lima, Peru. Negotiations were undertaken, but after 129 days, a tactical assault was launched by the Peruvian Government, resulting in the rescue of 71 of the remaining 72 hostages, and the death of two soldiers and all 14 rebels/hostage takers.

On March 17, 2000, Joseph C. Palczynski stormed into a Baltimore, Maryland, apartment and held three people hostage: a man, a woman, and a 12-year-old boy. Negotiations were immediately initiated by the local police. After five days of intense negotiation and no apparent progress, one of the hostages was able to surreptitiously slip a powerful anti-anxiety drug into Palczynski's drink during dinner. Later in the evening, both adult hostages escaped from the apartment. Led by two tactical officers armed with 9mm submachine guns, the SWAT (Special Weapons and Tactical) team entered the apartment and rescued the young boy. During the ensuing rescue, Mr. Palczynski was killed, having been shot a total of 27 times.

High Stakes—High Visibility

The Waco, Texas, tragedy garnered intense national attention in the United States, the Peru crisis siege was watched with much horror throughout the world, and the Palczynski saga riveted attention at the state and local levels. All three of these events clearly indicate the danger and difficulty of negotiating complex, conflict-laden interactions in crisis conditions. This challenge is perhaps best summarized by the cogent recommendation made by P.B. Heymann in a special U.S. Department of Justice report critiquing the events and outcome of the standoff at Waco: "It is important to have and be able to use a behavioral science component that can advise the tactical and negotiation groups about what to anticipate" (1993, p. 6).

Internationally, increasing behavioral science competence in crisis negotiation dynamics is critically important for peacefully resolving intergroup and interstate violence (e.g., ethnic conflict and disputes between nations). At the individual level, as people increase their travel to foreign cultures, international crisis negotiation competence becomes essential in a world of growing violence. In 1995, for example, 6,500 kidnappings took place in Latin America alone, compared to a total of 951 hostages taken between 1968 to 1982 throughout the world. Each year throughout the decade of the 1990s, an estimated 20,000 to 30,000 political and criminal kidnappings have been reported (Auerbach, 1998, p. 23).

In Iraq alone, the carnage is virtually an everyday occurrence. While we may be more aware of the 82 days of captivity and subsequent release suffered by the *Christian Science Monitor* reporter Jill Carroll in 2006, we may not be as cognizant of the fact that over 250 foreigners were kidnapped, with many killed, during the same year. Yet the slaughter of Iraqis by some 25,000 terrorist and guerrilla groups in the country is far, far greater (Cole, 2004). In one recent week alone, intracountry violence killed over 300 Iraqi citizens. To take one individual case, in June 2006, a kidnapping of three Iraqi brothers and a cousin was followed by a text message:

> Leave this area [you Shiites], or we will cut your necks so that the Americans can never help you. We are watching your every step. You are the tail of the occupation. (Peterson, 2006)

Some days later, the bodies of two of the three men were found floating in the Tigris River, each shot in the head. It is all too clear that the need for crisis negotiation capability is growing in importance within the United States and internationally.

Because crisis situations attract widespread media attention, these types of life-threatening incidents are "high-stakes/high-visibility" events that can have a critical impact on community relations, international affairs, national law enforcement mandates, political leadership, and subsequent law enforcement actions at the state, local, national, and international levels. Nor are these events rare; they erupt on a daily basis in many of our major cities throughout the world.

Tragedies on Thanksgiving Day

Two critical incidents took place in distant cities in the United States on Thanksgiving Day (November 23) in 2006. In Chicago, Illinois, Lance Johnson, age 21 took a 22-year-old woman, Tasha Cooks, as a hostage in his apartment building. Sometime during the day, Ms. Cooks called her great grandmother and told her she was being held and beaten inside the apartment. Negotiations were conducted over a 23-hour period of time during which no shots were fired either by the subject or the police. However, shortly thereafter, shots were heard. The SWAT team entered the apartment and discovered the hostage and the hostage taker mortally wounded. Because this situation ended in murder and suicide, one family member of the hostage commented, "knowing what kind of person they was dealing with up there, they should have went in. They gave him too much time to make up his mind to kill her and himself. They should have went in" (Associated Press, 2006).

However, sending in the SWAT team in a tactical assault in which negotiations were progressing and weapons had not been fired may have also resulted in the unintended death of the hostage and the hostage taker. Making the decision to tactically resolve vs. continue negotiations is one of the most difficult choices an incident commander makes. Contrary to the opinion of the grieving relative of the slain hostage, there was no way of knowing the kind of person Mr. Johnson was, nor is it obvious that a tactical assault was warranted.

On this same day, an armed cartoonist for the *Miami Herald* newspaper entered the newspaper building and demanded to see the editor of the newspaper's sister paper, *El Nuevo Herald*. For two hours, he held approximately 12 people hostage. Throughout negotiations, the cartoonist also did not fire any shots. In this case, the subject surrendered with no people killed or injured. Both the Chicago and Miami incidents involved an armed individual. Both used negotiations during which the subjects did not fire their weapons. Yet one incident ended tragically in the death of the hostage and the hostage taker while the other event ended with a peaceful surrender.

Today, there are increasing demands for effective and appropriate use of "crisis negotiation" strategies for peacefully resolving potentially violent encounters, including prison riots, criminal actions, terrorist acts, suicide attempts, and hostage-taking situations. As the events described above suggest, not all attempts at crisis negotiation result in a peaceful surrender of the subject. When negotiation fails to gain a peaceful surrender, people are at greater risk of being injured or killed, including hostages, law enforcement officers, innocent bystanders, and hostage takers.

THE CRISIS OF VIOLENCE

This book is most directly about the application of behavioral science theory and research concerning the negotiation of crisis (i.e., hostage, barricade, and suicide) incidents where the threat of violence is real and the situation involves a life-and-death struggle between a police negotiator and a hostage taker. At a more general level, this book also has relevance to the "crisis of violence" in our homes, communities, and nations. Connecting a particular focus on negotiating crisis incidents with a larger concern regarding the crisis of violence is the observation that violence in the form of injury and death is at unacceptably high levels in the United States and our world at large—and we must develop more effective negotiated approaches for resolving violent confrontations if we are to stem the rising tide of this ever-increasing level of mayhem. This unfortunate trend is sometimes reflected in the tendency of the media to sensationalize—if not glorify—crisis incidents that result in the deaths of individuals. The media's cryptic phrase, "if it bleeds, it leads" is, unfortunately, a telling commentary on the increased violence that occurs daily among human beings.

A Violent World We Live In

What is the status of global violence? Are we a more—or less—violent world? In the most comprehensive analysis of global violence, the World Health Organization (WHO) in 2002 conducted an extensive analysis of many forms of violence across our global community. WHO begins its summary of findings by stating that "violence is a universal scourge that tears at the fabric of communities and threatens the life, health and happiness of us all" (Krug, 2002). WHO defines violence as follows:

> The intentional use of physical force or power, threatened or actual, against oneself, another person, or against a group or community, that either results in or has a high likelihood of resulting in injury, death, psychological harm, maldevelopment or deprivation. (Krug, 2002)

The WHO report (Krug, 2002) paints a dismal picture of global violence in three areas: (1) self-directed violence, (2) interpersonal violence, and (3) collective violence. According to E.G. Krug (2002), 1.6 million people worldwide die as a result of violence: a rate of 28.8 percent per 100,000 people. Fifty percent of these deaths are due to suicide (self-directed violence), 33 percent to homicide (interpersonal violence), and 20 percent from armed conflict (collective violence) at the interethnic or interstate level.

Suicide

Violent deaths in the form of suicide are on the rise in our global community. The World Health Organization estimated that 815,000 people committed suicide in 2000 and 1 million people killed themselves in 2001, resulting in suicide being the 13th leading cause of death. For people 15–44 years of age, suicide is the fourth leading cause of death. Further, suicide is more common among men than women, with three male suicides for every one female suicide (Krug, 2002). Since the 1950s, global suicide rates have increased by 60 percent. In the United States, the statistics are equally grim: the suicide rate is 50 percent greater than the homicide rate (Buvinic & Morrison, 2000), with 300,000 suicides occurring each year and another 150,000 to 200,000 suicide attempts (Roberts & Dziegielewski, 1995). Suicide rates vary dramatically in different parts of the world. Suicide rates are 7 percent in Africa, 9 percent in the Americas, 12 percent in Asia, 20 percent in Europe, 6 percent in the Eastern Mediterranean region, and 22 percent in the Western Pacific region.

Homicide

According to M. Buvinic and A.R. Morrison (2000), homicide rates have rapidly increased over the last 30 years. During the 1970s, the world average was 5.9 for every 100,000 people. In the 1980s, that rate dropped slightly to 5.8. During the 1990s, however, the rate climbed to 8.86, representing an increase of more than 50 percent.

Homicide rates are much higher in selected areas of the world. For example, the homicide rates per 100,000 people are 22 percent for Africa (40 percent for sub-Saharan Africa), 19 percent for the Americas, 6 percent in Asia, 8 percent in Europe, 7 percent in the Eastern Mediterranean region, and 4.5 percent in the Western Pacific region.

Violence is a primary cause of death for people 15–44 years of age with 14 percent of the deaths occurring among men and 7 percent among women (Krug, 2002). The WHO report also indicates that 10–69 percent of all women worldwide have been physically attacked by an intimate male partner at some point in their lives. Individuals between the ages of 14–39 commit more than 90 percent of the murders, rapes, and assaults in our world community (Gilligan, 2001). In addition, those individuals who were victims of physical violence are also more likely to be subjected to multiple acts of violence over extended periods of time and suffer from multiple types of abuse (Krug, 2002). The cost of violence worldwide is estimated by WHO to exceed billions of dollars each and every year (Krug, 2002).

According to recent Bureau of Justice studies (Bureau of Justice Statistics, 2006) and recent findings from the FBI's semiannual uniform crime report for 2006, violent crime (defined as murder, forcible rape, robbery, and aggravated assault) in the United States had generally declined since the mid 1990s, but has significantly increased since 2004. In 1973, violent crime per 100,000 people was 4.7 percent, in 1980 it was 4.9 percent, in 1990 it totaled 4.4 percent, and by 1995, it was 4.6 percent. Similarly, homicide rates in the United States have also dramatically declined, returning to rates per 100,000 people comparable to the 1960s. For example, the homicide rate in 1968 was 7.3 percent, while in the 1980s it jumped to 9.6 percent and the 1990s was 10 percent. By 2002, the rate declined to 6.1 percent. However, the violent crime rate increased 1.3 percent from 2004 to 2005 and preliminary analysis by the FBI Uniform Crime Report for 2006 suggests violent crime has increased 3.7 percent, representing an increase since 2004 of 5 percent.

Yet, do these numbers reflect a true decrease in violent activity, or is this drop in violent crime and homicide rates, as some observers argue (e.g., Gilligan, 2001), a more accurate reflection of our nation's enhanced critical care capabilities in communication systems (e.g., 911 dispatch), quicker response times for police, firefighters, and emergency medical technicians to violent incidents, and technologically sophisticated emergency room procedures by which lives that would have been lost even a few years ago are today saved?

Regardless, for young men between the ages of 15 and 24, the homicide rate was 10 deaths per 100,000 people in 1965 and has more than tripled to 33 homicides per 100,000 people in the 1990s (Wethington, 1996). Between 1984 and 1994 alone, homicide rates tripled in the United States among 14- to 17-year-old boys (Gilligan, 2001). Compared to all other developed nations, the murder rates and the imprisonment rates in the United States are *five to ten times higher* (Gilligan, 2001).

These statistics provide consistent evidence that violence is at unacceptably high levels throughout our world community. It is not surprising, therefore, that law enforcement officers are increasingly being called upon to defuse potentially violent situations (e.g., domestic disputes) and other crisis incidents (e.g., hostage taking, barricade, and suicide).

ORGANIZATION OF CHAPTERS

Part I of the book provides an overview to the emerging area of hostage/crisis negotiation as a field of study and as a life-and-death practice most often undertaken by police negotiation teams. Chapter 1 provides an overview to the real-world consequences of inadequate negotiation responses to violent incidents. The chapter concludes with a brief explanation of each of the subsequent chapters as well as a summary of the demographic characteristics of four critical incidents that are analyzed later in the book (Chapters 7–10).

Chapter 2 presents an overview to the field of crisis negotiation. A conceptual overview to the conflict dynamics that characterize crisis situations is provided in order to directly situate the focus of the book within a conflict resolution framework.

Chapter 3 discusses the two primary conceptual templates of instrumental and expressive orientations that have traditionally been employed in understanding hostage-taker behavior. Strengths and weaknesses of these two orientations are examined. The chapter concludes by outlining a communication-based approach to crisis negotiation.

Part II presents an in-depth overview of the S.A.F.E. model, an applied, communication-based approach for de-escalating crisis situations and negotiating peaceful resolution of violent confrontations. In brief, the S.A.F.E. model focuses attention on four major conflict and crisis dynamics that impact escalation/de-escalation processes: **S**ubstantive demands, **A**ttunement (relational) issues, **F**ace (identity) issues, and **E**motional distress. Relevant research that supports the basic structure and formulation of the applied S.A.F.E. conceptual framework is reviewed in Part II. Chapter 4 reviews the core processes of the S.A.F.E. framework and then provides a detailed description of the first S.A.F.E. frame, namely, substantive demands. In this chapter, guidelines for tracking escalation and de-escalation patterns around substantive demand issues are discussed and strategies for negotiating substantive demand frame issues are delineated.

In Chapter 5, attunement (relationship development) and face frame negotiation dynamics are explained. In Chapter 6, the final S.A.F.E. frame element of emotional distress is presented, and specific strategies for engaging in supportive communication around intense, negative emotional experience are reviewed. Appendix A may be useful for researchers who wish to gain deeper insight concerning the underlying theoretical stance and core assumptions of the S.A.F.E. model for resolving critical incidents.

It is important to note that the initial formulation of the S.A.F.E. framework was a collaborative effort with Dr. Randall Rogan that resulted in a number of publications (Hammer, 1999, 2001; Hammer & Rogan, 1997, 2004; Rogan, 1997; Rogan & Hammer, 1994, 1995, 2002, 2006; Rogan, Hammer, & Van Zandt, 1997). The S.A.F.E. model as presented in Chapters 4, 5, and 6 in *Saving Lives* adds considerably to this initial body of work and the articulation of an applied formulation of the S.A.F.E. framework. Therefore, the S.A.F.E. model articulated in these chapters, including additions, elaborations, and/or modifications to the initial concepts of the S.A.F.E. framework presented in these earlier works are necessarily my own responsibility.

Part III presents extensive discourse analysis focusing on core aspects of the S.A.F.E. framework to four crisis/hostage incidents followed by a final chapter that discusses various ways the S.A.F.E. framework may be extended to situations outside the law enforcement, critical incident context.

Table 1.1 presents a demographic summary of each of the four critical events. These incidents are given pseudonyms in order to maintain the confidentiality of the individuals involved. For academic scholars and others who wish to know more detailed information on the methodology used in analyzing these incidents, Appendix B offers a detailed description of the specific "action implicative discourse" methodology used in analyzing these four incidents.

Chapters 7 and 8 analyze two incidents in which the final outcome was suicide by the hostage taker. Specifically, Chapter 7 summarizes results concerning an individual who previously killed his girlfriend, held hostages but released them, and ultimately killed himself ("The Alpha Incident: To Pay for One's Sins"). Chapter 8 reviews an incident in which the subject and his girlfriend previously had shot a police officer and attempt to rob a bank when the police arrive. They held hostages and subsequently released everyone. The incident ended when the subject kills his girlfriend and then commits suicide ("The Bravo Incident: The End of the Line").

Chapters 9 and 10 present findings concerning two incidents that ended with the peaceful surrender of the subject. Chapter 9 concerns an individual who previously had killed his father and had a long history of mental illness. No hostages were held. The situation ended when the subject surrenders to the tactical officers ("The Charlie Incident: A Russian Agent"). Chapter 10 involves a young man who hijacks an airplane. He is distraught and holds the pilot and the co-pilot hostage. He ultimately surrenders with no loss of life ("The Delta Incident: Deadline to Detonate").

Finally, Chapter 11 discusses the applicability of the S.A.F.E. framework in critical incident management for resolving major incidents (e.g., terrorist attacks using weapons of mass destruction). The chapter concludes by offering preliminary suggestions on how the S.A.F.E. model may be useful to resolve conflicts and solve problems within our families, organizations, and communities.

CONCLUSION

It is apparent that one critical competency in the next century is the ability to negotiate emotionally charged, conflict situations under crisis conditions. Crisis negotiation, as a developing field of study and practice, is increasingly being held accountable by domestic and international public institutions for

Table 1.1 Demographic Information on the Four Crisis Incidents

Incident Name	Incident Type	Gender: Perpetrator	Gender: Negotiator	Third Parties Involved	Violent Acts	Hostages	Time Negotiated	Outcome
Alpha	Domestic	Male	Male	None	Shot girlfriend before negotiation	Several hostages initially held, then released unharmed	7 hours	Suicide
Bravo	Criminal	Male for 1st hostage taker; Female for 2nd hostage taker	Male	Multiple 3rd parties involved in negotiation with both hostage takers	Shot police officer before negotiation; killed girlfriend at end of negotiation	Several hostages initially held, then released unharmed; girlfriend as co-conspirator	5.5 hours	Suicide
Charlie	Mental instability	Male	Male	None	Shot father before negotiation	None	6 hours	Surrender
Delta	Personal crisis/ substance abuse	Male	Male	Girlfriend involved in negotiation with subject	None	Two hostages (pilot, co-pilot) held,	4 hours	Surrender

identifying and effectively employing salient behavioral science theory and skills for peacefully resolving our most difficult and intractable conflict situations. It is my sincere hope that the conceptual framework and research findings advanced in the remaining chapters of this book contribute toward improved crisis negotiation theory and practice and assist in our fundamental calling—saving lives.

CHAPTER 2

The Growth of Crisis Negotiation

THE HISTORICAL ROOTS OF CRISIS NEGOTIATION

A Popular Topic

Today, crisis negotiation theory and practice have attained widespread public attention through such films as *The Negotiator* and *Inside Man;* television programs such as *Standoff* and *Dallas SWAT;* popular press publications, including *Facing Down Evil* (Van Zandt, 2006) and *Hostage at the Table* (Kohlrieser, 2006); and academic and professional books such as *Crisis Negotiations* (McMains & Mullins, 2006), *Crisis Negotiations: A Multiparty Perspective* (Giebels & Noelanders, 2004), and *Dynamic Processes of Crisis Negotiation* (Rogan, Hammer, & Van Zandt, 1997).

This growing public interest is grounded in a number of high-profile critical incidents, including the Branch Davidian siege in the spring, 1993, in Waco, Texas; the attack on December 17, 1996, at the Japanese diplomatic residence in Lima, Peru, by the Tupac Amaru in which 500 hostages were held for three months; the killing by Eric Harris and Dylan Klebold of 13 students and one teacher and the wounding of 23 others at Columbine High School in Colorado; and the terrorist attacks on the World Trade Center (Twin Towers) and the Pentagon in the United States on September 11, 2001, in which around 3,000 lives were lost. While hostage taking and crisis incidents may capture the attention of the media, the fact is that these high-risk situations are all too common throughout the world. Further, these types of events are not a recent phenomenon.

This chapter begins with a historical overview to the practice of critical incident management and hostage/crisis negotiation and the resultant varied definitions of crisis negotiations that characterize the field. Following this, insights are presented based on a number of surveys that have demographically profiled police hostage/crisis hostage negotiation efforts. The chapter continues with a detailed discussion of the role stress plays in critical incidents, the interactional dynamics involved in violent conflicts, and how crisis conditions can quickly escalate these types of dangerous encounters. The chapter concludes by discussing how hostage taking and barricade events can be profitably viewed within the broad, interdisciplinary field of conflict communication.

A Long History

Since ancient times, hostage taking has been used as a coercive technique for exerting geopolitical as well as domestic power (McMains & Mullins, 2006). One of the earliest recorded hostage-taking incidents is described in the Old Testament (Genesis 14) of the Bible (Soskis & Van Zandt, 1986). According to Biblical accounts, Lot, the nephew of Abram, was taken hostage by the armies of four kings. Abram responded by sending 318 of his men to secure Lot's release by means of an aggressive assault. As D.A. Soskis and C.R. Van Zandt (1986) comment, the rescue operation for Lot "may have been the first SWAT team [operation] in recorded history and serves to remind us that the tactical force option remains the preferred one in many circles" (p. 424). During the rule of the Roman Empire (27 B.C. to A.D. 476), Romans took hostages as guarantees of treaties (Call, 1999). Throughout history, pirates captured individuals for ransom, merchants were kidnapped to ensure that others would pay their debts, and politicians were held hostage to gain compliance from various nation-states (McMains & Mullins, 2006). In these and other kidnapping and hostage-taking situations, the hostages/victims were held against their will in order to coerce some kind of concession from the other party.

While hostage taking may well have a long and infamous history, employing *negotiation* as a method for resolution is a relatively recent occurrence. Prior to 1972, police strategy for resolving hostage situations essentially involved a demand for the hostage taker to release the hostages and surrender. And then, if the perpetrator did not surrender, the police SWAT unit was activated in a tactical assault aimed at rescuing the hostages (McMains & Mullins, 1996, 2006; Rogan et al., 1997; Russel & Beigel, 1979).

Flashpoints

Two incidents, one domestic and one international, played particularly important roles in challenging the widespread application of tactically dominated approaches to resolving crisis incidents. The first incident took place at New York's Attica Prison. On September 9, 1971, at 8:45 in the morning, a group of inmates overpowered correctional officers and proceeded to unlock all cellblocks. Within minutes, the inmates controlled the entire prison, holding 42 hostages. Shortly thereafter, they presented to New York State authorities a list of 32 demands that ranged from changes in diet to replacement of the prison superintendent. After three days of confused communication between prison officials and rioting prisoners, the order was given by New York Governor Nelson Rockefeller to regain control of the prison. At 10:00 A.M. on September 13, National Guardsmen, New York State Troopers, and prison guards stormed the prison. Fifteen minutes later, officers had killed 39 people and wounded 80 more. Of this group, 11 of the dead and 33 of the wounded were hostages and correctional officials. One officer and three inmates were killed by the prisoners during the three-day siege.

During the height of the 1972 Olympics, 13 members of the Black September Arab terrorist organization entered the Olympic village in Munich, Germany, and forced their way into the Israeli Olympic compound, killing two athletes and taking 11 hostages. Shortly thereafter, they demanded the release of 200 or so prisoners from Israeli prisons and transportation to the airport where they intended to fly to Egypt. After nearly 12 hours of communication with German authorities, the terrorists and their captives were transported to the municipal airport, where a tactical assault was launched. After an intense, 15-minute battle, 11 Israeli hostages, 1 police officer, and 10 hostage takers were killed. Three of the hostage takers were captured. These events captured significant attention both from the media as well as law enforcement. Both incidents were resolved through a tactical assault, the result of which was an unacceptably high rate of death and injury.

The "New York Plan"

These two incidents served as the impetus for law enforcement to reassess traditional, pre-1972, tactically based approaches for ending hostage-taking situations. The New York City Police Department, led by Dr. Harvey Schlossberg and Detective Frank Boltz, paid particular attention to the unsatisfactory outcomes to both the Attica Prison Riot and the Munich incident and developed by 1973 an approach for dealing with hostage-taking incidents that became known as the "New York Plan" (Boltz & Hershey, 1979; Butler, 1991; McMains & Mullins, 2006). This approach was subsequently implemented by the Federal Bureau of Investigation (FBI) Crisis Negotiation Unit in its own hostage-training programs at the FBI Academy in Quantico, Virginia, a few years later.

Schlossberg (1979) stated there are four approaches available to law enforcement to resolve incidents such as the Munich hostage-taking incident. These are (1) tactical assault, (2) sniper fire, (3) chemical agents, and a new alternative, (4) contain and negotiate. Schlossberg suggested that the fourth approach, contain and negotiate, was preferable as it represented the safest alternative to end a volatile situation. In fact, a study by Schlossberg (1979) revealed that in 78 percent of tactical assaults, hostages, law enforcement personnel, or hostage takers are killed or injured. Tactical resolution was thus deemed a high-risk solution to crisis incidents.

The development of the New York Plan spurred both scholars and practitioners to examine the usefulness of *negotiation* in peacefully resolving crisis incidents (Hammer & Weaver, 1998; Head, 1989; McMains & Mullins, 2006; Rogan & Hammer, 2006; Schlossberg, 1979). The New York Plan was based on the idea that a specialized team of police hostage negotiators should *contain and negotiate* crisis incidents rather than use force as the first response: a process of effective communication with the suspect, termed "dynamic inactivity" (Schlossberg, 1979, p. 211). Indeed, the New York Plan viewed tactical force as a complementary (rather than primary) option along with negotiation to resolve critical incidents (Butler, 1991).

The idea that negotiation can be effective in peacefully resolving such situations was initially articulated by Schlossberg (1979) in terms of four principles. First, the hostage has no intrinsic value, but is often used by hostage takers as a tool for getting attention. Second, it is in the best interests of the hostage taker to keep the hostages safe. Third, while hostage taking may be a "creative" act in response to high levels of frustration, the effort at negotiation is designed to move the hostage taking into an act of problem solving. Fourth, the goal of negotiation is to reduce the level of tension or frustration in the situation by offering the hostage taker the opportunity to emotionally "ventilate" in a supportive environment. In short, hostage/crisis negotiation was proffered as a new and complementary (to tactical intervention) means for peacefully resolving hostage taking and barricade incidents. It is important to note that the New York Plan did not view negotiation as an alternative or a replacement to the use of tactical force in these violent events. Rather, this approach emphasized the synergistic effect of tactical containment coupled with negotiation efforts.

By the mid 1980s, hostage negotiation teams, based on the New York Plan, were well established in police departments throughout the United States. In one survey, for example, 96 percent of police agencies agreed with the basic principles outlined in the New York Plan for hostage negotiation (Vasey, 1985). By the 1980s, the FBI hostage/crisis negotiation program had adapted the New York Plan to include greater emphasis on the psychological aspects of crisis negotiation (Fuselier, 1981a, 1981b). As the hostage/crisis negotiation field emerged, research attention began to focus on critical incidents, with particular interest in the interpersonal dynamics of crisis negotiation.

CHANGING DEFINITIONS OF CRISIS NEGOTIATIONS

An Early Focus on Terrorism

The terrorist hostage taking in Munich galvanized attention within law enforcement both within the United States and internationally. In addition, governments were keenly interested in preventing airline hijackings, which were relatively common in the 1970s. For example, 10 percent of all airline hijackings from 1931 to 1989 took place in one year: 1969 (McMains & Mullins, 2006). According to T.B. Feldmann and P.W. Johnson (1999), 528 airline hijackings took place between 1969 and 1982 (cited in McMains & Mullins, 2006, p. 40). It is not surprising, therefore, that initial definitions of crisis/hostage negotiations primarily focused on the resolution of terrorist incidents (see Boltz, Dudonis, & Schulz, 1990; MacWillson, 1992; Maher, 1977; Ochberg & Soskis, 1982). This early focus emphasized the more instrumental (bargaining) role hostages play in terrorist events. For example, H.H.A. Cooper (1981) viewed hostage taking as "a way of setting up a bargaining position that cannot be as conveniently or as well achieved by other means...[it] is a naked power play..." (p. 1).

A Broader View

Soon thereafter, crisis negotiators began to realize that most critical incidents faced by law enforcement did not involve terrorism (A.H. Miller, 1980). Rather, they tended to be suicide situations, domestic disturbances, and criminal activities. More recent definitions proffer a broader perspective toward hostage/crisis negotiation. M.J. McMains and W.C. Mullins (2006), for example, view crisis situations as "any incident in which people are being held by another person or persons against their will, usually by force or coercion, and demands are being made by the hostage taker" (p. 39). W.A. Donahue, C. Ramesh, and C. Borchgrevink (1991) define crisis negotiation as a communicative process that has, as its goal, the movement from crisis bargaining to more normative, problem-solving processes. F.J. Lanceley (2003) suggests that incident negotiations are a combination of crisis intervention (in which the hostage has no substantive value to the subject) and bargaining approaches (in which the hostage is used in order to gain a substantive demand). M.R. Hammer (2001) defines hostage/crisis negotiation within a conflict communication framework in which incompatibilities and interference between the hostage taker and the police negotiator give rise to perceptions of threat and negative emotions. From another definitional vantage point M.R. Hammer (1997) and M.R. Hammer and G. Weaver (1998) focus attention on the cultural differences that often are integral to crisis negotiation strategies.

R.G. Rogan and M.R. Hammer (2002, 2006) suggest a definition of crisis/hostage negotiation that blends both crisis intervention and bargaining approaches and permits a greater focus beyond terrorist events. Further, the definition presented below places hostage/crisis negotiation theory and practice more centrally located within a conflict communication frame:

> a unique form of conflict interaction in which law enforcement officers attempt to facilitate a (peaceful) resolution to an incident where an individual barricades him/herself, sometimes with a number of hostages, in an effort to

elicit some desired want or to communicate anger and frustration about a personal or social concern. (p. 229–230)

It is this view of hostage/crisis negotiation that grounds the conceptual development effort of the S.A.F.E. model and the analysis of incidents that provide evidence of the applicability of the S.A.F.E. framework as a negotiation approach for resolving critical incidents.

DEMOGRAPHIC ANALYSIS OF CRISIS INCIDENTS

Over the years, a number of surveys have been administered to law enforcement agencies that demographically profile hostage negotiation efforts. In 1983, V.S. Gettys surveyed 49 state and 49 municipal law enforcement departments. In 1988, one study (Fuselier, 1988) surveyed 34 police agencies, while another research team (Delprino & Bahn, 1988) sent questionnaires concerning the use of mental health professionals in crisis incidents to 193 municipal and 39 state police departments. In 1991, W.M. Butler (1991) surveyed all 50 state police agencies, 191 large municipal agencies, and a random sample (10 percent) of each state's small municipal police departments, from which 684 usable questionnaires were obtained. In 1994, M.R. Hammer, C.R. Van Zandt, and R.G. Rogan (1994) and R.G. Rogan, M.R. Hammer, and C.R. Van Zandt (1994) obtained responses from 242 crisis negotiation team leaders concerning negotiation practices.

More recently, the Crisis Management Unit at the FBI Academy created the Hostage Barricade Database System (HOBAS) in 1997 and began gathering information from law enforcement agencies throughout the United States. HOBAS collects data on incident characteristics as well as information on the subject and victims/hostages involved in the situation.

Results from these collective assessments provide a useful picture of key aspects of crisis incidents and the role and outcome of negotiation in resolving these situations. The most current HOBAS data set was examined. This data set consists of 4,784 critical incidents compiled on November 28, 2006. How effective is hostage/crisis negotiation in peacefully resolving violent confrontations? What role does behavioral science/mental health expertise play in a critical incident? What characteristics emerge regarding hostage takers and their hostages/victims? These and other questions were addressed primarily by researchers who "discovered" the crisis negotiation field in the 1980s and beyond.

Incident Outcomes

For 9½ hours on October 10, 1995, in Corpus Christi, Texas, Yolanda Saldivar held a 38-caliber gun to her head with the hammer cocked. During this time, Yolanda was determined to end her life. Police negotiators talked to her throughout this long period of time, asking her to drop her weapon and come out to face charges that she killed Tejano star Selena Quintanilla-Pérez. During this time, Yolanda repeatedly yelled that she wanted to die and begged the SWAT team to shoot and kill her. The negotiation team used a number of strategies to convince Yolanda to surrender, including an appeal to God and the Virgin of Guadalupe. They asked Yolanda to think about her family. Finally, Yolanda Saldivar put down her gun and surrendered peacefully (A. Turner, 1995). In this situation, negotiation practices helped prevent further violence.

Research shows that *negotiation is an effective strategy for resolving crisis incidents.* According to Butler (1991), in a survey of over 684 law enforcement agencies in the United States, 72 percent of crisis situations by 1991 were resolved through a negotiated surrender and 18 percent through a tactical entry and arrest. In fewer than 7 percent of the incidents is the perpetrator killed, while less than 6 percent of hostage takers and less than 9 percent of barricaded individuals commit suicide. In 3 percent of the incidents, the perpetrator kills the hostage and in 1 percent of crisis situations is the hostage killed or injured by the police. Finally, less than 1 percent of the time the hostage taker escapes.

Recent HOBAS data also confirm the overall effectiveness of negotiation as a key element of law enforcement's overall critical incident response capability. Of the 4,784 incidents, 57 percent of the incidents were resolved by negotiations only and an additional 12 percent were resolved with a combination of negotiation and tactical action. In only 20 percent of the incidents was tactical action the only resolution strategy employed. In 8 percent of the events, the incident was resolved through suicide and 2 percent by escape. Further, in 80 percent of the incidents, the victims were not injured or killed (14 percent were injured and 6 percent were killed by the subject). In 82 percent of the situations, the subject was not injured or killed (6 percent committed suicide, 10 percent were injured, 1 percent were killed, and 1 percent were killed through suicide by cop, i.e., subject-precipitated homicide). In 97 percent of the incidents, no bystanders or law enforcement officers were injured and in 99 percent of the situations, no bystanders or law enforcement officers were killed (Crisis Management Unit, 2006).

Use of Negotiators

A second observation is that from the 1980s forward, *police critical incident response teams have consistently included a crisis negotiation unit as part of the overall approach for resolving crisis incidents.* V.S. Gettys (1983) found that the vast majority (over 90 percent) of departments had specifically dedicated negotiators. Similar findings were obtained by both G.D. Fuselier (1988) and Butler (1991), although Butler's data suggest that significantly fewer small agencies employed a designated negotiator (30 percent) as compared to large agencies (96 percent).

Gettys's (1983) research also found that the main selection criterion for identifying crisis negotiators was primarily that an officer volunteers for the position. Other criteria, however (e.g., past negotiation experience, recommendations, fitness, and education), were used only by a minority of agencies surveyed. Further, only 14 percent or fewer of the agencies employed psychological testing or psychological interviews in selecting negotiators.

By the 1990s, the picture was considerably more complete. Butler (1991) found that by 1991, the major criteria in large agencies for selection remained volunteering (92 percent), although supervisor recommendation (70 percent) and negotiator recommendations (53 percent) were increasingly employed. In terms of selection tools, 55 percent of the large agencies used a panel interview while only 22 percent and 26 percent, respectively, relied on the Minnesota Multiphasic Personality Inventory psychological test or role plays.

Negotiator Training

In November 2006, Major Robert Beach and I, through my organization (Hammer Consulting, S.A.F.E. Hostage Operations), conducted a four-day, advanced workshop for police crisis negotiators from throughout the state of Delaware. This program focused on how to use the S.A.F.E. model and assessment materials to de-escalate and resolve critical incidents. During the program, the participants shared with us the fact that they conduct training for their teams virtually once a month and attend training programs (such as the S.A.F.E. program) as often as possible. In fact, for the participants in our program, training was well recognized as being essential to their ability to effectively negotiate actual incidents.

Research findings show that *police negotiation teams consistently receive training in crisis negotiation*. Gettys (1983) found that 100 percent of the agencies reported that their negotiators received basic crisis negotiation training. Other research by T. Strentz (1985) found that almost 75 percent of negotiators had received basic hostage negotiation training. Butler's (1991) research likewise confirms that over 90 percent of negotiators received crisis negotiation training, with an average of almost eight days of intensive instruction and that the FBI is the primary provider of this basic training (67 percent).

According to research conducted by Hammer, Van Zandt, and Rogan (1994) and Rogan, Hammer, & Van Zandt (1994), 35 percent of the crisis negotiation team leaders surveyed indicated their negotiators did not receive any basic crisis negotiation training, while 27 percent indicated their negotiators received, on average, five days of initial training. Almost half

(41 percent) of the teams did not engage in follow-up training activities. Finally, Rogan et al. (1994) report that negotiation teams identified the greatest training needs to be in the areas of (1) communication skills and strategies, (2) assessment of perpetrator emotional state and stability, and (3) resolution strategies.

Use of Mental Health Professionals

Fourth, overall data indicate that *mental health professionals are typically used in the minority of incidents and when they are employed, they are used for perpetrator assessment and postincident counseling and less for on-scene negotiation advisement.* Fuselier (1988) found that a little over half (58 percent) of the negotiation teams employ a mental health professional, primarily for assessment of the perpetrator (72 percent), postincident counseling of police (56 percent), and postincident review (39 percent). Yet, less than half (44 percent) of the mental health professionals received any training in hostage negotiation. In another, more comprehensive study, R.P. Delprino and C. Bahn (1988) found that while 44 percent of the respondents indicated a need for a mental health professional in crisis incidents, only 30 percent of the agencies actually used such a person in their incident call outs. According to Butler (1991), the variability in these survey findings are most likely due to differences among the investigators' survey respondents, which is the direct consequence of different sampling procedures.

Data from Butler's (1991) study suggest that 39 percent of the police departments surveyed use a mental health consultant, of whom 76 percent were doctoral level psychologists, 12 percent master's level psychologists, and 4 percent psychiatrists. Butler also found that 60 percent of the mental health consultants did, in fact, receive basic hostage negotiation training, representing a significant increase from earlier studies. However, Butler found that mental health professionals were actually called to only 23 percent of the total number of incidents negotiated. When called they were largely used for perpetrator assessment (88 percent), postincident counseling (69 percent) and advising on negotiation strategy (64 percent). Butler's data also indicate that agencies that employed a mental health professional had a statistically significant greater likelihood of their incidents being resolved by a negotiated surrender.

Research by Hammer, Van Zandt, and Rogan (1994) and Rogan et al. (1994) indicates that slightly over half (54 percent) of negotiation teams use a mental health professional with their greatest use in postincident counseling (82 percent), on-scene advising (60 percent), for negotiator training (44 percent), and negotiator selection (39 percent). Reporting a much lower figure, the FBI's HOBAS data suggest that mental health consultants are deployed during crisis incidents in only 15 percent of the cases. Overall, the survey data most consistently indicate that mental health professionals are used in a minority of crisis incidents, typically in activities outside the Negotiation Operations Center.

Mental Stability of Hostage Taker

A fifth observation is that *a small minority (10 percent) of hostage takers suffer from a diagnosable mental disorder*. Regarding perpetrator type, Strentz (1985) found that 52 percent of crisis incidents involve a person who is emotionally upset (e.g., domestic dispute, lost job, and/or depressive) and 40 percent involve a trapped criminal. Butler's (1991) data reveal that 69 percent of crisis incidents primarily involve a perpetrator who is emotionally upset (not necessarily suffering from a mental or emotional disorder) and 16 percent involve a trapped criminal. Research by Hammer, Van Zandt, and Rogan (1994) and Rogan et al. (1994) indicates that the most common type of incident are suicides, followed by barricades, domestic situations, hostage taking, criminal/high-risk situations, and kidnappings. Speaking most directly to the issue of mental illness among hostage takers, the HOBAS data indicate that 7 percent of the subjects had been previously committed to a mental facility prior to the incident (a clearer indication of an existing mental disorder condition). The HOBAS data also indicate that 10 percent of the hostage takers received some form of counseling following the incident with 1 percent sent for residential treatment. However, because respondents to this HOBAS question are able to "check more than one option," it is likely that, at most, 10 percent of the subjects may suffer mental illness. It is not clear, however, whether the mental illness of those hostage takers so identified actually emerged to a significant degree during the course of a crisis incident.

Additional Incident Characteristics

Collectively, the various surveys conducted throughout the 1980s to the present reveal additional information concerning crisis incidents. To begin, only 4 percent of incidents are classified by the FBI HOBAS data as a "true hostage" incident, while 96 percent are viewed as "nonhostage" incidents.[3] Of the nonhostage incidents, 49 percent are barricaded individuals, 9 percent are barricaded subjects holding victims, 36 percent are suicide or attempted suicide situations, and 2 percent are a combination of these typologies. Also, the majority of incidents (67 percent) last four hours or less, with the most common duration (37 percent) lasting two hours or less. In only 17 percent of the cases did law enforcement employ a third-party intermediary (TPI). In those incidents in which a TPI was asked to talk to the perpetrator, in 49 percent of the cases, the third party was a family member.

In terms of perpetrator characteristics, the majority (43 percent) are between the ages of 30 and 45, while 28 percent are between 18 and 29 years of age. Almost all (90 percent) are male. Fifty-seven percent were Caucasian, followed by 19 percent African-American and 9 percent Hispanic. A handgun (34 percent) or a shoulder weapon (22 percent) was most commonly used by hostage takers with 23 percent of perpetrators possessing no weapon at all. In 82 percent of the incidents, the subject was not injured or killed, while in 10 percent of the incidents, he or she was injured, in 3 percent of the incidents, the perpetrator was killed, and in 6 percent of the events, the subject committed suicide. In 5 percent of the incidents an existing restraining order was issued and in another 3 percent of the incidents a restraining order was previously issued.

The majority of victims/hostages were female (57 percent) and were primarily Caucasian (49 percent) followed by African-American (19 percent), and Hispanic (9 percent). In only 28 percent of the incidents, did the victim talk to the police negotiator (usually by telephone).

Finally, Butler (1991) found that 44 percent of incidents reported involved child hostages. In 6 percent of these incidents, the hostage was seriously injured, while in an additional 7 percent the hostage died. This compares to 1 percent of all incidents in which an adult hostage was either injured or killed. As Butler states, "a hostage is 14.9 times more likely to be seriously hurt or injured in hostage incidents involving a child hostage than in incidents that involve only adult hostages" (p. 53).

Clearly, some interesting findings from the various survey analyses of critical incidents have further informed both the practice and theory development of the nascent field of crisis negotiation. In this regard, there has been a slow but steady effort by law enforcement, hostage/crisis negotiation professionals, and by academic researchers to shorten the gap between theory and practice—in short, to support Kurt Lewin's vision of a "practical theory" (see Chapter 1).

CORE PARAMETERS OF THE EMERGING FIELD OF CRISIS NEGOTIATION

There is building evidence to suggest that a distinct, yet maturing field of inquiry is emerging in crisis negotiation, one that is characterized by increasing rigor in theory development and increased sophistication in crisis negotiation practice. There is little doubt that the development of this field has been driven by practitioners whose negotiation strategies and skills mean the difference between life and death. The literature of the field reflects this grounding, as it is centrally situated in the various "professional" journals (e.g., *FBI Law Enforcement Bulletin* and *Police Chief*), while basic theory and practice is passed on largely through specialized training programs conducted exclusively by law enforcement agencies for law enforcement negotiators.

Academic interest and contributions have significantly lagged behind. There is, however, evidence of increased academic attention to the practice of crisis negotiation (Giebels & Noelanders, 2004; Hammer, in press; Rogan & Hammer, 2006). While a handful of early books had been published on the topic of hostage negotiation (Boltz & Hershey, 1979; Miron & Goldstein, 1979), the first comprehensive textbook devoted exclusively to crisis negotiation was published in 1996 (McMains & Mullins) and most recently updated in 2006 (McMains & Mullins). In 2004, E. Giebels and S. Noelanders published an analysis of crisis negotiation dynamics involved in 35 incidents that took place in Europe. Nine of these events were classified as sieges, 16 cases involved kidnapping, and 10 cases were characterized as extortion. Similarly, several scholarly articles began appearing in academic journals (e.g., Donohue & Roberto, 1993; Hammer, 2000; Holmes & Sykes, 1993; Rogan & Hammer, 1994, 1995). In 1997, Rogan, Hammer, and Van Zandt produced an interdisciplinary survey of social science literature relevant to negotiating crisis incidents. More recently, specialized academic publications such as the *Journal of Police Crisis Negotiations* have arisen that directly focus on the dynamics of crisis negotiation.

As a maturing field of practice and theory development, there is growing consensus among both practitioners and researchers regarding the important role stress plays in critical incidents, the core interactional dynamics involved in violent conflicts, and the crisis conditions that can quickly escalate these types of dangerous encounters. It is to these conceptual concerns that we now turn.

THE CONFLICT COMMUNICATION PROCESS AND CRISIS CONDITIONS

Hostage taking and barricade events can be profitably viewed within the broad, interdisciplinary field of conflict communication. Indeed, communication is perhaps the most central concept associated with conflict and its resolution. Communication plays an integral role in how issues are defined and formed, how perceptions are framed, how intentions are signaled or masked, how information is shared, how influence is exerted, and how outcomes emerge (Putnam, 2006). Crisis/hostage events represent a particularly difficult form of conflict communication. These volatile situations are highly contentious interactions in which violence or the threat of violence exists, strong, negative emotions are often present, and communication is used to bring about a negotiated, peaceful resolution (Hammer, 2001, in press; Hammer & Rogan, 1997; Rogan & Hammer, 2006).

Incompatibilities and Disagreements

While many definitions of conflict have been proposed (Nicotera, 1995), two fundamental features of conflict are directly relevant to hostage-taking situations. First, conflict involves important *incompatibilities and disagreements* among contending parties. A number of writers emphasize this feature: (1) "expression of dissatisfaction or disagreement with an interaction, process, product, or service" (Costantino & Merchant, 1996, p. 4) and (2) "disagreements, differences of opinions, divergent interpretations, struggles for control, and multiple perspectives..." (Geist, 1995, p. 46). Other writers have emphasized incompatibilities, particularly focused on incompatible goals (Deutsch, 1973; Hocker & Wilmot, 1995). For instance, J.Z. Rubin, D.G. Pruitt, and SH Kim (1994) define conflict in terms of "divergence of interest, or a belief that the parties' current aspirations cannot be achieved simultaneously" (p. 5). Conflict then, is something more than a misunderstanding or misperception. Rather, conflict involves a substantive disagreement—and a disagreement that is framed and understood by the parties involved in terms of win/lose dynamics.

When applied to crisis incidents, the disagreements (i.e., substantive issues) between the hostage taker and the police negotiator involve more than a simple misunderstanding. For the subject, the very presence of the police is problematic. In fact, one of the first demands hostage takers often make is simply for the police to "go away." For the police, this is a demand that cannot be met for various reasons, including the fact that the subject has (or has been reported to have) a weapon within his or her possession. One of the first demands made by the negotiator is for the subject to put his or her weapon down and "come out." In almost all of the crisis situations encountered by police, the subject rarely complies with this demand immediately. From the subject's point of view, the demand to come out is incompatible with what the subject desires at that time. Thus, from the very initiation of contact between the subject and the negotiator, an incompatibility in substantive demands arises.

Interference, Stress, and Emotional Distress

A second element of conflict communication dynamics involves perceived *interference* by one or more parties in the goal-seeking capability of the other. Emphasizing this element, S. Fink (1986) describes conflict as "any social situation or process in which two or more social entities are linked by at least one form of antagonistic psychological relation or at least one form of antagonistic interaction" (p. 456). Similarly, J.P. Folger, M.S. Poole, and R.K. Stutman (1997) suggest that "conflict is the interaction of interdependent people who perceive incompatible goals and interference from each other in achieving those goals" (p. 4), while R.J. Fisher (1990) characterizes conflict as "a social situation involving perceived incompatibilities in goals or values between two or more parties, attempts by the parties to control each other, and antagonistic feelings by the parties toward each other" (p. 6). D.J.D. Sandole (1993) labels this process of interference under more violent conditions as a "manifest conflict process" that involves efforts at "undermining, directly or indirectly, the goal-seeking capability of one another" (Sandole, 1993, p. 6).

This notion of interference is central to critical incidents faced by negotiation teams. The sense often maintained by the hostage taker is that the police presence and actions (e.g., tactical deployment and/or negotiation strategies) directly interfere with the goals the subject has in this volatile situation. These goals are often quite varied, ranging from the desire to commit suicide, the need for face saving, and the demand for an automobile (for escape).

This creates conditions of increased stress and threat. Under these conditions, the subject's level of emotional distress often increases—sometimes to dangerously high levels. At times, although far less often, the police negotiator may also respond to these events with heightened levels of stress and emotional distress, creating increased likelihood of rapid escalation of the conflict.

Perceived incompatible goals coupled with interference, then, comprise two core aspects of a conflict dynamic evident in hostage taking, crisis situations (Hammer, 2001). Perceived incompatible goals and interference are the generative mechanisms (or triggers) that prompt cognitive appraisal of the situation and which elicit an affective reaction (e.g., hostility, anger, anxiety, and/or fear) to the perceived threat (Hammer, 2001). In this sense, the *interactional* dynamics involved in the conflict process revolve around the perception of threat and the associated emotional realities generated.

Clearly then, conflict is more than the rational assessment of the perceived interruption of one's goals; it is, rather, a highly emotional and dynamic phenomenon (Jones, 2001). In fact, it is precisely these conflict dynamics that often lead to contentious (win/lose) behavior between parties and that dominate an individual's information processing capabilities as evidenced by (1) hardening of ingroup/out-group distinctions, (2) reliance on stereotypes that exemplify either/or thinking, (3) sensitivity to insults toward one another's face or self-image, (4) attribution errors, and (5) mistrust toward the other party. Additionally, parties may also experience a reduced ability to empathize with one another and a tendency to employ zero-sum thinking (Fisher, 1990; Holmes & Fletcher-Bergland, 1995; Pruitt & Carnevale, 1993).

Crisis Conditions: Fuel to the Fire

Crisis situations exacerbate this already volatile conflict dynamic. The literature reveals five primary characteristics of a "crisis" that are associated with an individual's enhanced/exaggerated perception of threat and his or her resultant emotional distress. Hostage and barricade events are characterized by many, if not all, of these conditions. First, a decision-making point exists in which severely negative consequences can occur if the "wrong" decision is made. In a hostage situation, one of the most dangerous time periods is the arrival on scene of the critical incident response unit. During this time, there are typically multiple activities being undertaken, including setting up secure inner and outer perimeters, evacuation of people, SWAT team deployment, and setup of negotiation capability. One important characteristic of a hostage event is that from the moment police arrive, the subject often experiences a sense of pressure to make a "quick" decision to either end the event or to attempt to prevent the accompanying police actions.

Second, an element of surprise is present. Often the subject is not prepared for the arrival of police—particularly the large number of police officers who arrive on scene.

Third, the event is unexpected and is what K.E. Weick (1988) notes as a low-probability/high-consequence situation. The deployment of SWAT personnel communicates rather quickly to the subject that this is a "serious" and dangerous situation. In most cases, when subjects are interviewed following their surrender, they often remark that they really did not intend or expect "all of this to happen."

Fourth, conditions are inherently unstable, and the subject often perceives that the time period for coping with the situation is limited. Upon arrival to a critical incident, one of the first messages negotiators typically send to the subject is that the police are here to ensure the safety of everyone, including the hostage taker. Further, the negotiator will communicate to the subject that "we have all the time we want to talk and resolve this peacefully—so no one is hurt." The initial goal is to reassure the subject that time is not limited, and the intent of the police arrival on scene is simply to ensure people remain safe.

Finally, crises are characterized in terms of one or more of the parties experiencing a significant degree of stress and heightened emotional arousal in the form of extreme anxiety/fear (Fink, 1986; Herman, 1963; Holmes & Fletcher-Bergland, 1995; Weick, 1988). When this condition exists, the subject's stress level and emotional arousal are significantly heightened with the arrival of the police. The crisis event is inherently anxiety producing as both the subject and the police have weapons available to use.

Difficulty in Coping

The crisis conditions present during hostage/barricade situations are associated with increased relational mistrust, sensitivity to face or self-image concerns, and information processing errors (Rogan & Hammer, 2006). These factors reinforce conflict escalation as emotional arousal and contentious behavior increases (typically from the actions of the subject, but they can also occur as a result of anxiety-producing tactical actions of the police). Crisis conditions, coupled with a conflict dynamic of perceived incompatibilities and interference, often create a situation that challenges a hostage taker's ability to effectively and appropriately cope with the dangerous demands of the event.

In such high-stress situations the probability of violence increases as an individual may feel overwhelmed by intense fear, panic, or rage and respond in a dysfunctional and unpredictable manner. In crisis situations, parties often experience conflict as chaotic in structure and process, accompanied by strong, negative emotions and intense stress (Gladwin & Kumar, 1987). Taken together, these crisis features make a hostage/barricade standoff particularly difficult to de-escalate and challenging to resolve peacefully.

CONCLUSION

Critical incidents are one of the most difficult situations hostage negotiators face. The job of negotiators is no easy task. They face a subject who has a weapon and is often threatening to use it. The subject often experiences dangerously high levels of stress and consequently has heightened emotional arousal, culminating in emotional distress. The perceived threat (from police presence) can compromise the subject's ability to cope with the situation, resulting in information processes errors, biases, and difficulty in engaging in even minimal problem solving with the police negotiator. Further, the subject is in a state of mind in which he or she views the situation in win/lose terms and is committed to using violence (against himself or herself, hostages, or police) as a viable solution to his or her predicament.

The dynamics involved in these types of explosive confrontations are complex and important to understand. It is the goal of this book to further clarify the dynamics of crisis negotiation. More specifically, the next chapter focuses on traditional conceptual approaches taken in negotiating critical incidents. The theoretical underpinnings of these approaches are examined, highlighting the strengths and weaknesses of each approach and placing each approach in terms of its contribution to understanding patterns involved in negotiating with violent subjects.

CHAPTER 3

Traditional Approaches to Crisis Negotiation

INTRODUCTION

Consider three police negotiators in three different eras. Chris, a negotiator with a major metropolitan police agency arrives on scene and comments to the tactical officer, "What have we got, a crazy, a criminal, or a terrorist?" In another time and place, Bill, the police negotiator says through the telephone to the hostage taker, "come out with your hands up—or we will come in and get you!" Our third negotiator, Pat, again in another time and place, arrives on scene and begins negotiating with the subject by saying, "Hello, John, I'm Pat. What is the problem? I am here to help."

These are three very different statements by police negotiators and three very different approaches to crisis negotiation. Each of these statements has been used many times by negotiation teams, and each reflects a particular crisis negotiation model for resolving crisis incidents. Chris's statement reflects an approach to crisis negotiation that is based on "incident typologies." Bill's comments reflect a more instrumental model of negotiation, while Pat's effort to "help" the hostage taker is indicative of an expressive approach to crisis negotiation practice.

In this chapter, I discuss the three models (incident typologies, instrumental and expressive) that have been extensively relied upon in negotiating crisis situations. In discussing each of the approaches, I focus attention on the contribution each has made to the practice of crisis negotiation, noting their particular strengths and weaknesses. At the end of the chapter, I suggest that a communication-grounded framework, based on an accurate assessment of the communicative dynamics taking place between the hostage taker and the negotiator, represents a useful "fourth" approach for successfully negotiating crisis situations.

CATEGORIZATIONS OF CRISIS/HOSTAGE INCIDENTS

As stated earlier, following the Munich terrorist event, police negotiators both within the United States and Europe soon observed that the majority of critical incidents they faced did not involve a terrorist situation. As a result, there arose a need to more comprehensively identify and differentiate various types of crisis events. Initial efforts at conceptually defining hostage negotiations involved simple descriptive categorizations that were largely based on a mixture of both psychological and contextual characteristics in which the incidents occurred (Hammer & Rogan, 1997). These descriptive or typological models were the earliest templates negotiators relied upon for communicating with hostage takers.

Crisis Incident Typologies

The incident typologies were the first approach taken to classify the kinds of situations police negotiators face in a critical incident. The assumption with these typologies is that knowing how to classify an incident provides insight into the hostage taker's motivation, intentions, and possible behavior.

One of the earliest and most influential classifications of crisis incidents is provided by F.J. Hacker (1976) who viewed hostage takers as *criminals, crusaders,* and *crazies*. According to Hacker, criminals engage in terrorist acts for personal gain, crusaders are oriented toward prestige and power around an identified cause, while crazies are viewed as emotionally disturbed individuals. Similar to Hacker's categories, H. Schlossberg (1979) identified three types: *professional criminals, group oriented hostage takers,* and *psychos*. More recently, C.C. Combs (1997) employed Hacker's original conceptualization of crusaders, criminals, and crazies in describing terrorists.

Other, more elaborate categorizations described incidents according to particular traits of the perpetrator and his or her motivation (Cooper, 1981). Seven separate types of incidents were identified by H.H.A. Cooper, including *political extremists, fleeing criminals, institutionalized persons, estranged persons, wronged persons, religious fanatics,* and *mentally disturbed persons*. W. Middendorf (1975) offers a classification of hostage takers based on the following motives: (1) political, (2) escape, and (3) personal gain.

I. Goldaber (1979) and A.F. Maksymchuk (1982) identify three typologies of hostage takers. The *psychological type* is characterized as unpredictable and prone to violence at any time. Within this category are the *suicidal,* the *mentally disturbed,* and the *vengeance seeker*. The second category is the *criminal type* who is seen as a rationale, creative thinker who will surrender if there is no realistic way out. Within this group are the *cornered perpetrator*, the *aggrieved inmate*, and the *extortionist*. The third category is the *political type* who serves a particular cause and consists of the *social protestor*, the *militant ideological zealot*, and the *terrorist*. Using a similar set of categories, J.T. Turner (1986) suggests the most common types of hostage takers within the health care arena are the *criminal*, the *aggrieved individual*, the *estranged person*, and the *mentally ill individual*. More recently, T.B. Feldmann (2001) analyzed hostage and barricade incidents using the categories of *personal/domestic dispute, criminal acts, mentally ill, workplace violence, alcohol/drug related, and students*.

Finally, the Federal Bureau of Investigation (FBI) has embraced a four-part classification of hostage-taking incidents. These four types include hostage takings by *mentally/emotionally disturbed individuals, criminals* (hostage takings occurring during the commission of a crime such as a bank robbery), *terrorists*, and hostage takings during *prison* uprisings (Borum & Strentz, 1992; DiVasto, Lanceley, & Gruys, 1992; Fuselier, 1986; Fuselier & Noesner, 1990; Goldaber, 1979; McMains & Mullins, 1996, 2006; Soskis & Van Zandt, 1986).

Contribution of Incident Typologies

The primary contribution of these categorical approaches, as R.G. Rogan and M.R. Hammer (2006) observe, is "their utility in helping law enforcement to better understand the types of incidents that they encounter and some of the essential conditions associated with these incidents" (p. 455). Do these typologies provide insights, however, regarding the motivations and intentions of hostage takers? Do they explain the communication patterns that arise during a critical incident? Unfortunately, while these typologies provided an initial framework, these various classifications offer limited insight concerning the actual interaction dynamics involved in crisis situations.

Confusion among the Categories

Confusion arises due to the lack of conceptual coherency in the *relationship* between the proposed categories, mixing more psychological disorder categories with various situational typologies. Thus Hacker (1976) includes the category *criminal*, which is defined legally (i.e., someone is caught breaking the law); *crusader*, defined politically; and *crazies*, defined presumably through a psychological diagnosis of a mental disorder. This results in a lack of clarity concerning the conceptual distinctiveness among these proposed categories. Let us take an example. The police negotiation team arrives in a densely wooded area and sets up the Negotiation Operations Center. High up in a redwood tree is a militant environmental zealot who has chained himself or herself to a limb to stop further deforestation. Is our environmental zealot a "crusader" (i.e., someone who is acting on behalf of his or her beliefs) or a "criminal" (a person who is clearly breaking the law, perhaps for media attention)? Here is another example. James was released from a psychiatric institution one month ago. Since then, he has stopped taking his medication for the diagnosed mental disorder of paranoid schizophrenia. Today, James enters a food store and takes out a gun, yelling "give me all your money!" The store clerk immediately presses the hidden alarm button. A short time later, the hostage negotiation unit arrives. Upon seeing the police outside, James now "holds" the cashier hostage. Are police negotiators facing a "criminal" or "crazy" incident?

The question that arises is whether these classifications are useful as a framework for better understanding aspects of negotiation dynamics? The answer, unfortunately, is that these incident typologies are not as useful as they might be due to difficulty in consistently categorizing the incident. Further, the usefulness of these typologies is constrained due to the contradictory recommendations that have emerged for each typology presented.

Contradictory Negotiation Recommendations

Because of the conceptual confusion associated with these classifications, contradictory recommendations on how to effectively negotiate with these various types of hostage takers have been advanced (see Fuselier, 1988, for an early, cogent analysis of these contradictions). According to some authors, *political terrorists* (i.e., crusaders) have been identified as the *most difficult* with whom to negotiate peaceful resolutions (Soskis & Van Zandt, 1986) due to various reasons, including their high levels of commitment, planning, and use of power (Stratton, 1978), as well as their level of rationality, their sense of right and wrong, and strong loyalty to their group (Office of Security, 1983). Combs (1997) also suggests that crusaders are "the least likely to negotiate a resolution to a crisis" (p. 57) as negotiation would likely be seen as a betrayal of the cause.

Other writers have stated, however, that *criminals* are the *most difficult* with whom to negotiate peaceful resolutions because a trapped criminal is the most dangerous to hostages as well as law enforcement (Hassel, 1975). In contrast, Combs (1997) suggests that criminals are the *least difficult* to negotiate with because "their demands are quite logical (although often outrageous), and they are based in terms which can be met" (Combs, 1997, p. 58, e.g., money and/or safe passage).

Finally, *mentally disturbed individuals,* largely because of their psychological instability, have been cited by some writers as the *most difficult* in negotiating resolutions to crisis incidents (Maher, 1977). Goldaber (1979), for instance, suggests that the *vengeance seeker,* as a specific subtype of the mentally disturbed category, presents the greatest difficulty in negotiation and recommends this individual simply be seized as soon as possible. Yet other writers have concluded just the opposite regarding negotiation difficulties with mentally disturbed individuals. Combs (1997), for instance, argues that mentally disturbed individuals may be more likely to negotiate if the negotiator can understand the idiosyncratic motive of the hostage taker and offer some form of hope or alternatives.

Taken together, the various categorical approaches to understanding crisis situations have been valuable insofar as they provided an initial effort at bringing coherence to the developing field of crisis incident negotiation and as such served an important function in increasing scholarly attention to this neglected area of study.

For the crisis negotiation practitioner, these classification models provided a practical framework for answering the important question: "What kind of situation do we have here?" Lacking other frameworks to use to answer this question, the incident typologies were at least somewhat helpful, given the alternative was a general lack of any other relevant conceptual frameworks. However, their usefulness is constrained due to the inherent conceptual confusion among the categories as well as their limited insight in developing theoretically grounded, consistent, behavioral science insights for negotiating these types of high-stress events.

INSTRUMENTAL AND EXPRESSIVE BEHAVIOR

More contemporary interpretations of incident type focus almost entirely on the perpetrator's goals. Central to this approach is the work of MS. Miron and A.P. Goldstein (1979) who posited that the communication (language and behavior) of a perpetrator in hostage/crisis incidents ranges from instrumental to expressive. According to them, an instrumental orientation denotes a primary concern for satisfying some recognizable goal that is constructively beneficial to the perpetrator (e.g., obtaining money or the release of a fellow prisoner). Comparatively, an expressive communication orientation by a suspect refers to "those acts which serve only to display the power or significance of the perpetrator—acts which appear to be senseless in that there is no obvious way in which the perpetrator can stand to gain anything or in which the act is clearly self-destructive" (p. 10).

E. Giebels and S. Noelanders (2004) suggest that instrumental incidents contain relatively equal interaction patterns between the hostage taker and the police negotiator. Further, these situations typically involve perpetrators who are well prepared and who issue specific demands. In contrast, expressive incidents typically arise spontaneously and the subject and the victim/hostage are familiar with one another. Further, communication between the hostage taker and the police negotiator is more emotional and intense. These authors suggest that expressive situations are characterized as a form of counseling, where the subject has a problem and the negotiator helps the hostage taker work through his or her problem.

A Continuum, not a Dichotomy

Miron and Goldstein (1979), while differentiating the main features of instrumental and expressive goals in a critical incident, nevertheless emphasized that a subject's behavior can be simultaneously both instrumental and expressive. Further, they intended this continuum to be used as an interpretive framework for increasing understanding of the *meaningfulness* of hostage takers' behaviors, not as a tool for categorizing incidents as either instrumental or expressive in orientation. Practitioner interpretations, however, have tended to regard the notions of instrumental and expressive communication as two distinct types of critical incidents.

Hostage and Nonhostage Incidents

Using different terminology, but covering the same conceptual landscape, G.W. Noesner (1999) proposed a dichotomous classification of hostage and nonhostage situations. According to the author, a "hostage" situation is characterized by a suspect engaging in purposeful behavior for the attainment of some concrete outcome that denotes substantive value for the suspect. In this context, hostages serve as true bargaining chips that can be traded for something with the police. Alternatively, "nonhostage" incidents are marked by a suspect who engages in emotional and senseless actions (Noesner, 1999). Furthermore, any person held in a nonhostage event is really a "victim" to the perpetrator's anger and frustration, not as a bargaining commodity. Successfully identifying and labeling an incident as "hostage" or "nonhostage," according to the author, provides the negotiating team with a strategic template for managing the situation. In fact, the FBI's distinction between a hostage and a nonhostage incident essentially replaced the four-part incident classification the FBI had previously proposed (mentally disturbed subjects, criminals, terrorists, and prison uprisings).

Clearly, Noesner's (1999) classification scheme is grounded in Miron and Goldstein's (1979) instrumental-expressive behavioral motivation framework. In order for a negotiator to judge an incident as either hostage or nonhostage, he or she must first ascertain the functional value of the hostage(s) to the suspect, which requires a determination about the suspect's behavioral motivation. Briefly, Noesner's description of a true hostage situation is characterized by a suspect who demonstrates instrumental motivation and behavior (instrumental goal directedness), while nonhostage incidents involve suspects who have no substantive demands or whose demands are pragmatically unrealistic (i.e., expressive motivation).

In this sense, hostage incidents involve people who are held against their will for a substantive purpose, while nonhostage incidents involve "victims" held against their will for expressive reasons. Current practice, based on this distinction, posits that nonhostage incidents have greater risk to the safety of the victim compared to the risk to the hostage in hostage events (McMains & Mullins, 2006, p. 53), although evidence for this observation is unclear.

Overall, current crisis negotiation practice tends to assess a suspect's behavior as *either* instrumental *or* expressive, and, consequently, negotiation incidents are delineated as being *either* hostage/instrumental or non-hostage/expressive. This practice runs counter, however, to the original conceptualization of Miron and Goldstein (1979) who viewed instrumental and expressive behavior as existing along a continuum. As M.J. McMains and W.C. Mullins (2006) observe, both instrumental and expressive elements are involved in critical incidents and the "dichotomy seems artificial" (p. 54).

The Value of the Instrumental and Expressive Continuum

The two-part instrumental-expressive communication continuum developed by Miron and Goldstein (1979) nevertheless has been a useful distinction for negotiators in determining the type of crisis incident and appropriate strategy for communicating with the suspect (DiVasto et al., 1992; Fuselier, 1986; Lanceley, Ruple, & Moss, 1985; Noesner & Dolan, 1992; Van Zandt & Fuselier, 1989). This continuum, therefore, provides a valuable heuristic in identifying the general orientation present in a critical incident.

As a result of the influence of this continuum, two dominant crisis negotiation approaches have evolved from these early categorizations to help inform negotiators about the nature of crisis situations, as well as how to structure the communicative interaction. The "instrumental" model involves a variety of strategies that focus on more contentious, tactically driven actions and bargaining behaviors to convince the subject to surrender. The "expressive" negotiation model views negotiation dynamics as more psychologically driven, with an emphasis on therapeutic crisis intervention strategies in the context of diagnosed psychological pathology as a predominant approach for a peaceful, negotiated resolution. An important distinction between instrumental crisis negotiation models and expressive approaches lies in the very different use of tactical actions in escalating and de-escalating violent confrontations. In order to more fully understand the differences between instrumental and expressive approaches to crisis negotiation, a brief description of the relationship among crisis negotiators, incident command (decision making), and tactical actions is presented.

CRITICAL INCIDENT MODEL

The management structure of a crisis incident describes the overall elements involved in resolving potentially violent situations when law enforcement is involved. Essentially, there are three main elements of a crisis response team. The first element is Command. This consists of the designated Incident Commander who has overall responsibility for making decisions concerning the use of negotiation strategies and/or tactical options. In addition, the Incident Commander is responsible for the overall management of the event. Reporting directly to the Incident Command Center are the Negotiation and the Tactical Units (see Figure 3.1). The Negotiation team is responsible for maintaining communication with the perpetrator and negotiating the release of any hostages as well as the peaceful surrender of the barricaded individual. The Tactical team is responsible for developing tactical rescue and assault procedures in which the application of force is used to resolve the situation (McMains & Mullins, 2006).

In almost all critical incidents, the arrival of law enforcement on scene is itself conflict escalating insofar as armed police officers establish a secure perimeter and evacuate individuals from adjacent locations while tactical operations are initiated that include positioning of snipers and assembly of assault personnel. A key question in discussing various crisis negotiation models, therefore, is *the manner and degree to which the "tactical option" (i.e., use of force) is incorporated into the negotiation process*. As discussed below, there are very different answers, depending on whether a more instrumentally driven or expressive crisis negotiation model is employed.

INSTRUMENTAL CRISIS NEGOTIATION

Police strategy for resolving hostage situations prior to 1972 did not involve negotiation to any significant degree. This approach typically employed a planned assault directed toward the rescue of the hostages (Hammer & Rogan, 1997; Russel & Beigel, 1979). As negotiation was introduced in the 1970s, there emerged a model or approach for conducting negotiation that can be described as more instrumental in focus. This instrumental model emphasized the bargaining of substantive (instrumental) demands as a preferred method of communicating with the subject and resolving the incident. These demands focus on objective, situationally relevant wants or demands, as well as those objective, situationally unrelated

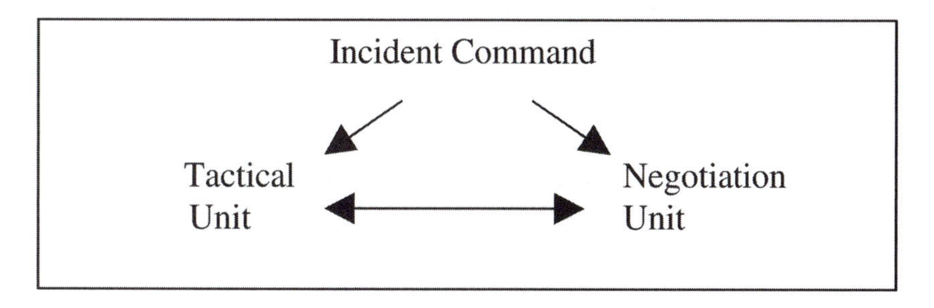

Figure 3.1 Critical Incident Management Model

wants or demands made by the subject, as well as demands made by the negotiation team (Hammer, 1997).

More generally, instrumental concerns represent the commodity goals (e.g., money, goods, and/or services) of the individual negotiator (Roloff & Jordan, 1992). A hostage taker's demands for a "getaway" car would be considered an instrumental demand (i.e., it is a situationally related request), while a demand for delivery of a pack of cigarettes would also be considered an instrumental demand, although one that is less directly related to the situation (Hammer, 2001). That is, the demand for a pack of cigarettes, while instrumental in nature, is not necessarily directly related to the situation, as one does not need to hold another person hostage to obtain cigarettes. However, the demand for cigarettes may be considered substantive, insofar as it is an objective want or need expressed by the subject.

Bargaining

At a more general level, one key feature of the instrumental approach is its emphasis on bargaining in which the efforts of each party involved in the conflict are dedicated to dictating or clarifying their individual instrumental concerns. Basic to this approach is the presumption that individuals enter into the interaction with their goals predetermined and relatively stable (Wilson & Putnam, 1990). Consequently, the challenge in this type of interaction is to attempt to modify an opponent's commitment to key instrumental objectives.

An underlying assumption for instrumentally focused negotiations is that conflict is a consequence of goal interference within an interdependent relationship and that both parties to the conflict are concerned about maximizing their rewards and minimizing respective costs (Folger, Poole, & Stutman, 2000; Northrup, 1989). This theoretic orientation is grounded in social exchange theory that posits people's primary motivation in negotiation is self-interest (Thibaut & Kelly, 1959).

Briefly, this instrumentally grounded approach holds that conflict interaction is characterized by (1) individuals who are aware of their respective costs and benefits, (2) costs and rewards can be objectively evaluated, (3) parties are cognitively aware of their options for various outcomes, and (4) behavioral decision making is based on a rational weighing of costs and benefits (Northrup, 1989; Roloff, 1981). This instrumentally focused negotiation process, according to MR. Hammer and R.G. Rogan (1997), involves "rational discourse between contending parties (i.e., where each party focuses on instrumental, substantive issues and makes logical cost/benefit choices" (p. 10). This rational discourse process has been variously described in the broad field of conflict resolution as problem solving, bargaining, and constructive conflict management (Boardman & Horowitz,

1994; Bush & Folger, 1994). In this way, rationality assumes dominance with bargaining or problem solving being the benchmark of instrumentality.

When applied specifically to crisis/hostage negotiation, resolution is attempted through bargaining that is typified by a quid pro quo interaction (Hammer, 2001). As noted in J.L. Greenstone (1995), this approach includes such specific negotiating tactics as making the perpetrator work for everything he gets, using time to one's advantage, not relinquishing too much too soon to a perpetrator, and getting something for everything given.

Tactically Driven Actions

In addition to bargaining or problem solving as a core concept of the instrumental model as applied to hostage/crisis situations, a second feature is an *active use of tactical force*. That is, a more instrumental approach to crisis negotiation is often anchored in the view that the effectiveness of bargaining (i.e., engaging the hostage taker in quid pro quo exchanges to obtain his or her peaceful surrender) is dependent on law enforcement's strategic use of tactically driven, anxiety-producing, contentious actions designed to convince the hostage taker that it is in his or her own best interests to surrender. FBI guidelines for negotiation in the 1970s and 1980s and early 1990s leaned heavily toward a tactically driven, instrumental model of negotiation. For example, one FBI guideline is that negotiators should attempt to manipulate anxiety through such activities as cutting off electricity and power to the hostage taker (McMains & Mullins, 2006). In addition to cutting off power, there are a variety of other general anxiety-increasing, contentious tactics, including threats, harassment, positional commitment, persuasive argument, and physical force that can be used in critical incidents (Pruitt & Carnevale, 1993; Van de Vliert, 1997).

More specific to the critical incident context, visible displays of weaponry, firepower, personnel, and environmental control are often viewed as central, from a more instrumental perspective, in communicating to the subject the disproportionate odds with which he or she is confronted. Often such anxiety-stimulating tactics as the playing of loud or obnoxious music, shining of bright lights at night, and helicopter flyovers are used to harass the suspect and to produce conditions of deprivation, as well as heightened anxiety (Miron & Goldstein, 1979). Noesner (1999) recommends that in hostage (instrumental) situations, law enforcement should use highly visible (e.g., anxiety enhancing) tactical containment, use delay tactics, have the hostage taker work hard for everything he or she receives from the police, and point out the benefits of surrender compared with the risk of death or injury with a tactical resolution. It is important to realize that the instrumental assumption (albeit not always in awareness) is that the perpetrator is presumed to be rational and his or her emotionality is a variable to be manipulated by the police (A.H. Miller, 1980).

Branch Davidian Siege in 1993

Two situations stand out as examples of this more instrumental approach. During the 1993 cult confrontation with the Branch Davidians in Waco, Texas, the FBI attempted to increase the anxiety of David Koresh, the cult leader, by playing music by Alice Cooper, Andy Williams, Mitch Miller Christmas songs, Tibetan chants, and Muslim prayer calls. Other efforts designed to break the will and disrupt the sleep patterns of David Koresh included amplified sounds of dentist drills, rabbits being killed, and a train crashing. The use of blinding lights and various tactical actions to "constrict the environment" of the subject were also used under the rationale that it is important to demonstrate control and to increase the subject's discomfort.

Confrontation in Roby, Illinois

Another situation arose on September 22, 1997, when sheriff's deputies knocked on the door of 51-year-old Shirley Allen in Roby, Illinois. They were called there on behalf of the family to bring Shirley for a psychological examination. She refused to leave, meeting the deputies at the door with a shotgun. At this point, the critical incident began. From September 22 until October 30, police used tear gas, pepper spray, played loud music throughout the day and night, shot bean bag bullets at her and into her home, and cut off her water and electricity, all in an effort to coerce her cooperation. On one occasion, the authorities sent into the house "J.D.," a police German shepherd. Shirley promptly shot the dog (which subsequently recovered). Finally, on October 30, 1997, as Shirley stepped out on her porch, tactical officers apprehended her. She was not injured.

Central to the instrumental approach in hostage/crisis negotiation is the belief that when presented with such an array of force, all of which serves to highlight the suspect's vulnerability, the perpetrator will be rational enough to decide to surrender. The job of the negotiator, therefore, is to convince the suspect that if he or she surrenders peacefully, he or she will not be harmed (A.H. Miller, 1980).

In the instrumental approach, tactical options play a strong role in determining negotiation strategy. From this perspective, it is the systematic application of tactical actions (e.g., increasing the physical "presence" of SWAT personnel and snipers and firing rounds of "rubber" bullets into the window) that function to coercively "convince" the perpetrator that it is in his or her own best interests to surrender.

This instrumental model, therefore, proposes that crisis negotiation involves a judicious use of contending tactics coupled with a bargaining focus such that the hostage taker will weigh the costs (e.g., possible loss of life) and benefits (e.g., to continue to live) and rationally "work out" a peaceful surrender ritual with the law enforcement negotiator.

Limitations of the Instrumental Approach

While contentious tactics can be useful in some situations in forcing reluctant adversaries to rethink their positions and getting them to the negotiation table, they more often than not fail to produce the positive results desired. The principal limitation of tactically driven, instrumental bargaining is that such behaviors by one party often prompt reciprocal actions by the other. According to D.G. Pruitt and P.J. Carnevale (1993), this often leads to escalatory spirals, with each party retaliating against the other party, resulting in a continual growth in hostility.

Within the instrumental approach, concern for expressive (i.e., emotional and relational) needs is minimized. In fact, within this bargaining framework, emotion is generally regarded as an addendum to the primary instrumental/rational orientation of the subject and the police negotiator (Hammer, 2001; Jones, 1997). This represents one of the most critical limitations of the instrumental model. Further, by focusing primarily on instrumental concerns, other critical relational and identity goal concerns may be overlooked and relegated to secondary status, important only when they impact on instrumental objectives.

Effectiveness of the Instrumental Model

The instrumental approach may be useful when (1) the hostage taker is focused on his or her substantive demands, (2) is willing to bargain to reach an agreement, and most importantly, (3) is ignoring the police presence or is under such a low level of stress and anxiety that he or she is not motivated to move the situation to resolution. Under these conditions, introducing increased tactical presence along with targeted bargaining/problem solving may help convince the hostage taker that, indeed, it is in his or her best interests to negotiate surrender.

However, these conditions are not commonly found in most crisis/hostage negotiations. For example, in a study by W.B. Head (1989), it was discovered that perpetrators made no demands in one-quarter of the 137 incidents analyzed, while in those situations in which demands were communicated, those demands went unsatisfied 57 percent of the time. Unlike other types of nonviolent, instrumentally focused negotiations (e.g., purchasing a home), participants in crisis negotiations rarely, if ever, come to the table with well-developed goals and a willingness to engage in good faith bargaining (Rogan, Donohue, & Lyles, 1990). Rather, crisis/hostage negotiations are most commonly noted for their high levels of uncertainty, anxiety, emotional arousal, and emotional instability. In fact, according to D.A. Soskis and C.R. Van Zandt (1986), most hostage negotiation incidents are the consequence of an individual failing to effectively manage a life-stressing event.

As mentioned earlier, in virtually all of the critical incidents police respond to, the initial arrival of armed police officers and SWAT rescue personnel and camouflaged snipers dramatically increases the stress and anxiety of the hostage taker. Therefore, it is unlikely that manipulation of anxiety should be a primary focus of negotiation efforts. However, should the conditions listed above arise later during an incident, a more tactically driven negotiation (bargaining) strategy may be appropriate.

Most Incidents Are not Instrumentally Focused

A set of recent surveys of hostage negotiation team leaders in the United States reveals that the majority of incidents negotiators actually manage are not what might be classically viewed as instrumental insofar as they involve suicides, barricaded subjects, and domestic disputes (Hammer, Van Zandt, & Rogan, 1994; Rogan, Hammer, & Van Zandt, 1994). Other evidence reported by Noesner (1999) indicates that 86 percent of all incidents can be classified as expressive (i.e., nonhostage). Similarly, McMains and Mullins (2006) note that 82 percent of all police negotiations deal with incidents other than actual true hostage takings. They further suggest that of the 18 percent that did involve a hostage, a notable percentage were "pseudo-hostage-takings" in which the suspect was more intent on making the hostage a victim than using him or her as a bargaining resource (p. 41). Finally, Giebels's (1999) survey of crisis negotiation practice in Europe indicates that 40 percent of crisis incidents can be classified as instrumental and 60 percent as expressive.

As stated earlier, crisis negotiation fundamentally involves an interaction pattern of contentious communication, high emotional arousal, and strong, realistic perceptions of threat (Hammer, 2001). The instrumental model simply does not account well for these types of communicative dynamics. As R.G. Rogan, W.A. Donohue, & J. Lyles (1990) comment regarding the nature of crisis negotiation, "if the interactants reach an impasse, they cannot table the discussion until the following day and return to a more convenient time" (p. 79).

It is precisely within this context that volatile interaction dynamics centered around relational and identity concerns become preeminent. As such, instrumental crisis negotiation approaches that are tactically driven are limited in comprehensively conceptualizing the resolution process of most hostage negotiations. It is this realization that prompted a reconceptualization of hostage negotiation as primarily expressive interaction and crisis interventionist in focus. This conceptual realignment is the basis for the expressive approach of crisis negotiation.

EXPRESSIVE CRISIS NEGOTIATION

The expressive approach to negotiation is principally grounded in psychology (Miron & Goldstein, 1979; Schlossberg, 1979) and human relations theory (Folger, Poole, & Stutman, 1997). Basic to this approach is the presumption that quality interpersonal relationships are critical to effective conflict management, as are the expressive needs of the parties involved. As such, this model focuses on the expressive end of the instrumental-expressive continuum.

According to Schlossberg (1979), a critical characteristic of expressive-based hostage incidents is that the hostage serves no instrumental value to the perpetrator. Rather, the taking of hostages is done for the purpose of drawing attention to the needs or plight of the suspect himself or herself. Similarly, in those incidents in which no hostage is taken (e.g., suicides and barricaded subjects), the goal of the suspect is to gain attention to his or her situation (McMains & Mullins, 2006; Schlossberg, 1979). In this way, the negotiator has nothing that the suspect wants, in a material/instrumental sense. Therefore, attempts to negotiate with the suspect about substantive wants and demands will likely not produce the desired results of a negotiated surrender.

An Emphasis on Emotion

Contrasted with the instrumental approach, the expressive model emphasizes the central role of emotion to incident resolution (Miron & Goldstein, 1979). In fact, managing the suspect's emotional arousal is viewed as central to successful incident resolution (Noesner & Webster, 1997; Rogan & Hammer, 2002). According to Schlossberg (1979), the heightened levels of emotional excitation that characterize perpetrators in these incidents can negatively impact the potential for a negotiated resolution as heightened emotional arousal can lead a perpetrator to react in either a flight or fight response (Cannon, 1929) rather than a more problem-solving direction (A.H. Miller, 1980).

Tactical Actions Support Containment

Because a core goal is to reduce the level of tension by helping the hostage taker "ventilate" in a safe and supportive communicative environment (Hammer & Weaver, 1998), tactical activities in the expressive model function in a far more passive capacity focusing on maintaining secure containment of the situation compared to their active, anxiety-enhancing use in instrumental bargaining approaches. The use of contentious tactics from the perspective of the expressive model is seen as generally increasing the level of anxiety (which is already felt to be high) of the subject and therefore making the incident more—not less—difficult to peacefully resolve.

According to Schlossberg (1979), the tactical function should engage in passive containment, in which a secure environment is maintained such that "an individual who is seeking help can be in a controlled atmosphere..." within which therapeutic dialogue can take place with negotiators (p. 209).

There are two core features of the expressive model as applied to crisis negotiation practice: (1) the important role of crisis intervention skills for dealing with heightened levels of emotional instability and (2) the elevation of psychological disorder (pathology) diagnosis to a privileged position as the basis for interacting with the perpetrator in a crisis incident.

Emotional Instability and Crisis Intervention

The expressive approach to crisis/hostage negotiation focuses attention on the subject's emotional state, particularly his or her level of emotional instability. With this foundation, the expressive model emphasizes the application of therapeutic crisis intervention skills and strategies to effectively help the perpetrator manage potentially dysfunctional levels of anger, fear, and frustration. From this perspective, hostage takers are characterized as experiencing a psychological "crisis" in which the individual is in a state of emotional distress and unable to effectively cope through more customary problem-solving mechanisms (Caplan, 1961; Roberts & Dziegielewski, 1995).

Indeed, this perspective has gained considerable influence in the field with the only textbook devoted specifically to hostage negotiation defining negotiation largely in terms of crisis intervention (McMains & Mullins, 2006). Crisis intervention is designed to address the psychological needs of an individual in distress by helping the person identify more adaptive means of coping with a specific crisis (Roberts & Dziegielewski, 1995). As such, the role of the negotiator becomes one of crisis intervenor rather than instrumental "deal maker."

A Focus on Incident Stages

The expressive model is "stage" focused, in that a number of authors suggest that there are predictable phases that characterize crisis incidents. A.R. Roberts (1991), for example, posits the following seven stages: (1) assess lethality and safety needs, (2) establish communication and rapport, (3) identify primary problems, (4) provide support and deal with feelings, (5) explore alternatives, (6) develop an action plan, and (7) provide follow-up. While some of the crisis intervention stages are appropriate for counseling trauma victims, others are not as applicable to hostage-taking events (e.g., provide follow-up).

McMains and Mullins (2006) identify four central stages of crisis intervention. The first stage is the precrisis phase and represents "business as usual" for both the negotiator and the hostage taker. That is, emotions are under control, stress levels are manageable, and both parties are coping reasonably well with their situation. In the crisis stage, emotions are high, stress is high, and the individual's ability to effective cope is compromised. It is this stage in which crisis negotiation typically begins. The third stage is accommodation in which the hostage taker is able to consider more appropriate (nonviolent) solutions to the crisis situation and problem solving emerges in a more consistent manner. Finally, in the resolution stage, the hostage taker and the negotiator commit to a specific course of action that works out the solution to the crisis.

Empathy and Active Listening Skills

In order to successfully reach the resolution stage, negotiators should work to elicit the concerns and feelings of the suspect and thereby convey an empathic understanding of the perpetrator's (crisis) condition in order to achieve resolution (Rogan et al., 1990). According to G.W. Noesner and M. Webster (1997), the objective of creating an empathic relationship with a perpetrator is ultimately to enable the negotiator to influence the suspect's behavior. This is accomplished by reducing the subject's level of emotional arousal (distress) and then facilitating rational problem solving (Donohue & Roberto, 1993). J.G. Stratton (1978) was one of the first authors to characterize this relationship between emotion and reason, which he viewed "as a teeter-totter where initially emotion is high, reason is low; and as time passes, these two dynamics can move toward a more equal level" (p. 124).

In order to reduce emotional excitation and distress, negotiators learn within the expressive approach crisis intervention techniques that focus on active listening (McMains & Mullins, 2006; Noesner & Webster, 1997; Slatkin, 1996). Active listening skills (e.g., paraphrasing, minimal encouragers, reflecting feelings, mirroring, open-ended questions, and "I" messages) are often regarded as the linchpin in helping perpetrators vent and dissipate pent-up anxiety, thereby enabling a decrease in emotional distress, resulting in more rational problem solving focused on surrender (McMains & Mullins, 2006; Noesner, 1999; Noesner & Webster, 1997).

A number of writers have identified specific guidelines consistent with the more expressive model of crisis negotiation. Noesner (1999) suggests that police should use passive or low visibility tactical deployment, demonstrate patience and empathy toward the hostage taker, be willing to make small concessions (to build trust), use active listening skills to understand the perspective and feelings of the hostage taker, and offer peaceful options for resolving the situation (rather than emphasizing the consequences of a tactical assault). T.N. Davidson (2002) summarizes, largely from an expressive model platform, negotiation guidelines that include (1) slow the process down, in order to calm the hostage taker, (2) stall for time, communicate self-disclosure, be empathic, communicate warmth toward the subject, and minimize the subject's crimes and consequences in order to build rapport with the hostage taker, and (3) avoid lying, try not to say "no" to the subject's demands, and try to be as honest as possible for the duration of the incident in order to build trust.

From the perspective of the expressive model, one of first steps in crisis intervention recommended to crisis negotiators is a psychological assessment of the subject (Hoff, 1989). Building trust between negotiator and suspect (through the application of crisis intervention skills) is considered a critical aspect for de-escalating the situation. This process can be hindered, however, by the psychological state (mental stability) of the perpetrator.

An Emphasis on Psychological Disorder

It has been estimated that the majority of incidents that negotiators actually confront involve a perpetrator characterized by a mental or emotional disorder. This surprising observation was reported by G.D. Fuselier (1981a). Fuselier, based on unpublished research conducted by the FBI (Strentz, 1985), *reported that 52 percent of all negotiation incidents are perpetrated by suspects who have clinically diagnosed mental disorders, involving antisocial personality, depression, paranoia, and inadequate personality.* This finding was quite persuasive to crisis negotiators and clearly pointed to an uncharted need: how to understand the personality disorder and attendant behavioral patterns of hostage takers.

Consequently, a rather sizable body of literature has been devoted to understanding the psychological and personality traits of perpetrators, as well as strategies for negotiating with suspects who exhibit behavior patterns consistent with specific mental and emotional disorder typologies (Borum & Strentz, 1992; Fuselier, 1981a, 1981b; Lanceley, 1981; Lanceley et al., 1985; Office of Security, 1983; Strentz, 1985).

Since this finding was reported, crisis negotiators have increasingly used psychological categories to diagnose the mental health of hostage takers. According to R. Borum and T. Strentz (1992), "this classification allows negotiators to understand the 'style' and motivation of the subject, and therefore, choose a negotiation strategy appropriate for the situation" (p. 6). Thus, for example, the actual needs of a hostage taker who has a borderline personality disorder are considered more expressive than instrumental, with a strong desire for support and recognition rather than money or escape. Negotiators are admonished to provide therapeutic communication that empathizes with and supports this psychological type (Borum & Strentz, 1992).

Fuselier (1981a) indicates that a hostage taker with an inadequate personality demonstrates ineffective behavior to social, physical, and emotional pressure, often has not completed high school, and generally feels that he or she is a failure. For this personality disorder, the taking of hostages may likely reflect the subject's desperate effort to demonstrate competence and success. Fuselier suggests that negotiators communicate sympathy, understanding, and acceptance of the subject and his or her situation. Further, the negotiator should not try to use third-party intermediaries such as family and friends due to a likely animosity toward intimates. Finally, Fuselier argues that the negotiator should present the surrender process in a way that does not make the hostage taker feel he or she has failed again. T. Strentz (1983) offers similar recommendations, suggesting that the negotiator should permit the subject to vent emotions, look to build trust, and provide the hostage taker with basic needs such as food and water.

Quite different assessment and advice is offered when negotiating with a subject who has an antisocial personality disorder. This type of disorder is characterized as a lack of conscience and is considered a psychopath or sociopath. This individual is concerned first and foremost with himself or herself and obtaining, through any means necessary, his or her own demands. Negotiators are advised to avoid lying and be on guard for being deceived by the hostage taker (Fuselier, 1981a; Lanceley, 1981). Antisocial personality types also, according to Strentz (1983), can become easily bored; therefore, he recommends against stalling for time as the hostage taker may vent his anger and violence directly on the hostages.

The United States Department of State suggests specific negotiation strategies for the paranoid schizophrenic, the psychotic depressive, the antisocial personality, and the inadequate personality. For example, when negotiating with the psychotic depressive type, it is recommended that (1) friends and relatives should *not* be brought to the incident site, (2) use directive and explicit communication, and (3) repeat assurances and express confidence that the individual's problems can be solved (Office of Security, 1983, pp. 14–15).

In general, negotiation recommendations are heavily weighted toward the application of crisis intervention listening skills when negotiating with individuals who have these psychological disorders. Even finer distinctions are made within this literature, including the recommendation by G.D. Fuselier (1986) that problem-solving strategies are considerably more useful with a paranoid personality compared to a paranoid schizophrenic.

Undeniably, the expressive model of negotiation has contributed significantly to our understanding and management of crisis/hostage negotiations. The expressive approach focuses attention on crisis intervention skills (e.g., active listening) in order to develop an empathic relationship with a perpetrator. As the emotional distress of the subject is diminished, the negotiator can begin to facilitate problem solving and a more "normative bargaining" mode typified by enhanced deliberation (Donohue & Roberto, 1993). The expressive model also brings attention to the influence of psychological disorders among hostage takers and the role these can play in crisis incidents.

LIMITATIONS OF THE EXPRESSIVE APPROACH

The dichotomization of rationality and emotionality proposed by Stratton (1978) serves, unfortunately, to reinforce an interactionally false separation of instrumentality and expressiveness, wherein an expressive approach to negotiation is employed only to reduce emotionality and thereby facilitate rational problem solving. Further, this position tends to relegate emotion to being an addendum to rationality that must be dealt with only in those incidents noted as expressive and in which it directly impacts on instrumental issues (Hammer, 2001; Putnam, 1994). This artificial separation of rationality and emotion and the presumption that "emotion management" is important only to the extent that rationality can again emerge in the hostage taker is problematic. The separation of rationality and emotionality ignores the observation that crisis situations are more accurately represented as a fluid movement between problem solving or bargaining and empathic communication focused on reducing emotional distress.

Further, the emphasis in the expressive model on a more psychopathological diagnostic approach tends to lead to a static trait operational philosophy when negotiating with hostage takers. Research by Head (1989) reinforces this view, when he concludes the following:

> It is apparent that law enforcement agencies do implicitly and explicitly rely upon typologies of hostage takers in formulating responses to hostage situations. [There seems to be] a clear preference on the part of responding agents to be able to classify a hostage taker into a predisposed category. (p. 144)

As a result, psychopathological diagnostic categories tend to frame negotiators' understanding of the crisis negotiation dynamics solely in terms of the "abnormal" perpetrator. Once so categorized, negotiators run the risk of attempting to communicate to the supposed disorder rather than attending and responding to the interactional dynamics that take place between the hostage taker and the police negotiator.

This is critical, as debates about the validity of personality constructs and their importance in explaining and predicting human behavior have been going on for years (Daly & Bippus, 1998). For example, questions have been raised about the cross-situational consistency of behaviors associated with traits (Mischel, 1968); the situational relevance (person-by-situation interaction) of traits, wherein personality constructs are applicable only in certain situations (Mischel, 1999); and the general relevancy of traits across individuals (trait relevancy) where the importance of a trait varies differentially for individuals (Britt & Sheppherd, 1999). In an attempt to answer these questions, research has attempted to explore the precise nature of the relationship between various individual personality traits and communication/behavior (Daly, 2002).

While researchers have concluded that individual personality traits do affect how people communicate/behave in various contexts, we are warned to be cautious about focusing too extensively on any one single trait, as people possess multiple characteristics, all of which interact to form a behavioral predisposition (Daly, 2002).

Inattention to Interaction

A person's personality can and does affect the general behavior of another person and specifically conflict management practices (Wilson & Waltman, 1988). However, by focusing on the pathology of the individual subject, attention to the interactive nature of human communication/behavior in crisis events is minimized. As J.S. Docherty (1998) cogently suggests, "the other party to the interaction (the police) remains unexamined and the interactive process itself is largely ignored as a possible cause of the subjects' behavior" (p. 94). As evidence for this claim, Docherty's (1998) analysis of the negotiation dynamics present during the Branch Davidian siege in Waco, Texas, indicates that "FBI negotiators continued to pursue this [psychopathological] diagnostic approach even when the wildly contradictory diagnoses offered by the experts rendered the formulation of a coherent negotiation strategy extremely difficult, perhaps impossible" (p. 96).[4]

Further, diagnosing a hostage taker's psychological disorder (assuming this can be done on scene, which itself is a problematic assumption) simply does not provide sufficient information or predictability for negotiators to rely on when selecting strategies for resolving the situation peacefully. According to Docherty (1998), crisis negotiation simply is far more of an "interactive improvisation" than a scripted event (p. 87).

Far-Reaching Effects

This emphasis in crisis negotiation theory and practice on the psychopathology of the hostage taker has had far-reaching effects. In addition to the limitations of accurate assessment of hostage takers in terms of their psychopathological makeup, police departments rapidly added hostage negotiation team "consultants" who were predominately (if not exclusively) from the "mental health" profession, notably psychologists (Butler, 1991) whose specializations typically were in abnormal psychology or clinical psychology. Absent from this development were, for example, communication experts, social psychologists, and intergroup dynamics scholars. Given the apparent prevalence of mental disorders among hostage takers, however, the prioritization of abnormal and clinical psychology mental health professionals seemed warranted. But how prevalent are mental disorders in crisis incidents?

ARE PSYCHOLOGICAL DISORDERS AMONG HOSTAGE TAKERS OVERESTIMATED?

There is no question that research conducted by the FBI from the late 1970s to the early 1980s was most influential in launching crisis negotiation theory and practice toward an examination of mental disorders in hostage taking. One of the most influential research efforts was conducted by the FBI. This study examined 245 hostage-taking incidents that involved 292 perpetrators between the years 1976 and 1983. While the results from this research were unpublished (Strentz, 1985), one of the most frequently cited statistics from this work is that somewhere between 52 percent (Borum & Strentz, 1992; Fuselier, 1986, 1988; Strentz, 1983) and 59 percent (Soskis & Van Zandt, 1986) of hostage incidents involve mentally disturbed individuals. Further, this research (Strentz, 1985) is also cited as the basis for the finding that "the persons who most frequently take hostages in the United States can be divided into four major psychiatric classifications paranoid schizophrenic, depressed categories,. . .antisocial and inadequate personalities" (Strentz, 1983, p. 363) (see also Fuselier, 1981a, 1981b).

Other writers suggest that the figures of 52 to 59 percent of hostage takers suffer from a diagnosable mental disorder may be considerably higher. Borum and Strentz (1992) suggest that "the actual figure may be much higher because hostage takers with mental disorders frequently exhibit the characteristics of more than one classification and may be classified according to the circumstances of the situation" (p. 6). Borum and Strentz (1992) go on to give the example that an individual with an antisocial personality disorder who takes hostages while robbing a business may be classified as a "trapped criminal" rather than a mentally disturbed hostage taker.

This seminal research by the FBI (Borum & Strentz, 1992; Fuselier, 1986, 1988; Soskis & Van Zandt, 1986; Strentz, 1983, 1985) was very influential in bringing psychologists and a focus on the psychopathology of hostage takers into crisis negotiation practices within the expressive approach. Yet a review of the actual "coding" that was completed in this original research on the 245 hostage incidents casts doubt regarding the pandemic mental disorders of hostage takers.

The actual item (in the questionnaire) that was employed to determine the categorization of hostage takers consisted of five response categories: (1) trapped criminal, (2) emotionally disturbed, (3) political, (4) inmate, and (5) combination. From a social science methods perspective, it is somewhat problematic that a limited set of a priori categories were used rather than determining the codes of the overall hostage taker "type" by a close, unrestricted analysis of each incident. A more detailed and perhaps more useful set of discriminatory categories would likely have emerged from this type of verifiable analysis than the five general types listed above.

Emotionally Disturbed Is not Emotionally Disordered

Of more importance, however, is the definition of the category "emotionally disturbed," which actually consisted of *any emotional reason* for the incident (e.g., a domestic dispute, being fired from the job, and/or being depressed or psychotic) (Butler, 1991). In this seminal study of hostage incidents between 1976 and 1983, the FBI reported that 52 to 59 percent of the incidents were identified, therefore, as fitting the emotionally disturbed category, of which presumably, some additional inferences were drawn to further specify that the following four psychological disorders comprised the category of emotionally disturbed: depressive disorder, psychotic disorder, antisocial personality, and inadequate personality. In other words, if "any emotional reason" constitutes the category of emotionally disturbed (which was then interpreted as emotionally disordered), then any subject who has some level of emotional upset during an incident could be classified as emotionally disturbed. It is not surprising, therefore, that such a high number (59 percent) of subjects would be so classified. However, there is no evidence offered in the response options to the questionnaire in this early research study that the subjects, in fact, suffered from a diagnosable psychological *disorder*.

It should also be noted that in this original study, actual verification of the information obtained from the research questionnaire was limited to the self-reported statements of the respondents (predominately police officers) who submitted their responses to the survey. Therefore, it is questionable whether police negotiators had sufficient background to make valid judgments concerning the mental health of the hostage takers.

Based on the reported research method of this seminal study, no systematic effort was undertaken to "objectively" determine if any of the hostage takers were actually diagnosed as suffering from any psychological disorder either prior to or immediately following the hostage-taking incident. This is of central importance when classifying incidents or perpetrators as suffering from mental instability or identified mental disorders. Clearly, the task of providing an accurate psychological assessment is often difficult due to lack of sufficient prior information, inability to conduct sufficient follow-up interviews to determine an accurate diagnosis, and the perpetrator's actual behavior during the course of the incident. For example, with such "objective" data on the mental state of the subject, it is almost impossible to determine whether a subject's behavior is more reflective of a mental disorder or simply heightened levels of stress.

Because of these and other difficulties, four objective, behavioral criteria for classification of a perpetrator's mental state during the time of a crisis incident are warranted in evaluating the veracity of mental health diagnosis: (1) evidence of prior diagnosis of identifiable mental disorder, (2) postincident psychological assessment that documents specific mental disorder (using in-depth interviews and standard testing), (3) evidence of psychotropic medication prescribed to the perpetrator prior to the incident and evidence the individual was no longer using such medication during the incident, and (4) evidence, via systematic discourse analysis of the diagnosed mental illness patterns made manifest during the incident (e.g., hallucinations and delusions). None of these criteria were employed in this original research project; *thus, the accuracy of the conclusion concerning the high prevalence of mental disorders among hostage takers is not supported.*

Perhaps of most concern is that the category of "emotionally disturbed" was not defined *at all in terms of diagnosable mental illness.* Rather, any emotional reason, including a domestic dispute, references the broader category of expressive behavior delineated by Miron and Goldstein (1979). It is widely recognized that emotional upset is a core characteristic of conflict, even more so during violent confrontations. As such, all persons involved in such highly charged interactions as crisis negotiations are likely to manifest heightened levels of emotionality (Rogan, 1997). Therefore, simply because the hostage taker evidenced behavior reflective of being emotionally upset does not at all suggest that he or she is exhibiting behavior reflective of a psychological disorder.

A Reinterpretation

Thus, a reinterpretation of the 1983 reported research by the FBI (Strentz, 1985) may be in order. Accepting the somewhat dubious conclusion that individual police responses to the questionnaire were reasonably accurate in reporting whether hostage takers experienced some level of emotional upset, it is not surprising that over half of the reported incidents involved an emotionally distraught hostage taker (i.e., he or she is upset about something). However, *there is no evidence that a subject who may be emotionally upset is suffering from any mental disorder whatsoever.*

A similar caution can be made concerning research reported by Feldmann (2001). In this study, 12 hostage/barricade incidents originally developed by the Department of Psychiatry and Behavioral Sciences at the University of Louisville School of Medicine were examined. Assuming some level of generalizability, Feldmann (2001) reports 19 percent of the perpetrators displayed primary signs of mental illness.[5] This figure is based on the criteria that individuals operated "under the influence of significant psychopathology such as delusions, paranoid or grandiose thinking, or hallucinations" or "those with major depression, unrelated to an interpersonal problem, accompanied by strong suicidal impulses" (p. 23). With these more behaviorally articulated criteria specified, these data suggest mental illness is far less prevalent in crisis incidents than the reported 50 to 60 percent figure cited in the earlier, seminal study (Strentz, 1985) conducted by the FBI.

Feldman (2001) goes on to report, however, that psychiatric diagnoses were found in *97 percent of all the incidents* using DSM-IV (*Diagnostic and Statistical Manual of Mental Disorders,* 4th ed.) guidelines, with the most common being depression (22 percent), antisocial personality disorder (20 percent), borderline personality disorder (9 percent), polysubstance abuse and dependence (7 percent), alcohol intoxication (6 percent), schizophrenia (6 percent), conduct disorder (6 percent), and cocaine abuse and dependence (6 percent). The author concludes, not unexpectedly, that "given the high levels of psychopathology among hostage-takers, the complex dynamics of the negotiation process, and the levels of stress inherent in such situations, mental health professionals should be utilized as consultants by police hostage negotiation teams" (p. 30).

How accurate, however, is the finding that *97 percent of all incidents* involved hostage takers who suffer from mental illness? First, a number of the "psychiatric" categories are not clear insofar as whether they actually reflect psychopathology. For instance, it is unclear in the study whether substance *use* (e.g., alcohol and cocaine) was assessed or whether long-standing substance *abuse* that is made manifest in the behavior of the hostage taker throughout a crisis event was assessed. Unfortunately, the author does not provide explanations for how these types of psychopathology diagnoses were made, particularly in those incidents that were *not* categorized as involving mentally ill hostage takers.

In terms of the assessment of mental disorders of depression, antisocial personality, borderline personality, and schizophrenia, it is notoriously difficult to make such a diagnosis either during an incident or "after the fact" unless extensive interviewing and standardized testing is conducted. Therefore, restricting such inferences of these types of mental illnesses to more observable criteria discussed earlier (prior diagnosis, postincident diagnosis, behavioral patterns evidenced during the incident, and psychotropic medication) is warranted. While it is unclear how these diagnoses were actually completed, the author reports findings from one such objective measure, namely, whether the subject was taking psychotropic medication at the time of the incident. Again, only 17 percent of the subjects evidenced mental illness through this more objective measure.

Thus, the author's conclusion that mental health professionals *specifically* are needed as incident advisors because of the high degree of mental illness among subjects is not supported in his own data. Rather, some of the stronger evidence for the presence of mental illness within his sample suggests a range from 17 percent (indicated by use of psychotropic medicine at the time of the incident) to 19 percent (categorized as mental illness using stated criteria). The author's incorporation of these two, more objective criteria represents a valuable contribution to understanding the role of mental illness in crisis events.

HOBAS Data on Mental Illness of Hostage Takers

Recent data obtained from 4,784 crisis incidents collected by the FBI through the Hostage Barricade Database System (HOBAS) project (Crisis Management Unit, 2006) provides, again, a much lower estimate of the degree to which perpetrators suffer from mental disorders compared to the 52–59 percent figure of the original FBI study (Strentz, 1985). While the HOBAS questionnaire is typically completed by the submitting police officer and therefore suffers from the same difficulties in determining veracity and reliability of responses as the earlier FBI study, the questionnaire items in the HOBAS questionnaire are more behaviorally focused than items from the seminal FBI survey reported by T. Strentz (1985).

One particular question from the HOBAS survey directly addresses the issue of whether subjects experienced mental health difficulties. To this question, respondents selected from the following response options: (1) committed in past to state mental health facility, (2) no known current problems, (3) no known prior(s), (4) other, (5) receiving counseling/therapy, and (6) residential treatment facility. Unfortunately, the respondents are instructed to "select all (options) that apply." This instruction makes it difficult to accurately estimate the number or percentage of incidents in which the hostage taker suffered from mental health problems (multiple checks are possible for the same incident). With this in mind, a cautious interpretation of responses to this question reveals that 7 percent of the responses indicated the subject was committed in the past to a state mental facility and 1 percent of the responses indicated subjects had residential treatment (both objective measures of mental disorder problems). Further, only 10 percent of the responses indicated any counseling or therapy given to the hostage taker (it is unclear whether this response option refers to counseling given prior to the incident or following the event). Overall, assuming some minimally acceptable level of accuracy with these data, the HOBAS data seem to suggest that the percentage of hostage takers who are actually suffering from a mental disorder is much lower than the figures reported by Fuselier (1981a) and Strentz (1985) in the original FBI research.

With this in mind, the HOBAS data, along with the more objective data from the Feldmann (2001) study, suggest that it is more likely that *7–19 percent of crisis incidents involve individuals who have a diagnosed mental disorder*. This number is a far cry from the early estimates that 52–59 percent of hostage takers suffer from a mental disorder.

Implications

The implications from this reinterpretation of past studies are quite substantial. First, it appears that the emphasis on psychological pathology as a critical concern in crisis negotiation, while clearly important, is nevertheless vastly overrated. While the recent HOBAS data collected by the FBI reveal that a substantial number of crisis incidents can be characterized as expressive in focus, *far fewer crisis incidents involve hostage takers who are suffering from a diagnosed mental disorder.*

Second, because of the overextended focus on hostage taker's psycho pathology, sufficient research and theory development has *not* been directed toward understanding the interactive dynamics involved in crisis situations.

Third, psychologists have increasingly been the "consultant of choice" for crisis negotiation teams. As Soskis and Van Zandt (1986) comment, "clinicians are sometimes called in as consultants in such situations, either because they have a direct knowledge of the hostage taker or because they are familiar with the disorder from which he suffers" (p. 425). The data suggest that the hostage taker does not suffer a psychological disorder nearly to the degree psychologists contend. This is not to say, however, that the contribution of clinical and abnormal psychologists to hostage negotiation teams has been unimportant (Butler, 1991). In fact, around issues of postincident stress debriefing, emotional stabilization of possible third-party intermediaries, and review of mental health records of a hostage taker (or hostages/victims) obtained during an incident, mental health professionals make an invaluable contribution.

The result from this overstatement of the prevalence of psychological disorders among hostage takers is, at times, an effort among negotiation teams and their mental health advisors to overpathologize the observed behavior patterns of the subject. This can result in an inaccurate labeling of a hostage taker as "antisocial" when there is no firm evidence to support such a diagnosis. This occurred, for example, during the Waco siege, reflected by the FBI's unproductive obsession with figuring out a psychological diagnosis at the expense of focusing more attention on understanding the interactional dynamics present in the situation (Docherty, 1998).

Another outcome from this psychopathologizing of hostage-taker actions is that other behavioral and social science trained experts (e.g., in communication, conflict resolution, and intergroup relations), who may have a broader set of capabilities and consequently more targeted contributions concerning human behavior in crisis contexts, have not been generally incorporated as incident advisors by crisis negotiators.

The dominance of a psychological (particularly a psychopathology) framework is institutionalized in recommendations to hostage negotiation teams across the United States through the National Council of Negotiation Associations (NCNA). This national organization is comprised of representatives of the major crisis/hostage law enforcement organizations in the United States. In the NCNA guidelines for effective crisis negotiation practice, it offers recommendation #7: "Negotiation teams should consider establishing a consultative relationship with a *mental health professional (s)* to serve as team advisor, participate in negotiation team training, respond to team call outs, focus on behavioral assessment of the subject, and assist in team de-briefings" (NCNA Guidelines, 2001, p. 3). This recommendation would seem to explicitly exclude other behavioral science expertise from providing useful advisement to critical incidents. Rather than frame this recommendation in terms of mental health professionals only, the recommendation should actively incorporate a wider lens, namely, behavioral science expertise *and* mental health professionals. This would be in keeping with P.B. Heymann's (1993) recommendation from the Justice Department's review of the Branch Davidian siege, "It is important to have and be able to use a behavioral science component that can advise the tactical and negotiation groups about what to anticipate" (p. 6).

Overall, it is argued that the emergence and dominance of the expressive model (grounded in psychopathology diagnosis) among crisis negotiators and the unwarranted exclusion of other behavioral sciences in consultancy and advisory capacities has arisen based in part on a small set (10 percent) of crisis incidents in which hostage takers may manifest a specific psychological disorder while the incident is unfolding. This has led to a concomitant neglect of the more complex, interactive context in which conflict escalates and de-escalates in crisis incidents more generally.

In order to correct a possible misinterpretation of the analysis presented in this chapter concerning the limitations of the expressive model, let me state unequivocally that overall, the expressive approach, with its focus on a therapeutic crisis intervention approach, has been a welcome and significant contribution to the crisis negotiation field. The expressive approach clearly broadens the focus and skills of negotiators beyond traditional terrorist and other more instrumentally oriented incidents. The expressive model draws attention to more effective suicide response options, allows for tactical options to focus more on containment rather than solely on manipulating anxiety, and helps police negotiators better empathize with the situation of the hostage taker. Further, the expressive model has provided valuable information regarding patterns of thought and behavior associated with particular psychological disorders, which are relevant in some critical incidents, albeit in far fewer (10 percent) than assumed.

Landover Mall Siege: An Exemplar of Expressive Negotiation Practice

One of the pioneers in expanding negotiation practice beyond tactically driven, instrumental bargaining is William Hogewood. As a police hostage negotiator and trainer, Officer Hogewood has been a leader in developing and applying crisis intervention skills for negotiators that are useful across a wide range of incidents. As a crisis negotiator, he faced one of the most harrowing situations a police officer can encounter on February 9, 1983, in the Landover Mall in Hyattsville, Maryland, just outside Washington, D.C. This incident was resolved peacefully because of Hogewood's effective application of negotiation strategies grounded in the expressive model.

Upon arriving on scene, Hogewood was told that a 21-year-old man, Lennie Dunmore, was holding 12 people hostage. Lennie was sitting on a chair in a room with a briefcase in his lap. Around his neck was a leather collar with two pipes connected by wires to the briefcase. He kept his finger on a switch. Clearly, Dunmore appeared to have a bomb. Further he gave the police a list of demands. In addition, police found bomb-making materials in Dunmore's home along with an explosive charge hidden in his brother's electric razor.

On the surface, this incident might appear to be a terrorist incident and therefore would fit a more instrumental focused negotiation approach. In 1983, while many negotiation teams still depended on a strong show of force in order to coerce the hostage taker to consider his options and surrender (i.e., the instrumental model), Hogewood sensed that this more tactically driven approach would not be successful in this situation and a more expressive focused strategy was more appropriate. Rather than look for ways to manipulate the hostage taker's anxiety level, the negotiator (Hogewood) was concerned about making sure Dunmore did not become more upset.

How was this accomplished? First, the negotiator made sure that tactical presence was minimized. This is not to suggest, however, that the tactical squad remained passive—far from it. Rather, the SWAT members worked to cut a hole through the side wall and carefully removed all of the hostages to safety. While this action was taking place, the negotiator was calming the subject and assuring Dunmore that he was concerned for Dunmore's safety. At one point, Hogewood said to the hostage taker, "Lennie, I know you're upset; I don't want you to get hurt" (Gregg, 1983). Hogewood used active listening skills to hear Dunmore's story and to empathize with his concerns. Further, a search of Dunmore's health records revealed he had been previously diagnosed as a paranoid schizophrenic. One negotiation strategy adapted by Hogewood was to maintain respect for Dunmore's space needs, consistent with observed behavior patterns associated with paranoid schizophrenia.

Two hours into the negotiation, Hogewood offered Lennie coffee and cigarettes. At that point, Hogewood said he was concerned Lennie would harm himself with the bomb and how it was important that they trusted one another. Shortly thereafter, Hogewood asked Lennie if he was ready to come out. A few minutes later, Dunmore disengaged the bomb and peacefully surrendered. This incident is a powerful example of the contribution the expressive approach to crisis negotiation has made—and continues to make—in resolving violent situations.

Insofar as the social sciences are continually gaining more knowledge concerning human behavior, so it is with theory development and practice in crisis negotiation. The contributions of incident typologies, instrumental, and expressive models are substantial in increasing understanding of critical incidents and assisting negotiation efforts at resolving such events. As contributions are realized, additional questions emerge. One core concern is that the three models discussed do not focus sufficient attention on the identification of deeper interaction goals that emerge and define the negotiation dynamic between hostage takers and negotiators. In short, attending to the instrumental demands or the emotional state of the hostage taker is only part of the negotiation process and must be integrated with other equally salient aspects of negotiation.

A COMMUNICATION-BASED APPROACH

It is clear that the development of "theory" in crisis negotiation is in its infancy. Nevertheless, in spite of the cautions identified in this chapter, emerging insights concerning the relevance and application of incident typologies, instrumental strategies, and expressive crisis intervention techniques in the service of peaceful resolution of violent confrontations has been important and will continue to play a role in negotiating the complex array of crisis incidents police negotiators face each and every day.

The communication-based approach articulated in the remainder of this book is based on the view that instrumental and expressive approaches should not be characterized as a dichotomous set of behaviors, but a confluence of emotion and rationality, wherein emotion is a critical dimension of all decision making and behavior (Adler, Rosen, & Silverstein, 1998; Goleman, 1995; Rogan, 1997). Conceptually integrating insights concerning instrumental and expressive negotiation dynamics is particularly useful for both theory development and practice.

It is the contention of this book that an analysis of the actual discourse of crisis negotiation, based on a communication framework, can help identify those specific aspects of crisis conflict dynamics that are central to conflict escalation and de-escalation processes and the peaceful resolution of these emotionally and instrumentally difficult interactions.

PART II

The S.A.F.E. Model for Negotiating Critical Incidents

CHAPTER 4

The S.A.F.E. Model: Negotiating Substantive Demands

FROM THEORY TO PRACTICE

The development of the applied, S.A.F.E. model that crisis/hostage negotiators can use on scene as a critical incident unfolds demands a perspective toward inquiry that fluidly moves between theory development and the chaotic world of experience of the hostage negotiator. This takes two forms in my own work in articulating the S.A.F.E. model in the next two chapters. On the one hand, for a number of years, I have been fortunate to be part of hostage negotiation teams in the Washington, D.C., area where I helped develop negotiation strategies to de-escalate and resolve these violent situations. Thus, every theoretical "concept" of the S.A.F.E. model had virtually instant "real-world" application and testing of its usefulness to these types of events. On the other hand, I have been conducting various analyses of audiotaped incidents, again, to more precisely refine particular S.A.F.E. concepts or to test in discourse the applicability of these concepts.

The result of my continual efforts to marry "theory with practice" in this book is the identification of four carefully selected actual crisis negotiation "cases" that are reviewed in Chapters 6–9. The discourse analysis I conducted on the four cases provides a social scientific basis for the S.A.F.E. model both in terms of its theoretical concepts and applied negotiation strategies to resolve violent situations.

"We're Still Trying to Figure out What Happened"

On Tuesday, March 14, 2006, Aleksandrin Bozhilov, age 30, stopped at an Exxon gas station and pumped gas into the tank of his green Ford Escort. The total came to less than $20. When he went inside the station, he did not pay this small amount; rather, he grabbed the cashier and held her captive for four hours, during which time sheriff's deputies surrounded the gas station and hostage negotiators attempted to communicate with Mr. Bozhilov. However, he often hung up the telephone, although at one point he told negotiators he would surrender. Yet another time, he indicated he wanted to kill the hostage and himself. At 8:20 P.M., Mr. Bozhilov exited the front door with the cashier firmly held in front of him, holding a scissors to her throat. Her shirt and neck were covered in blood. A police sniper then fired a shot, killing Mr. Bozhilov.

Police authorities at first thought this was a robbery. However, this explanation did not seem very likely as a police officer was present, with lights flashing, at a car accident that had happened on the road just in front of the store. Sheriff Simpson commented, "It was not really a scene you're going to look for when you're going to commit a robbery" (Brulliard, 2006, p. B01). Authorities thought Bozhilov might have known his hostage, but there was no prior relationship. Police negotiators during this ordeal were not able to determine a motive for Bozhilov's actions. This incident ended in the saved life of the hostage. It also ended in a death. "We're still trying to figure out what happened—why he did this. Just nothing worked," said Sheriff Simpson (Brulliard, 2006, p. B01).

In Part II, I present a detailed discussion of the S.A.F.E. model, an additional tool police authorities can use in situations like the one involving Mr. Bozhilov. In this chapter, I review the conceptual stance of the model, focusing on the underlying assumptions and some key theoretical foundations. In Chapter 5, I present an in-depth explanation of the four frames of the S.A.F.E. approach, emphasizing how police negotiation teams can track key elements of each S.A.F.E. frame and what specific communication strategies negotiators can use to de-escalate these volatile situations.

From F.I.R.E. to S.A.F.E.

It was in the mid 1990s that Dr. R.G. Rogan and I began publishing our work on a communicative approach to crisis/hostage negotiation (e.g., Rogan & Hammer, 1994, 1995). At that time, a four-part framework began to emerge as a promising line of investigation regarding escalation and de-escalation patterns of crisis incidents. We initially termed this framework the F.I.R.E. model (e.g., Hammer, 1997, 1999; Rogan, 1999; Rogan, Hammer, & Van Zandt, 1997). The acronym F.I.R.E. represented *F*ace, *I*nstrumental demands, *R*elationship, and *E*motion. In presenting this early framework, police negotiators welcomed the four dimensions as useful to think about as they negotiated with a subject.

However, some negotiators commented that the acronym F.I.R.E. might be problematic. They stated that the F.I.R.E. acronym could be misinterpreted outside law enforcement as a more "tactical" approach for resolving incidents, rather than the "negotiated" approach advocated by Dr. Rogan and me. Based on this feedback, we changed the acronym to S.A.F.E., a better symbol of the approach we were developing.

I mention this example because it illustrates how the practical experiences of crisis negotiators played an important role in the development of the initial statement of the S.A.F.E. framework. Further, the experiences of negotiators continue to play an integral role in further refining the S.A.F.E. model presented in this book.

The Cart before the Horse

The overview of the S.A.F.E. model presented in Part II, in one sense, is "putting the cart before the horse." That is, the "cart" in this case represents the deductive formulation of the S.A.F.E. model (which includes the theoretical statement as well as the applied analytical templates and negotiation strategies), while the "horse" alludes to the inductive process of incident analysis that is captured in summary form in Chapters 7–10. In other words, the actual work reported in this book was inductively derived and focuses on deep analysis of the four crisis incidents. During the course of this analysis, various tentative "hypotheses" emerged, which were then "tested" in subsequent discourse episodes. This resulted in the more formal statement of the S.A.F.E. theoretical framework presented in Part II.

I decided to "put the horse before the cart" in order to enable a more coherent reading of the discourse analysis presented in subsequent chapters. With the more detailed and expansive formulation of the S.A.F.E. model presented first, discourse episodes from the four incidents are identified and the analysis articulated in ways that demonstrate specific elements and formulations of the S.A.F.E. theory.

Researchers interested in reviewing the philosophical basis, delineation of the assumptions, and the metatheoretical stance taken in developing the S.A.F.E. model are encouraged to review Appendix A. Further, Appendix B provides a detailed summary of the discourse analysis methodology used in the study. In this current chapter, the S.A.F.E. model is introduced, followed by an in-depth discussion of the substantive demand frame.

A Communication Perspective

It has been only since the late 1980s that researchers began to explore the communicative dynamics of crisis negotiation. Contrasted specifically with the instrumental and expressive approaches, where relatively stable qualities and behaviors of the perpetrator are emphasized, a communication-based approach focuses on the functional meaning of communicative messages and symbols as they emerge during interaction between the subject and the crisis/hostage negotiator.

A communication perspective toward crisis negotiation is grounded in four principles. First, focus is directed toward microanalysis of verbal and nonverbal behavior. Second, attention is given to how meaning is constructed in social contexts. Third, discourse elements are viewed as core skills for conflict analysis and conflict-resolution practices (Folger & Jones, 2004; Jones, 2006). Finally, frames are the interpretive structure within which meaning is constructed and behaviorally enacted. That is, frames enable individuals to perceive and respond to others in their social environment. Within an interpretive frame are specific "conflictual issues" that emerge during a critical incident. The S.A.F.E. model suggests that the police negotiator and the subject "negotiate" conflictual issues (topics) that are "framed" around substantive demands, attunement, face, and emotional distress.

The S.A.F.E. model identifies key features of how issues are viewed by the subject within each frame and provides guidelines for *tracking* substantive demand, attunement, face, and emotional distress issues. In addition, the S.A.F.E. model identifies various substantive demand, attunement, face, and emotional distress *strategies* police negotiators may employ to de-escalate the situation when communicating with the subject in the identified frame of the hostage taker.

It should be noted that the specific information presented on the S.A.F.E. model is not sufficient for police or other negotiators or crisis interveners to competently implement when a crisis or critical incident arises. In order to ensure the S.A.F.E. approach is appropriately used, law enforcement critical incident teams and individuals who have need for this training attend an in-depth training program entitled *Using the S.A.F.E. Model in Crisis Incidents* (for more information, go to www.hammerconsulting.org). During this program, participants receive targeted, applied resources for effectively using the S.A.F.E. approach, including a S.A.F.E. field guide (Hammer, 2005b), a set of S.A.F.E. assessment tools (Hammer, 2005c), and S.A.F.E. analysis worksheets that can be completed as a crisis unfolds (Hammer, 2005d).

THE S.A.F.E. MODEL AND CRISIS NEGOTIATION STRATEGY DEVELOPMENT

The S.A.F.E. model is designed to support critical incident management protocols through the development of more comprehensive negotiation strategy. Crisis negotiation strategy, from the S.A.F.E. perspective, is a communication plan to influence the behavior of the subject to peacefully surrender or assist in a tactical resolution of the incident (Hammer, 2005b).

The development of a crisis negotiation strategy is important for a number of reasons.

Increased Understanding of Subject's Behavior

First, a strategic approach in negotiation permits increased understanding and predictability of the subject's (and hostage/victim's) behavior. Therefore, both tactical actions and negotiation messages can be more effectively aligned with the predominant orientation of the subject.

Aids Incident Command Decision Making

Second, a crisis negotiation strategy aids incident command in decision making. Crisis negotiation teams have, historically, lagged behind their tactical brothers and sisters in the development of a critical incident resolution strategy. Traditional "instrumental" model approaches largely view negotiation strategy in terms of bargaining for demands, while the "expressive" approaches primarily equate negotiation strategy to the use of active listening skills as a way to understand and ultimately influence the subject. In both of these traditional approaches, little attention is directed toward understanding escalation and de-escalation patterns that arise as the incident develops.

This lack of a clearly articulated negotiation strategy has historically been a problem when incident commanders request input from the tactical and negotiation teams. Tactical input is usually presented as a detailed strategic plan that identifies entry points, obstacles, and assault team actions. In contrast, the negotiation "strategy" often is phrased as "we'll keep talking to the subject." Without a more clearly delineated negotiation strategy, incident command may find the tactical team's detailed rescue strategy more compelling when, in fact, negotiation is sufficiently progressing toward a peaceful resolution.

Strategic Response to Public Challenges

Third, a negotiation strategy is important when public and legal challenges are lodged against police response to a critical incident, particularly when a tactical resolution is implemented. In this regard, G.W. Noesner (1999) suggests that incident commanders should ask three questions about which strategies to employ in a crisis event: (1) Is the action necessary? (2) Is the action risk effective? (3) Is the action acceptable? Unfortunately, these three questions are not always addressed at the command level during crisis incidents.

Today, there is increased public scrutiny of these types of high visibility/high stakes events. Various government agencies, citizen review boards, community activist organizations, and the media often ask three questions about a tactical resolution: (1) Did the police have to use a tactical approach? (2) What changed in the situation to warrant a tactical response? (3) What was the negotiation strategy used? (Hare, 2004).

The S.A.F.E. model identifies escalation and de-escalation patterns in an incident and proposes possible negotiation strategies. As such, the S.A.F.E. framework is explicitly designed to generate a more comprehensive response to the question, "what is our crisis negotiation strategy?"

Current negotiation practices, however, rely on various lists of incident "indicators" to assess escalation and de-escalation patterns in an event. For example, T. Strentz (1995) suggests ten indicators of incident de-escalation:

1. Hostages have not been killed since the start of the incident.
2. Threats toward hostages have decreased.
3. The subject has been talking for longer periods of time (to the negotiator).
4. Demands have been moving from instrumental substantive to expressive.
5. The subject has been using a lower tone of voice and talking slower.
6. The subject has been talking about the hostages in more individual terms.
7. Deadlines have passed without action by the subject.
8. Exchanges have taken place without problems.
9. Hostages have been released since the incident began.
10. The police negotiator has developed a more trusting relationship with the subject.

While these lists are clearly helpful and likely reflect generally useful indicators of de-escalation in a crisis incident, there is little guidance for the negotiation team in using these indicators to make a strategic assessment of whether a situation is escalating or de-escalating, particularly when conflicting evidence arises around these indicators. For example, in a particular incident, a hostage taker may not have killed anyone since the start of the incident, and the negotiation team also notes that the subject's demands are becoming more expressive. Both of these are proposed indicators of de-escalation. However, the negotiator also reports that threats to the hostages have increased and the subject is becoming more agitated (higher tone of voice and talking faster and louder), both possible signs of escalation. Is the situation escalating or de-escalating?

S.A.F.E. INTERACTION PROCESS

Before discussing in detail each of the four S.A.F.E. frames, the S.A.F.E. model suggests three core interactive processes for police negotiators to engage. The first process is the *identification of the predominant S.A.F.E. frame of the subject and the police negotiator*. Is the subject communicatively framing his or her interaction with the police negotiator in terms of bargaining or problem-solving expressed demands (substantive demand frame), relational trust or mistrust toward the negotiator or others (attunement frame), sensitivity to how he or she is being perceived by the negotiator or others (face frame), or how upset, angry, sad, etc., the subject is (emotional distress frame)? Is the police negotiator communicating with the subject from a substantive demand, attunement, face, or emotional distress frame?

The second interactive process is for the police negotiator to *match his or her communication to the predominant S.A.F.E. frame of the subject.* That is, the negotiator needs to engage the subject within his or her primary S.A.F.E. frame. This means engaging in strategic negotiation of relational trust and mistrust if the subject is largely in an attunement frame, or negotiating emotional distress if the subject is experiencing heightened emotional difficulties that are interfering with his or her ability to cope with the current, volatile situation. How this is accomplished is discussed later in Part II for each of these frames.

The third process is for the negotiator to *shift the subject to another S.A.F.E. frame after achieving some "progress" in de-escalating the situation* and addressing the underlying needs of the subject within his or her predominant frame. This frame-shifting process enables the police negotiator to exert influence with the hostage taker and can lead to further de-escalation and a peaceful resolution (Hammer, 2001, 2005b, 2005c). Figure 4.1 graphically portrays this three-part process.

The S.A.F.E. approach highlights the interactive dynamics around these four frames in the following ways:

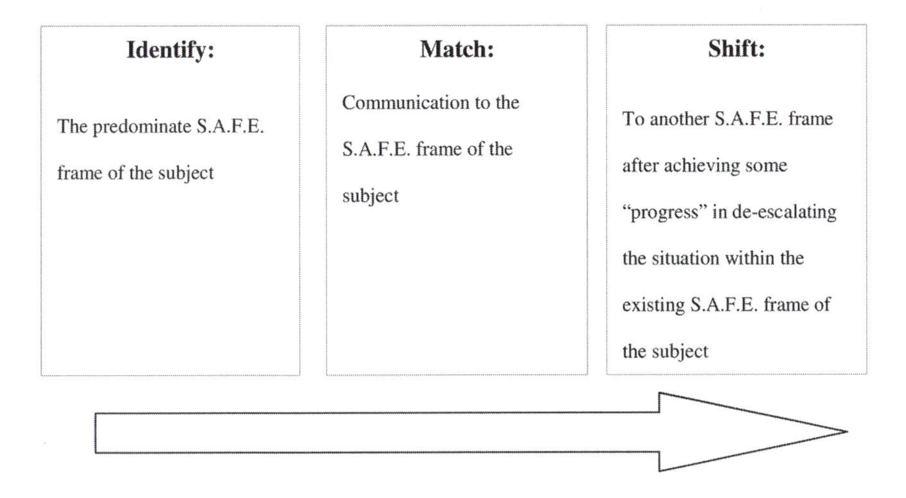

Figure 4.1 S.A.F.E. Process Guidelines

1. Subjects and police negotiators do not necessarily operate within the same frame when negotiating with one another.
2. When subjects and negotiators are operating in divergent frames, misunderstandings increase and there is greater likelihood for escalation.
3. When subjects and negotiators communicate with one another within the same frame, there is greater likelihood for de-escalation.
4. The basic interactive process for police negotiators communicating with subjects, therefore, involves identification of the predominant frame of the subject and shifting negotiation strategies to this identified frame of the subject.
5. As the concerns (conflictual issues) of the subject are addressed within his or her predominant S.A.F.E. frame, a sense of progress is experienced by the subject.
6. When this occurs, the police negotiator has a greater likelihood of success in shifting with the subject to another frame and a set of issues within this new frame that is more conducive to resolution of the incident (e.g., a substantive demand frame for discussing surrender).

Substantive demands, attunement, face, and emotional distress are the basic interpretive frames through which the police negotiator and the subject shape their negotiation discourse and respond to one another. Each frame acts as a "trigger" for escalating or de-escalating crisis situations. The S.A.F.E. model focuses on "tracking" or assessing escalation/de-escalation patterns and then identifies possible negotiation strategies designed to de-escalate or resolve the event. Each of the frames is discussed in greater detail in subsequent chapters, beginning with the substantive demand frame.

SUBSTANTIVE DEMAND FRAME

Within crisis incidents, there emerges an interactive frame through which the hostage taker interprets events and responds to the actions and communication messages of the police tactical and negotiation teams that is grounded in the substantive demands each party makes of one another. This instrumental demand frame is consistent with earlier conceptualizations that focus on an individual's concern for objective and generally tangible wants and demands (Roloff & Jordan, 1992; S. Wilson & Putnam, 1990). Within the context of crisis negotiation, substantive demands are situationally related, objective wants or needs. There are a number of features of substantive demands that are important to track in order to assess escalation and de-escalation when the subject is operating primarily within a substantive demand frame.

TRACKING SUBSTANTIVE DEMAND FRAME ISSUES

Subjects are interpreting events from a substantive demand frame when they are focused on obtaining that which is requested (demanded) from the negotiator. Subjects are operating in this frame when they consistently focus on or return to the topic of what they want or need. The goal for the police negotiator when the subject is in a substantive demand frame is to "match" the substantive frame of the hostage taker and look for ways to address the substantive demands made by the subject and the demands presented by the negotiator to the subject (Hammer, 2005b).

Central vs. Peripheral Substantive Demands

The S.A.F.E. framework points to a number of key features of demands. First, demands are understood as statements made by the subject that request something he or she wants or needs (similarly, the police negotiator also expresses demands as well, e.g., for the subject to surrender). Two fundamental types of demands are identified: central substantive demands and peripheral substantive demands. Briefly, central substantive demands refer to those requests made by the subject that are considered *most relevant* by the subject to his or her current situation. Peripheral substantive demands are concerned with wants that are considered by the subject to be secondarily related or dependent on the current event.

An example can illustrate how different types of demands can function as a critical incident arises. The police arrive and immediately surround a bank as a result of a silent alarm being set off by a bank employee. Harry is holding hostage ten people inside the bank. The would-be bank robber, "Harry," begins talking to the police negotiator. Fairly quickly, Harry tells the police negotiator that he wants a car and he wants to take two hostages with him as he flees the bank. Once clear of the police, he promises to release the hostages, unharmed. Is this request for a car a central or peripheral substantive demand?

Simply by knowing the content of the demand (a car) does not provide sufficient information for determining whether the demand is central or peripheral for the subject. By listening carefully to how the subject presents his demand for a car, the negotiation team is better able to identify the type of demand. If the subject indicates, through his or her discourse, that the demand for a car is in some ways more important, more urgent, or more valued than other demands or concerns he or she has at this time, it is likely the demand for the car is a central substantive demand.

However, a demand for a car could also operate as a peripheral (secondary) demand. How might this work? The hostage taker in our same example has been unwilling to surrender, and it is now 14 hours into the event. At this point, the subject says, "Hey! I told you I wanted a car! When is it coming?" The next statements from the hostage taker are, "It has been over 12 hours! We really need some food and something to drink in here! If you don't get me some food and beer within 30 minutes, I am going to start shooting people! Do you understand?"

Harry, our hostage taker, has now reiterated his demand for a car and also added a second demand—food and beer. Further, he now attaches a threat (to start killing the hostages) and a deadline to the demand (30 minutes) for food and beer. As a negotiation team, which demand do you determine is central and which one is peripheral? While the "messages" from the subject are short, you notice that, based on the discourse of Harry, he is communicating to you, the negotiator, that the food and beer are now more important to him than the car. You might notice that the food and beer demand has a threat and a deadline attached while the car that is requested has no threat or deadline. You might conclude, therefore, that the car has become a more peripheral demand for now and his need for food and beer is more important. In short, food and beer are now a more central substantive demand.

This approach to central and peripheral demands is in contrast with current conceptualizations of what is called "substantive" demands vs. "nonsubstantive" demands (FBI, 1996). Substantive demands are viewed in current definitions as objective and situationally related, while nonsubstantive demands are objective but situationally unrelated. From this perspective, a subject's request for a car is considered a substantive demand, while a request for pizza and beer is a nonsubstantive demand. The reason pizza and beer are viewed as nonsubstantive is that the subject did not have to hold people hostage in order to order a pizza (i.e., situationally unrelated). The hostage taker certainly could do better with a pizza delivery service rather than engaging the hostage negotiation and rescue units of the police.

The determination of the "value" of the demand is, therefore, made from the perspective of the negotiator rather than the hostage taker in this traditional view and is not interactively dependent. That is, substantive vs. nonsubstantive distinctions function as cross-situational categories. A "car" is always seen as a substantive demand, and food and water are treated as a nonsubstantive demand across critical incidents. The difficulty with this traditional (but current) categorical system is that it does not account for the fluid change in demands that often occurs during a crisis event. Further, some demands often move from more important to the subject (central substantive demands in S.A.F.E. terminology) to less salient (peripheral substantive demands). Therefore, the S.A.F.E. models proffers a view of demands in terms of whether they are central or peripheral, rather than substantive or nonsubstantive.

How Demands Are Asserted by the Subject

The S.A.F.E. model proposes that negotiation teams track not only the types of demands made by the subject as central vs. peripheral, but also assess how the subject asserts his or her own demands (and how the subject "receives" demands expressed by the police negotiator). The S.A.F.E. model suggests that the police negotiation team track how the subject asserts his or her demands in terms of whether the demands are increasing or decreasing in number and whether the demands are hardening (becoming more extreme and/or positional) or softening.

In addition, demands should be tracked in terms of whether the subject attaches a threat and/or a deadline to demands. Further, the negotiation team should note whether an attached threat is "offensive" or "defensive" in nature. Threats are viewed as messages that present the unfavorable consequences that can occur from a failure to comply with an asserted demand (Hovland, Janis, & Kelly, 1953). A threat is offensive when it threatens harm if the demand is not met. For instance, a hostage taker says, "If you don't let my children talk to me, I will kill their mother." A threat is defensive if it is issued in response to a perceived threatening act by the other party and threatens harm if the perceived threatening behavior continues or escalates. For example, a subject may shout, "If you SWAT guys don't stop coming closer, I will kill the hostages."

While any threat issued is escalatory and dangerous, an offensive threat is considered more potent than a defensive threat. That is because when a subject issues a defensive threat (e.g., stop coming closer), the police have the option of more directly influencing the hostage taker's commitment to carry out the threat by simply having the SWAT team members remain in position. In contrast, when an offensive threat is made, the hostage taker's commitment to carry out the threat is based on whether his or her demand can or will be met.

Talladega Prison Standoff

Dr. Rogan and I analyzed how demands and threats were used during the negotiation that took place during the 1991 Talladega prison siege (Hammer & Rogan, 2004). On August 21, 1991, a prison uprising took place in the Alpha Unit at the Federal Correctional Institution in Talladega, Alabama. Over 100 Cuban detainees held 8 Bureau of Prison (BOP) staff members, 3 Immigration and Naturalization Service staff members, and 18 American inmates. On August 30, the incident was resolved when FBI, SWAT, and BOP Special Operations Response Teams assaulted the Alpha Unit, rescued the hostages, and took the inmates back into custody. No one was injured.

An analysis of the types of demands and threats made by the prison detainees indicates a generally de-escalatory pattern among the inmates throughout the siege. Specifically, while some of the demands were physical (e.g., medicines) and issue focused (request for an attorney), a number of demands were environmental in nature (e.g., closeness of FBI tactical equipment and turning off very bright lights shown throughout the night hours toward the detainees). An increase in environmental demands (e.g., move back the equipment and turn off the lights) resulted in "direct response to the FBI/BOP tactics for stimulating anxiety and reducing the comfort levels of the detainees" (Hammer & Rogan, 2004, p. 51).

Most of the threats issued by the detainees were not explicitly attached to specific demands. Further, the detainees tended to make specific threats "more when the hostage takers themselves felt threatened than as a reinforcement of the seriousness of their demands" (Hammer & Rogan, 2004, p. 52). Overall, these findings suggest that the way in which demands and threats were asserted were more defensive in orientation than offensive in purpose. Further, these more defensive-oriented threats generally indicated a desire to achieve a negotiated settlement by the detainees and suggested a de-escalatory pattern within a substantive demand frame. In short, the evidence from tracking how substantive demands functioned in this event indicates a pattern of de-escalation in spite of more aggressive tactical actions.

How Demands Are Received by the Subject

Another important consideration is how the subject is receiving demands made by the police negotiator. The negotiation team should track whether the subject ignores or rejects the demands made by the police negotiator, or whether the hostage taker considers or accepts the negotiator's requests. Often, de-escalation takes place with subjects who may not "back down" on their demands, but more willingly comply with demands made by the police negotiator (e.g., picking up the telephone, talking longer, using less offensive language, and releasing hostages).

Systematically addressing these questions provides a basis for a determination as to whether the situation is escalating or de-escalating around substantive demand concerns (Hammer, 2005c, 2005d).

STRATEGIES FOR NEGOTIATING SUBSTANTIVE DEMAND FRAME ISSUES

Quite a number of negotiation strategies are available to police negotiators, depending on their assessment of demand type, threats, deadlines, how the subject presents his or her demands, and how the hostage taker responds to the negotiator's demands. The main criterion for "matching" negotiation strategy to substantive demands assessment is the degree to which the strategy directly addresses the frame of the subject.

Ignore or Downplay Subject's Substantive Demands

There are three core strategies relevant to this S.A.F.E. analysis. The first and simplest strategy is to ignore or downplay the subject's substantive demands. By ignoring the demand, the negotiator is essentially refocusing the subject to topics away from the request. This can be done if the subject does not continue to assert his or her own demands, or if the subject is no longer attentive to or committed to having his or her demand(s) met. When this occurs, the negotiator may simply try to move the dialogue with the subject to topics more relevant to the police negotiator (e.g., release of hostages).

Similarly, if the subject attaches a threat and a deadline to a demand, the negotiator may be able to "talk through" a deadline. This strategy may be appropriate if the subject is no longer focused on the threat or deadline. A second option is to "wait through" a deadline. This involves ending the conversation with the subject before the deadline and then initiating conversation after the deadline. This option may be appropriate if the subject remains fixated on getting his or her demand met (Hammer, 2005b; McMains & Mullins, 2006).

A strategy for *downplaying* the subject's demands is a task/activity breakdown, or what M.J. McMains and W.C. Mullins (2006) term "making demands into sub-demands" (p. 133). This strategy may be appropriate when the subject demands something that either cannot be met or cannot be met easily. This might involve a demand that needs a "higher" level of decision making to approve, takes time to meet the demand, involves multiple arrangements to ensure safety needs, or requires information or approval from an outside "third party" who may not be immediately available. An example of the latter would be a situation in which "Bill" has barricaded himself in his home and demands to speak with his children who are currently living with his ex-wife.

Why is this strategy effective for negotiating substantive demands? To continue with the last example, Bill has barricaded himself in his house and has asked the police negotiator to talk with his two boys, Jim, age 10, and Al, age 12 (who are now living with his ex-wife). When presented with such demands, police negotiators often reply, "we are working on that" or "look, you are asking a lot here, I am not sure we can do all that" or "we have not located your children yet" or "I don't know, my boss needs to review the situation." Each of these common statements does not substantively respond to the demand frame of the hostage taker. Therefore, these responses often communicate stalling, deception, or lack of consideration toward the subject. They fundamentally communicate a lack of cooperation in working with the subject in his substantive frame.

How might the negotiator respond differently? The negotiation team should generate, according to McMains and Mullins (2006), a list of tasks or activities that need to be accomplished in order to make progress in meeting the subject's demand. In our example, some of the activities would include the following:

- Determine the reason the subject wants to talk to his children. For example, he may wish to say a "final goodbye" to Jim and Al before he commits suicide. In this case, having the subject actually talk to his children is not recommended.
- Obtain Bill's ex-wife's name, phone number, and address.
- Locate the school the children may be attending at this time.
- Contact other police officers to locate his ex-wife and children.
- Talk with Bill's ex-wife to find out if she is willing to have her children talk to the subject.
- Provide technical telephone hookup for a possible conversation between the subject and his children.

With the task/activity list in hand, the police negotiator now has more information available to directly respond to the subject in a substantive demand frame. When Bill again asks to talk to his kids, the negotiator can say, "here is what we are doing" and then review some of the steps the police are taking. The negotiator can ask Bill for some information, such as the city and address of his ex-wife. The negotiator can educate the subject about the complexity in meeting his demand. These messages, rather than communicating stalling or deception, actually communicate cooperation. This strategy can help the subject see the police negotiator as someone who is sensitive to the demands being made (McMains & Mullins, 2006).

Bargain Substantive Demands

A second primary strategy is for the police negotiator to bargain substantive demands. This strategy can be used when the subject remains focused on getting his or her demands met and the subject is willing to trade for something he or she wants for something the police negotiator wants. Bargaining, or quid pro quo exchanges, is often done when the police negotiator trades a peripheral demand (providing the subject with food and water) for a central substantive demand (release of hostages). Another kind of trade that is often made is allowing the subject to talk to his wife or children after he puts the gun down and peacefully surrenders (McMains & Mullins, 2006).

While the general guideline is for police negotiators to exchange peripheral wants for central demands, in some circumstances, police negotiators may need to trade central substantive demands with the hostage taker. For example, in a terrorist with WMD (weapons of mass destruction) scenario, police negotiators may need to release prisoners for disarming a WMD or provide safe passage out of the country for turning over a WMD. This possible situation may challenge current practices that "some demands are simply not negotiable and it makes no sense to enter into a discussion concerning those demands" (McMains & Mullins, 2006, p. 127).

Problem Solving Underlying Interests

A third strategy is problem solving underlying interests. The S.A.F.E. model incorporates many of the specific applied negotiation tactics associated with various "problem-solving" approaches found more generally within conflict-resolution theory and practice in negotiating central and peripheral substantive demands (R. Fisher & Ury, 1991; Folger, Poole, & Stutman, 2000; Pruitt & Carnevale, 1993). A problem-solving strategy is appropriate to use if the subject or the police negotiator is unwilling to ignore, downplay, or bargain substantive demands. Oftentimes this strategy is called for when the police negotiator is not willing to exchange, for instance, weapons for the release of hostages.

Positions vs. Interests

Adapting a problem-solving strategy is grounded in distinguishing between the demand "position" vs. the demand "interest." Positions reflect the individual's stated want or request while interests identify underlying needs or concerns upon which the position is based (R. Fisher & Ury, 1991). In crisis situations, a number of positions advocated by hostage takers are appropriately viewed as not bargainable, in the sense of compromising, from the perspective of the police negotiation team. For example, the hostage taker may request a car and a bulletproof vest. It is unlikely law enforcement is going to be willing to compromise on these demand positions (unless extraordinary circumstances arise such as WMD incidents).

From a substantive frame perspective, however, these central substantive demands of the subject can be reframed in terms of underlying interests. This is typically done by asking, "Why do you want the car and vest?" It may be that the hostage taker is afraid he may be killed by the tactical team if he should surrender and therefore wants a car for escape and safety along with the bulletproof vest. Substantively, it is now possible to negotiate in a way that meets the hostage taker's underlying interest (to not be killed if he surrenders). This may involve making available to the subject various options for surrender, including having an attorney present. In this way, the police negotiator is able to meet the underlying interests of the subject but not compromise on the demand position.

McMains and Mullins (2006) suggest that A.H. Maslow's (1954) hierarchy of needs offers one useful template for identifying possible underlying interests of a hostage taker's demand position. Maslow argues that human beings have a set of basic needs that must be met for an individual to function within society. At the most basic level are those biological needs for survival (e.g., food, water, and shelter). At the next level are safety needs (e.g., physical security). The third level consists of social needs (e.g., relationships). The fourth and fifth levels are ego needs (e.g., recognition) and self-actualization (realize one's potential in the world). When applied to crisis incidents, the underlying interests of many of the subject's demands (position) are concerned with biological, safety, and social needs.

Identify Common Goals

Other problem-solving strategies police negotiators can use include asserting common goals with the hostage taker. For example, the negotiator may tell the hostage taker that "no one needs to get hurt. Neither one of us wants that to happen." Shifting the conversation from expressing demand positions to mutual problem solving (how can we resolve this situation by working together?) enables the subject to consider alternatives for resolution that go beyond compliance with his or her demands. Problem solving enables more creative solutions to emerge and creates a cooperative interaction pattern between the police negotiator and the subject. Problem solving, along with ignoring, downplaying, and bargaining strategies can be employed to demonstrate progress in the substantive demand frame, which supports overall de-escalation of the crisis event.

SUBSTANTIVE FRAME PATTERNS

The S.A.F.E. model posits the following substantive frame patterns. First, the number, type, and relative rigidity of demands communicated during a crisis negotiation are related to conflict escalation and de-escalation. Briefly, increased expression or increased "positional commitment" (Pruitt & Carnevale, 1993) of peripheral substantive demands and greater expressed positional commitment to previously communicated central substantive demands are posited to be associated with conflict escalation. That is, an increase in central substantive demands reflects an escalating pattern between interactants as these demands, because they are situationally relevant, are oftentimes considered "rational" and obtainable from the perspective of the hostage taker. Similarly, the central substantive demand of the police negotiator for the hostage taker to surrender is also considered to be rational and obtainable.

However, peripheral substantive demands, because they are not seen by the subject as relevant or important compared to central substantive demands, function somewhat differently. That is, while an increase in peripheral substantive demands is associated with escalating conflict dynamics, this escalation is often more centrally related to the attunement interpretive frame than the substantive demand frame.

Contention over peripheral demands, because they are not viewed as relevant or important by the subject, typically become the lens through which power and trust issues between the negotiator and the perpetrator are negotiated. That is, peripheral substantive demands, while clearly situated within the substantive demand frame, can communicatively function as the relational battleground between the subject and the police negotiator. This arises in hostage events because perpetrators who experience frustration with negotiators around power and trust issues tend to create additional, yet peripheral, substantive demands through which the power dynamics are played out in an increasingly contentious manner. In contrast, increased expressed flexibility toward central substantive wants and a reduction in the number of peripheral substantive demands is related to conflict de-escalation.

The S.A.F.E. model posits that incidents that end in a peaceful resolution are characterized by the emergence of the substantive demand frame oftentimes later—as opposed to earlier—in the incident. This frame is critically important as various agreements need to be reached with the hostage taker concerning how the surrender will actually take place (what is termed the surrender ritual).

CHAPTER 5

Negotiating Attunement and Face Frames in Crisis Incidents

ATTUNEMENT FRAMES

Within a critical incident, a second interactive frame arises through which the hostage taker interprets events and responds to the actions and communication messages of the police tactical and negotiation teams. This frame is grounded in the degree of relational attunement (concern) each party experiences toward one another. Attunement is concerned with the quality of the relationship between parties and has been characterized under such conceptual umbrellas as "trust" and "affiliation." Attunement-framed communication is important not only because it immediately impacts current interaction, but future relations as well. As J.P. Folger, M.S. Poole, and R.K. Stutman (2005) point out, "relational communication has its most profound effects through influencing future interaction. How people interact in conflicts is colored by their assessments of others—judgments about things such as the others' trustworthiness, intentions (good or bad), and determination to win" (p. 35).

In the case of the critical incident, attunement refers to this relational dimension between contending parties. More specifically, attunement reflects the degree of interpersonal closeness and distance between the subject and the police negotiator and/or third-party intermediaries (TPIs) (Hammer, 2005b).

Using Third-Party Intermediaries

The S.A.F.E. model posits that attunement can and often must be developed between the subject and the police negotiator. However, there may be times when the subject is unwilling to trust the police negotiator sufficiently to complete the surrender. In those situations, attunement can be successfully built with someone other than the police negotiator, who is termed a third-party intermediary (Romano, 1998). This person could be, for instance, a family member or a friend of the subject. The S.A.F.E. model suggests that in a crisis event, when the subject is operating in an attunement frame, it is important for the subject to experience sufficient trust (attunement) toward a key individual in the event, such that the subject will be influenced to surrender because of the trust gained with this key person, whether that individual is the police negotiator or a TPI.

Further, the S.A.F.E. model indicates that TPIs can productively be used when the subject is operating not only in the attunement frame, but also when he or she is communicating with the police negotiator around substantive issues (substantive demand frame) by reassuring the subject that the agreements made with the police will be honored. Also, the TPI may act as a guarantor of instrumental agreements made between the subject and the police negotiator (e.g., the presence of an attorney at the time of surrender). The TPI may also be helpful if the hostage taker is operating in a face frame by supporting face-saving actions by the subject or having the subject surrender to a TPI rather than the police negotiator (Romano, 1998). Finally, TPIs may also be useful if the subject is experiencing significant emotional distress. In this case, the TPI may be able to help calm the subject through empathic listening (Hammer, 2005b, 2005c).

Of course, whether to use a TPI to converse with the subject is a decision made by the negotiation team based on a number of factors (McMains & Mullins, 2006). Nevertheless, the S.A.F.E. framework posits that attunement can be productively addressed by a TPI when necessary and under the correct conditions. The correct conditions are critically important when introducing a TPI into a crisis situation. For example, it is well known among negotiators that subjects who are potentially suicidal often request to talk with spouses or other family members (McMains & Mullins, 2006). While, on the surface, this may seem to be a demand the police should honor, the reality is that often suicidal subjects wish to say "one last word" to a TPI (often a spouse or family member), after which they are more likely to complete the suicide act. For this reason, police negotiators rarely allow a suicidal subject to talk to a TPI if they believe this may not aid in producing a peaceful surrender.

Attunement as Trust and Affiliation

Under the guise of relational trust, attunement is often viewed as the single most important aspect of a good relationship (R. Fisher & Brown, 1988). At a general level, attunement or trust has been variously defined in terms of a vulnerability one party extends to another party (e.g., Cupach & Canary, 1997; Rousseau, Sitkin, Burt, & Camerer, 1988) and an "expectation that the other party will cooperate in the future" (Pruitt &

Carnevale, 1993, p. 133). Under the guise of affiliation, W.A. Donohue (1998) views attunement as the degree of attraction, liking, respect, trust, and a desire to cooperate with the other party. Thus, attunement consists of a sense of vulnerability and an expectation of cooperation in some future act as well as a liking toward and consideration for the well-being of the other party (Hammer, 2005b).

Cooperative Behavior and the Rule of Reciprocity

Behaviorally, how is attunement developed? What is the basis of attunement in interaction? Fundamentally, the attunement frame is grounded in the degree of *competition vs. cooperation* between the contending parties (Deutsch, 1973). In this sense, while social conflict situations contain both competitive and cooperative patterns, one or the other of these frames predominate for interpreting behavior within conflict episodes.

The main reason cooperative behavior is so powerful in building attunement is the basic human response captured in the rule of reciprocity. This rule states that like behavior tends to be reciprocated. That is, cooperation breeds cooperation. Unfortunately, contentiousness also tends to elicit competitiveness from the other party. By framing actions and communication messages in terms of "cooperative behavior," the police negotiator is gaining attunement "influence" with the subject.

M.J. McMains and W.C. Mullins (2006) identify three features of the rule of reciprocity that underlie the effectiveness of cooperative actions and messages. First, this rule is very powerful. In fact, the rule of reciprocity is particularly impactful when the parties do not know or even like one another, a characteristic quite applicable to a critical incident involving a hostage taker and a police negotiator. Second, the rule of reciprocity "attracts uninvited debts" (McMains & Mullins, 2006, p. 239). What this means is that freely offered cooperative acts by the police negotiator are powerful inducements to the subject to repay the debt through reciprocal cooperative behavior. Finally, the rule does not demand a "tit-for-tat" exchange of cooperative actions. In one critical incident, a police negotiator offered to accompany the subject to the police station upon surrender. This one cooperative act influenced the subject's decision to release the hostages, put his gun down, and surrender to the tactical squad.

The goal, therefore, of the police negotiator, when the subject is operating within an attunement frame, is to engage in cooperative behavior in order to gain increased relational closeness vs. distance (Hammer, 2005b). This is accomplished through cooperative actions and communicative messages. Yet this is a difficult objective. With the arrival of police SWAT officers, stress and the perception of threat are heightened in the subject. The result is that in the vast majority of critical incidents, the hostage taker begins the interaction with the police negotiator from a position of relational distance (i.e., low affiliation and trust). Thus, attunement is typically a predominant frame that needs to be "negotiated" as the event develops.

In a general sense, attunement is grounded in perceptions of gains and losses, where a person's gains or losses are dependent on the actions of the other party (Johnson, 1997). Attunement in the crisis event is defined from the S.A.F.E. model in a more constrained manner. Progress in the attunement frame is achieved when the subject believes future actions of the police negotiation and tactical teams will not be harmful to himself or herself and the negotiator has consideration for the well-being of the subject. In essence, police negotiators are focused on building trust and affiliation (attunement) with a subject such that when the subject is willing to put down his or her weapon and surrender, the subject believes that when he or she steps out of his or her own safety zone, the tactical officers will not kill or harm him or her. Decreases in attunement result in the hostage taker "moving away" or interpersonally distancing himself or herself from the police negotiator cognitively, affectively, and behaviorally (Cupach & Canary, 1997; Johnson, 1997).

Various studies have consistently shown that when we say we trust someone, we are less critical, we require less information, we share more aspects of ourselves, and we give people the benefit of the doubt (Folger et al., 2005). Other studies have shown that trust increases information exchange about values and priorities between parties and makes it easier for the parties to reach a satisfactory agreement to end their conflict (Kimmel, Pruitt, Magenau, Konar-Goldband, & Carnevale, 1980; Lindskold & Han, 1988).

Within the context of crisis negotiation, attunement (interpersonal closeness) is typically absent at the beginning of negotiation between the suspect and law enforcement. In attempting to address these concerns, negotiators do not begin their interaction with a suspect in the attunement frame at ground zero, but rather at a deficit (i.e., in a competitive, relational distance frame) (Rogan, 1990; Rogan, Donohue, & Lyles, 1990). For example, in attempting to establish trust, negotiators must often overcome the suspect's distrust of the police. Nonetheless, the importance for negotiators to attend to such interpersonal issues and to develop a positive relationship with the perpetrator has been acknowledged as critical factors in incident resolution. While police negotiators are asked to create a trusting relationship with the suspect, little has been written about the dynamics of relationship development within the context of crisis negotiation to help explain this interactive challenge.

Recently, Donohue and his colleagues (Donohue, 1998; Donohue & Roberto, 1993; Drake & Donohue, 1996) have examined relationship-building dimensions in hostage-negotiation events from the perspective of Relational Order Theory (ROT). ROT views conflict parties as engaging one another through their discourse in creating and negotiating the parameters of their relationship (Donohue, 1998).

Of particular relevance to this book is that a key relational dimension is the extent to which individuals communicate attraction, liking, respect, trust, and a willingness to cooperate with one another (Donohue, 1998; Donohue & Roberto, 1993).[6] Such information and knowledge is important to the relationship because it helps the subject and the police negotiator to decide how much and what kind of information to share, how to structure their developing relationship, and whether or not to continue the relationship development process (Donohue & Roberto, 1993). In sum, a fundamental aspect for negotiating the attunement between the hostage taker and the negotiator is concerned with the level of relational distance (competition) and relational closeness (cooperation) between interactants.

Research by W.A. Donohue and A.J. Roberto (1993) highlights the importance of attunement in crisis situations. Donohue and Roberto discovered that the creation of a stable relational pattern of either interpersonal closeness or distance early in the negotiation interaction remained fairly constant throughout the negotiation between the police negotiator and the subject. In those incidents where the subject and the negotiator maintained greater interpersonal distance, they were less able to establish any consistent consensus upon which to resolve substantive concerns, whereas in cases of interpersonal closeness conditions, the hostage taker and the police negotiator were better able to focus on instrumental issues oriented toward resolving the situation.

TRACKING ATTUNEMENT FRAME ISSUES

The core interactive process identified in the S.A.F.E. model for "negotiating" attunement involves efforts at engaging in and encouraging reciprocal cooperative actions between the police negotiator and the subject. The overall focus for the negotiation team is on identifying specific cooperative vs. uncooperative acts taken by the subject and by the police SWAT and negotiation units. Cooperative acts can include both behavioral actions (e.g., releasing hostages) and communicative messages.

The S.A.F.E. model emphasizes that police negotiation teams should pay close attention to microbehaviors that can be tracked as "cooperative." For instance, the police insert a "throw phone" into the location of the subject.[7] The police negotiator now attempts to call the subject. The throw phone rings 50 times before the subject answers. Over the next hour, the subject's behavior changes to the point where he or she is picking up the throw phone within five rings when the negotiator calls. Noting this change is important as the police negotiator can then express his or her appreciation of the subject's willingness to talk (framing the subject's actions as cooperative). Thus, a reciprocal attunement act is completed. The hostage taker picks up the throw phone sooner (cooperative act) after which the police negotiator thanks the subject for his willingness to talk (cooperative act reciprocated).

Tracking cooperative actions and communicative messages of the subject and the negotiator are important insofar as attunement is built slowly, through repetitive, microbehavioral steps that are framed as cooperative. Unfortunately, attunement can be quickly and dramatically decreased through one significant, uncooperative act. As D.W. Johnson (1997) comments, "trust is hard to build and easy to destroy" (p. 75).

Of particular attention to police negotiators in terms of tracking behavioral actions is to note those situations when the subject is faced with contradictory actions between the tactical and negotiation teams. For example, a verbal message of "we are not here to harm you, we only want to resolve this peacefully" is sent by the primary negotiator to the subject. At the same time, the subject observes that the SWAT unit is "taking ground" by slowly moving some of the snipers closer. The verbal message communicates cooperation while the SWAT actions are likely to send a clear message to the subject of escalation and threat: in short, a message of competition (noncooperation). Tracking these kinds of contradictory attunement actions is important.

In terms of tracking communicative messages, one aspect negotiation teams are advised to note is patterns of increased vs. decreased time communicating with the subject, and to list statements made by the subject of trust/mistrust toward the negotiator or TPIs. Further, negotiation team members can note those topics of conversation that are more social vs. more contentious with the subject and track whether there is an increase or decrease in social vs. contentious dialogue. Police negotiators should also list the outcome (positive/negative) when the hostage taker's demands are met as a means of building trust.

STRATEGIES FOR NEGOTIATING ATTUNEMENT FRAME ISSUES

There are quite a number of possible attunement frame strategies to use in negotiating with a subject when the subject is predominantly focused on issues of trust with the police negotiator. Two main approaches police negotiation teams have at their disposal are (1) to demonstrate through strategically framed actions that the negotiator is cooperating in trying to resolve this volatile situation peacefully and (2) to send communicative messages of cooperation to the subject.

Cooperatively Framed Actions

Some of the more cooperatively framed actions negotiators can employ are to strategically offer to meet one or more of the subject's peripheral demands as an effort to build trust (attunement). For example, offering the subject, after eight hours of negotiation, some water, when framed in terms of the police negotiator's concern for the well-being of the subject, acts as an attunement "credit" that slowly builds "interest" as the event continues. Other demonstrations of cooperative behavior the police may engage in with the subject can include ensuring that tactical actions support attunement goals: for instance, maintaining appropriate "containment" tactical deployment rather than deliberate efforts to heighten the anxiety of the subject (e.g., tear gas insertion). Second, the police negotiator may request that the SWAT team reduce its tactical "presence" without compromising containment and safety concerns. Again, this type of strategic act may be called for when the subject is functioning in the attunement frame—where he or she is so focused on issues of mistrust toward the police that this type of tactical demonstration of cooperation might be significant in building sufficient attunement with the negotiator that the subject now seriously considers surrender rather than violent actions.

Cooperatively Framed Communication Messages

There are a number of communication strategies identified in the S.A.F.E. model police negotiators can employ to build trust when the subject is operating within an attunement frame. One approach is to shift the conversation to those social, more cooperatively oriented topics and away from those topics that make the subject more angry, depressed, etc. (i.e., more contentious topics). Second, the police negotiator should look for opportunities to express concern and consideration toward the hostage taker and his or her needs. Also it is important to express concern toward people important to the subject. A third strategy is to discuss commonality in beliefs, experiences, and opinions with the subject. When the subject and the police negotiator "connect" to one another through the discovery of some common experience (e.g., both served in the 101st Airborne Division), the assumed commonality serves to build attunement influence (McMains & Mullins, 2006, p. 243). A fourth strategy is to use communication skills of active listening (e.g., paraphrasing, reflecting emotion, summarizing, and minimal encouragers), questioning (e.g., open-ended questions and probes), informing (e.g., "I" messages, explanations, advice, and instructions), and disclosure (e.g., background, interests, and goals) (McMains & Mullins, 2006).

The Language of Cooperation

Other strategies relevant to building attunement involve the language that police negotiators use. Moving from more formal language to more informal language increases relational closeness between the police negotiator and the subject. For example, a negotiator might begin talking to the subject by saying, "Hello, Mr. Smith, I am Officer Jones. What seems to be the problem?" Somewhat later, Officer Jones can then say, "Mr. Smith, I would appreciate it if you just call me Jim." This strategic language switch from the formal to informal communicates to Mr. Smith increased attunement (relational closeness) from the police negotiator. This move to more informal language encourages Mr. Smith to then say, "You can call me Bill." Alternatively, if the subject does not reciprocate the move from formal to informal, the police negotiator can ask, "Mr. Smith, would you mind if I called you by your first name?" Again, this communicative move of the police negotiator builds attunement with the subject.

Another strategy is to use the language of relational closeness vs. the language of interpersonal distance. Relevant to the attunement frame are the efforts of Donohue and Roberto (1993) at identifying language markers of relational closeness and distance. Their work, based on the verbal immediacy analysis posited by M. Weiner and A. Mehrabian (1968), identifies specific language elements that increase relational closeness between individuals compared to language that increases interpersonal distance. These language "signs" are oftentimes unconsciously used to communicate interpersonal distance or closeness toward another party. For example, former President Bill Clinton, during the Monica Lewinsky scandal, made the famous statement: "I did not have sexual relations with *that* woman." President Clinton's use of the term "that" woman reflects a linguistic choice that distances him from the event and from Monica Lewinsky. In contrast, the use of the term "this" in a sentence indicates relational closeness rather than distance. For example, to say, "Do you think *this* idea is worth considering?" reflects a higher level of attunement than the statement "Do you think *that* idea is worth considering?" Police negotiators are encouraged to use the following language attunement markers:

Relational Closeness Marker	Relational Distance Marker
This	That
These	Those
Our	Mine
Here	There
Present tense	Past tense
We	I

Other research (e.g., Bargh, Chen, & Burrows, 1996) shows how this type of language "priming" unconsciously yet powerfully influences behavior. In their work, these researchers found that when individuals are linguistically primed with thoughts of cooperation, they subsequently behave in a more cooperative manner. Further, the subjects in the research were not aware that they were systematically "primed" toward cooperative actions.

ATTUNEMENT FRAME PATTERNS

Overall, the S.A.F.E. model posits the following attunement patterns. Crisis negotiation situations are oftentimes initiated within a competitive, relational distance frame. This relational distance frame escalates conflict as it reflects mistrust and lack of consideration toward the other party. Further, this relational distance frame will remain fairly stable unless specific cooperative messages and behavior are initiated and reciprocated by the subject and the police negotiator (or TPIs). Increased attunement (relational closeness) is associated with conflict de-escalation, and as relational closeness increases, substantive demands become more negotiable. Finally, a peaceful resolution of crisis incidents is more likely when attunement increases.

FACE FRAMES

As crisis situations develop, there often emerges an interactive frame through which the hostage taker interprets events and responds to the actions and communication messages of the police tactical and negotiation teams that is grounded in a concern for face, or one's self-image as perceived by the other party. The notion of face is a core aspect of human interaction and has a strong history of investigation across cultures (Ting-Toomey & Kurogi, 1998; Ting-Toomey & Takai, 2006). In fact, the concept of face can be traced to the fourth century B.C. in China, where it originally reflected a concern with *lien,* meaning good character, and *mien-tzu,* indicating reputation (Folger et al., 2005; Littlejohn & Domenici, 2006). At a general level, face is "a set of coordinated practices in which communicators build, maintain, protect, or threaten personal dignity, honor, and respect" (Littlejohn & Domenici, 2006, p. 228). Further, these authors suggest that people generally desire to present a positive face to others and will similarly support a positively presented face of the other party as well (Littlejohn & Domenici, 2006, p. 229).

Within the context of conflict interaction, face is a critical concern to disputing parties (Donohue & Kolt, 1992; Littlejohn & Domenici, 2006; Northrup, 1989; Ting-Toomey, 1988; Ting-Toomey & Kurogi, 1998). In fact, research has indicated that individuals will sacrifice rewards in an attempt to maintain face (Brown, 1977). Further, when conflicts arise, individuals often believe they must insist on their stated demands or positions. If they do not consistently do this, they feel they will appear weak in the view of the other party. This predominant focus on face and face-saving "can encourage people to keep arguing for a position even though they no longer believe in it or to back down because they realize it is not contributing to a workable resolution to the conflict" (Folger et al., 2005, p. 36).

Face has been identified as a critical factor in crisis negotiation for both perpetrators and negotiators (Miron & Goldstein, 1979; Rogan &

Hammer, 1994). The S.A.F.E. model, then, views face as the projected self-image or reputation held by an individual (Hammer, 2005b), which is grounded in interaction (Hammer & Rogan, 1997). In crisis/hostage incidents, the hostage taker and the negotiator oftentimes experience heightened sensitivity to face issues (Hammer, 2001; Lanceley, Ruple, & Moss, 1985; Miron & Goldstein, 1979; Rogan & Hammer, 1994). The arrival and deployment of the SWAT unit in a critical incident inherently makes these types of incidents face-threatening to the hostage taker. Further, given the publicly confrontational nature of crisis negotiation, face is a constant concern throughout the duration of a crisis incident. Therefore, police negotiators have the challenging task of attempting to not only manage their own face (e.g., self-image and reputation) concerns, but more importantly to satisfactorily address the face needs of the perpetrator.

Three Features of Facework

Face can be conceptualized as varying along three dimensions: (1) locus of concern (is the face message directed toward self or other?), (2) facework valence (does the face message honor or threaten the self-image of self or other?), and (3) temporality (does the face message function to proactively protect against possible future face threats or retroactively restore face loss?). This produces six types of face messages: (1) *defend self face* behaviors are self-focused messages that are face-honoring in nature and are designed to guard against possible future face-attack messages from the other party (e.g., "I can take care of that situation if I want"), (2) *attack self face* messages are statements one makes against one's own self-image (e.g., "I have never been able to handle the stress of working a job"), (3) *restore self face* behaviors are messages that restore one's own self-image by countering a perceived face-attack message from others (e.g., "I may be confused, but I am not stupid"), (4) *restore other's face* behaviors are messages that honor the face needs of the other party (e.g., "You may have made some mistakes in the past, but you sound like you want to make better decisions in the future"), (5) *defend other face* messages protect the other's self-image from potential future attack or loss (e.g., "You are a sensitive person in the way you are handling your family situation"), and (6) *attack other face* messages are behaviors that directly threaten the face attributes of the other (e.g., "You are not using your head right now. Where is your mind?") (Rogan & Hammer, 1994, 2002).

The S.A.F.E. model views face within E. Goffman's (1967) seminal conceptualization, which defines face as "the positive social value a person effectively claims for himself [or herself] by the line others assume he [or she] has taken during a particular contact" (p. 5). Accordingly, face is conceptualized as a concern for one's projected image within a social interaction. In short, face is about how an individual wishes to be seen by others.

Individual concern for face is grounded in a desire to maintain a positive social expression of one's self. As such, face (identity) is an abiding sense of self and who one is in relation to the world (Northrup, 1989). In this way, individual face does not exist independent of the communicative event, but rather is innately tied to the social interchange.

The goal in the S.A.F.E. model is for the police negotiator to validate the face concerns of the subject (Hammer, 2005b). The S.A.F.E. model suggests that face-threatening acts, when reciprocated, escalate conflict, while face-honoring acts de-escalate conflict. Also, face needs that are not addressed (e.g., ignored) or are perceived to be rejected escalate conflict, while face needs that are honored and are perceived to be validated de-escalate the situation. In addition, consistent attack self face acts may be possible indicators of suicidal intentions (Rogan & Hammer, 1994).

Two Characteristics of Face

The S.A.F.E. approach draws from social identity theory and identifies two types of face that are particularly central to crisis negotiation: social/group identity and individual identity (Tajfel, 1978, 1981). According to M.R. Hammer and R.G. Rogan (1997), "Personal identity is based on an individual's unique perceptions of his/her own attributes (e.g., strong, weak, intelligent) while social identity consists of those characteristics and their emotional significance that is attached to one's membership in social group(s)" (pp. 15–16).

The importance of these two types of face can vary from incident to incident, as well as over time within an incident. For example, R.G. Rogan and M.R. Hammer (1994) conclude that personal identity concern is central in those negotiations involving a suicidal person. Comparatively, social identity seems to be of greatest concern in negotiations with members or leaders of certain social groups, cults, or particular national organizations (Hammer, 2001). Regardless of the specific face concern, communication that attacks or threatens another's face tends to escalate conflict, while face-honoring messages seem to result in conflict de-escalation. Overall, then, both individual and/or group face needs can be salient in a crisis situation and when not validated, equally escalatory.

TRACKING FACE FRAME ISSUES

It is important for police negotiation teams to track the expressed personal face and/or group face characteristics of the subject. When the face frame is dominant for a hostage taker, he or she is actively engaged in explaining those characteristics of his or her self-image that are important. In essence, the subject is asking the police negotiator to validate (i.e., to acknowledge) that the negotiator understands how the subject sees himself or herself as the crisis incident develops.

For some individuals, group face characteristics are more salient than personal characteristics. Some group face needs include nationality, ethnicity, sexual orientation, and membership in various organizations or institutions. For example, for some hostage takers, it is important to them that their self-image of being a valued member of the military be validated (acknowledged) by the police negotiator.

For others, personal face characteristics are more salient to the subject. Personal face characteristics include individual qualities such as friendly, honest, a liar, doing poorly in school, a "kick-ass" kid in school, or a poor father. For example, in 1996, an 80-day siege occurred between the FBI and the Freemen group outside of Jordan, Montana. The Freemen were a group of ranchers who believed that the government had no authority over their "sovereign" territory. They believed that American society was in disarray and their rights to govern themselves came from such documents as the Bible and the Magna Carta.

Federal authorities became involved when the group issued bad checks, received stolen goods, and refused to leave land they had lost due to foreclosures. During the 80 days of the standoff, the FBI talked directly to Mr. Clarke, the leader of the Freemen, and used a large number of TPIs in an effort to peacefully resolve the situation. Face issues were a central concern for the Freemen. At one point, Mr. Clarke told the FBI negotiator, "my word is my bond." This comment spoke deeply and directly to a core personal face characteristic of this person. When the Freemen finally surrendered, he turned to the police negotiator and commented, "I told you my word is my bond" (Romano, 1997).

It is also important for the police negotiation team to track whether face characteristics expressed by the subject are viewed by him or her as positive or negative features of his or her self-image. Finally, the S.A.F.E. model guides the negotiation team to track the following four core face behaviors of the subject and the police negotiator:

1. Attack self-behavior (e.g., "I am no good."),
2. Attack other face behavior (e.g., "You're stupid if you think I am coming out."),
3. Honor self face behavior (e.g., "I'm good with cars."), and
4. Honor other behavior (e.g., "I know you want to help me.").

STRATEGIES FOR NEGOTIATING FACE ISSUES

The police negotiator should recognize that face needs are not bargainable. That is, a subject cannot "trade" 50 percent of his or her self-image for 50 percent of something else. What can be done in negotiating within the face frame is to validate the face needs of the subject. A number of strategies can be employed to accomplish this goal and therefore demonstrate progress in the face frame. First, listening skills, discussed earlier, can be used to encourage the subject to talk about his or her situation and himself or herself. Listening skills can validate both personal and group face needs of the subject.

Second, subjects often attempt to explain their situation and how they got into various difficulties by justifying their actions through the use of verbal qualifiers. Verbal qualifiers are language markers for salient face concerns. They are used by a hostage taker as a way to "plus up" his or her self-image to the police negotiator. They are used as a "face-saving" mechanism by the subject and reflect face needs that can be validated or acknowledged by the police negotiator.

Verbal qualifiers are words or phrases that typically precede what is said and reflect a concern for one's own projected self-image, often attempting to present oneself in a "better light." Work by R.G. Rogan and M.R. Hammer (1994) suggests that subjects who operate predominantly within a face frame, and engage in substantial self face attack behavior, are attempting to present their self-image in a "negative light." This effort may indicate an increased likelihood for suicide.

Nevertheless, when hostage takers verbally qualify their situation or their actions, they are likely operating within a predominant face frame. The following is a short segment of dialogue between a police negotiator and "Bill" that illustrates how important face is to Bill:

> *Neg:* I need for you to tell me exactly what precipitated this incident.
>
> *Bill:* All right, it basically started, a couple of weeks ago maybe. You know, I went out, had a couple of drinks, all right. People do that, couple of drinks, nothing wrong with that. I got in a little trouble with the law, you know, got caught drinking and driving. That happens, people get caught drinking and driving sometimes.
>
> *Neg:* Right, happens all the time.
>
> *Bill:* My school just slipped off the handle; I've been working for them for 18 years. Eighteen years I gave those people down there, and they are going to call me down there; they didn't even let me finish my first period class. Called me down to the office and kicked me out. They kicked me out of the school, that's what they did. Tell me I'm suspended.

Bill's primary S.A.F.E. frame is face. He feels his reputation and self-image are threatened, and he is embarrassed about the DUI and the school suspension. He uses "verbal qualifiers" to minimize his own actions (and responsibility) in order to present himself in a better light (honor self face). The verbal qualifiers Bill uses in telling his story are listed in italics:

- "You know, I went out, had a couple of drinks, all right. *People do that,* couple of drinks, *nothing wrong with that.*"
- "I got in *a little* trouble with the law, *you know,* got caught *drinking and driving.*"
- "*That happens, people* get caught drinking and driving *sometimes.*"

Police negotiators also can use verbal qualifiers, in this case, to honor the face of the subject. Following are some examples of face-honoring statements (verbal qualifiers are in italics):

- *I know you are upset about how long it is taking to find your girlfriend;* we are trying very hard to locate her.
- *I know this is hard to hear right now;* we have a problem. The people inside with you are needing medication. Can you send them out?
- *You are doing great;* now if you put the gun down on the table, we can make sure when you come out that you will be able to talk to your kids.

FACE FRAME PATTERNS

Allowing the subject to talk about himself or herself is a way to acknowledge or validate face needs. By validating face needs, progress is made within the face frame, thus reducing the likelihood of escalation. How the police negotiator responds to the subject's face behavior contributes to either escalation or de-escalation of the incident. For example, when a subject engages in self face attack behavior (e.g., "I have been a lousy father to my kids"), the negotiator can respond by first acknowledging (through listening) that the negotiator understands how the subject may see himself as a poor father. Once acknowledged, the police negotiator may then focus on a positive face characteristic of the hostage taker with a face-honoring statement (e.g., "You did provide for your family, though, right?").

In critical incidents, face frames often emerge during the surrender ritual where subjects may demand a face-saving exit (e.g., "I don't want to go down on my knees after I come out"). When subjects are operating in the face frame, the negotiation team should look for ways to honor the face-saving requests of hostage takers, providing those demands do not compromise safety concerns.

CHAPTER 6

Negotiating Emotional Distress Frames

EMOTIONAL DISTRESS FRAMES

A Death on Christmas Day

Army Reservist James Dean had recently returned to his home in St. Mary's County, Maryland, after an 18-month tour of duty in Afghanistan. Upon his return, he was depressed and was soon diagnosed with post-traumatic stress disorder (PTSD) and was prescribed medication. In early December 2006, he received orders to deploy to Iraq in January 2007. He told his father that he did not want to go to war the first time, and he did not want to go again. On Christmas day, 2006, Mr. Dean seemed to "snap" according to his family, threatening to kill himself. He drove to his father's home, seized some weapons, and barricaded himself inside. For 14 hours police negotiators attempted to convince Mr. Dean to peacefully surrender.

He fired shots at police cars outside. At some point, police tactical units began firing tear gas into the home to force Dean to come out. Dean then stepped outside and apparently pointed his gun at a police officer, at which time another officer fired and killed Mr. Dean. Mr. Dean was emotionally distressed, suffering from PTSD, and fearing a return to battle. He likely created a "suicide by cop" (Van Zandt, 1993) situation on Christmas day. For Mr. Dean, his level of emotional distress paralyzed his ability to effectively cope with the situation (Greenwell, 2006).

The Central Role of Emotion in Crisis Negotiation

Within crisis incidents, there emerges an interactive frame through which the hostage taker interprets events and responds to the actions and communication messages of the police tactical and negotiation teams that is grounded in the level of emotion (emotional distress) experienced by the subject. From the perspective of the traditional instrumental negotiation model, emotion and emotional distress are of little direct concern to incident resolution efforts. With the emergence of the expressive model, however, the centrality of emotion to crisis negotiation is more clearly articulated. With increased attention devoted to the expressive motivation of the perpetrator, a suspect's emotional state becomes a crucial ingredient in determining the success or failure of a negotiated outcome (Miron & Goldstein, 1979).

As such, the crisis interventionist focus delineated in the expressive model views emotional distress as compromising the individual's ability to process information and effectively problem solve critical issues and concerns. Active listening and empathic communication skills are identified by many authors (Carkhuff, 1981; Howell, 1982; Johnson, 1997; Lawyer & Katz, 1985; McMains & Mullins, 2001, 2006; Noesner & Webster, 1997) as essential in dealing with an individual's heightened level of emotional excitation and as the means for reducing the potential for negative and violent (fight/flight) reactions (Cannon, 1929). The general premise of this approach is that by reducing the subject's emotion through active listening, the negotiator will facilitate rationality and normative bargaining in the interaction.

While the desire to facilitate a reduction in emotional arousal and promote enhanced rational decision making is inherently central to resolving crisis interactions, the view of emotion as an undesirable "side effect" to normal conflict interaction and, therefore, a hindrance to effective incident resolution is flawed (Jones, 2000; Rogan & Hammer, 2002). This artificial separation of rationality and emotionality often results in an inadequate and an incomplete understanding of the role of affect in conflict interaction. Rather, emotion is viewed from the S.A.F.E. framework as a core element by which a person frames a conflict interaction.

Core Aspects of Emotion

Research is surprisingly limited in specifically examining the role of emotion in critical incident management and crisis negotiation. Yet, the crisis negotiation literature is not alone. General interpersonal and organization conflict and negotiation literature is likewise alarmingly devoid of any sizable body of research into emotion in conflict dynamics (Jones, 2001; Rogan, 1997).

Nevertheless, there are a number of consistent observations that can be made concerning the role of emotion in conflict interaction. First, communication dynamics are central to understanding emotion, and conflict is inherently an emotional process. Second, emotions emerge from individuals' interpretations of their social environment. That is, emotions arise from some sort of appraisal process (Jones, 2001, 2006). Third, conflict involves varying levels of emotional intensity, with critical incidents (where violence or the threat of violence is present) typically eliciting levels of emotional intensity that can more accurately be described in terms of emotional distress. Fourth, while emotions can be elicited in situations where social interaction is absent (e.g., viewing a sunset), the kinds of emotional distress experiences that characterize subjects in crisis situations are overwhelmingly generated from interpersonal communication events (Andersen & Guerrero, 1998). This emphasizes the role emotion plays as a barometer of peoples' social experiences. Sixth, emotional communication involves an interaction of verbal and nonverbal exchanges between individuals that can either intensify or reduce emotional distress (Andersen & Guerrero, 1998).

Defining Emotion

The importance for crisis negotiators to effectively deal with intense emotions of hostage takers is highlighted in a nationwide survey of police hostage/crisis negotiators I conducted with Dr. Rogan. The two most cited needs were assessment of hostage taker's emotionality and improving communication skills (Hammer, Van Zandt, & Rogan, 1994; Rogan, Hammer, & Van Zandt, 1994).

What is emotion? While researchers do not agree on a number of aspects of emotion (Ekman & Davidson, 1994), emotion generally is understood to involve three interrelated processes. The first process is the physiological. The physiological component focuses on the neurobiological reactions of the body, such as various amino acids and peptides that are produced in response to external emotion-eliciting stimuli. The second process is the cognitive, or the subjective, experience of emotion. The cognitive element refers to the mental appraisal processes of both internal somatovisceral fluctuations, which are posited to denote discrete emotional experiences (Lewis, 1993), and the cognitive assessment of environmental stimuli as they have meaning for the well-being of the individual (Lazarus, 1984, 1991). The third process is the behavioral. This component denotes the action tendencies, including the linguistic and paralinguistic means by which an individual conveys an emotional experience (Guerrero & La Valley, 2006; Pittam & Scherer, 1993).

These elements interact with one another in systematic ways. First, emotions arise in response to stimuli that threaten or enhance one's goals. Emotional responses are often tied to precipitating events, and those events are construed along a continuum from dangerous to self to supportive of self. Second, affect is a core characteristic in defining emotion. Affect is concerned with the subjective experience of emotion and refers to the positiveness or negativeness (valence) of one's feeling state. Thus, anger and sadness are valenced as negative emotional states, while happiness and joy are positive emotions. Third, emotional responses are typically expressed through physiological changes, with more intense emotions related to a higher degree of physiological changes (e.g., heart rate and perspiration). Fourth, cognitive appraisals act to interpret emotional experience. That is, whether an initial emotional reaction to an event is positively or negatively experienced depends on how that event is understood or cognitively appraised. More specifically, emotion as appraisal entails a cognitive assessment of one's environment and the factors that tend to block and disrupt one's goal achievement (Lazarus, 1984, 1991; Smith & Pope, 1992). Finally, emotions are accompanied by specific action tendencies or behavioral imperatives associated with specific emotional experiences. These action tendencies provide a map for how an individual may likely respond to heightened emotions. These action tendencies are critically important in crisis situations, where the subject may be experiencing emotional distress (i.e., highly intense emotions) (Guerrero & La Valley, 2006).

Crisis Incidents and Emotion Markers

Undeniably, crisis incidents are marked by heightened levels of emotional excitation. Consequently, accurate assessment of a suspect's emotional experience is essential to achieving a peacefully negotiated incident resolution. Historically, the expressive model has relied upon developing a suspect's psychological and personality profile as a means to predict affective and behavioral propensities (Borum & Strentz, 1992; Lanceley, Ruple, & Moss, 1985). Numerous social psychologists, however, warn against such profiling as it tends to minimize the interactive nature of most emotional experiences (Miller & Leary, 1992).

There is reason to believe that accurate assessment or tracking of the emotional experience of the subject (and police negotiator) can be accomplished by attending to the verbal and nonverbal cues expressed by the interacting parties. In one study, Dr. Rogan and I (1995) examined emotional distress messages in hostage/crisis incidents by focusing not only on the nonverbal display of emotion states, but also on the communicative dimensions of language in terms of emotional intensity (degree of strength/weakness) and emotional valence (degree of positive or negative emotion) as manifest in a subject's linguistic cues (words). We quantitatively analyzed these two dimensions of emotional distress communication in three separate incidents (representative of the three most typical incidents negotiated): a suicide, a mental/emotional instability incident, and a domestic hostage situation.

Across all three incidents, the subject's subjective emotional experience became negatively intense shortly after the negotiators initiated contact. This reflects a common point at which the perpetrator realized the full severity of the situation and responded by escalating his behavior into increased competition and aggressiveness. Following this initial period, the perpetrator's negative affect began to decrease.

However, as negotiators began to move the interaction to problem-solving negotiation, differences between the types of incidents began to emerge. In the suicide situation, the subject's verbal behavior began a steady increase in negative intensity. This pattern continued throughout the remainder of the interaction to the point where he committed suicide. Comparatively, the domestic hostage incident was marked by an up-and-down progression to the point at which the perpetrator reneged on a plan to surrender. The emotional and mental instability situation was characterized by a continual increase in positive intensity up through the perpetrator's surrender.

Two findings from this study are relevant. First, the negotiator in the suicide incident characterized the perpetrator as being unemotional throughout the entire incident. The negotiator based this assessment primarily on the general tone of the perpetrator's voice. Yet, as evidenced by our coding of the perpetrator's verbal messages, we detected an increase in positive affect up to the point at which the negotiator refocused the interaction on negotiating the problem (shifting from expressive/emotional to instrumental/rational issues), which was marked by a continual increase in negative affect and ultimately the perpetrator's suicide. Second, this study indicates that verbal messages can be evaluated for important information about a speaker's emotional state and behavioral propensity. Subsequent research by W. Bilsky, J. Muller, A. Voss, and E. Von Groote (2004) examined this metric with that of the Gottschalk-Gleser hostility scale and found mutual validity, reliability, and usefulness of both assessment protocols. Therefore, attending to the content of verbal messages can provide negotiators with critical insight into the perpetrator's mind.

TRACKING EMOTIONAL DISTRESS ISSUES

The S.A.F.E. model defines emotional distress as "intense, negative emotions that compromise an individual's coping ability" (Hammer, 2005b, p. 11). Subjects are operating within this frame when negative emotions dominate their behavior. The police negotiator's goal, when subjects are experiencing emotional distress, is to "help the subject cope with these negative feelings so he/she can re-assess the situation and peacefully surrender" (Hammer, 2005b, p. 11).

The S.A.F.E. model identifies five essential emotional distress states that are posited as particularly dangerous in a critical incident and a sixth emotional (positive) state of happiness or joy. The emotional distress states are sadness, fear, disgust, anger, and shame. These emotions are also identified by a number of researchers as fundamental to the human experience. The S.A.F.E. model highlights the emotional meaning, what R.S. Lazarus

(1994) identifies as core relational themes and the action tendencies of these negative emotional experiences (Andersen & Guerrero, 1998; Scherer & Wallbot, 1994; Shaver, Schwartz, Kirson, & O'Connor, 1987).

Sadness is viewed as a sense of loneliness, rejection, and discouragement based on an experience of a significant loss in one's life. The action tendency emphasized in the S.A.F.E. model is to disengage from the loss and seek help in coping with the loss. Fear is a sense of apprehension, uncertainty, and danger based on a perceived threat that can physically or psychologically hurt oneself. The action tendency of fear is to avoid or escape from the perceived threat. Disgust is a sense of distaste or revulsion toward something or someone (including oneself) that is viewed as spoiled or deteriorated. The action tendency of disgust is to get "rid of" or "wash away" the offending emotion. Anger is a sense of being physically or psychologically restrained based on a view that another has unfairly interfered with one's attainment of some goal. The action tendency of anger is to attack the offending party. Shame is a fundamentally intense, painful sense of dejection and a feeling of being rejected by others. Shame involves a desperate occupation with one's view of self as inadequate, inferior, and separated from one's social place (Retzinger, 1993). The action tendency for shame is to hide, disappear, or die. The sixth emotion is happiness or joy. This is an important, core positive emotional state and is experienced as elation with being with people. The action tendency for happiness is to approach or embrace.

Emotional Contagion

The S.A.F.E. model views "emotion work" with an emotionally distressed subject as involving a stabilization of his or her emotional experience and efforts at transforming negative, emotionally distressed states toward more positive (e.g., happiness) emotional experiences. This is important as more positive emotional experiences are associated with an increased willingness to explore new ideas, more effective problem solving, increased responsiveness to suggestions, and less extreme (and violent) risk-taking behavior.

Further, a more positive emotional state of a subject can help facilitate emotional matching, or what is more commonly referred to as emotional contagion (Andersen & Guerrero, 1998). Emotional matching helps create a positive emotional climate between parties. Commenting on happiness, K. Oatley and P.N. Johnson-Laird (1987) state, "the social communication of emotions leads each actor to become aware of the other's euphoric feelings, and a euphoric mutual emotion is created" (p. 46). Of course, negative emotions can also be matched as well. For this reason, the S.A.F.E. model prepares police negotiators to express their understanding of the situation to the subject, but not to inhabit the negative emotionally distressed space of the subject.

Emotional contagion most often becomes salient during a crisis event at the time of the surrender ritual. At that time, the police negotiator has obtained the agreement of the subject to finally "come out." When this happens, there is often a visible sigh of relief that occurs in the Negotiation Operations Center. However, the goal of the police negotiator should not be to encourage the subject to emotionally "match" this downturn in emotional energy. Rather, the S.A.F.E. model recommends that police negotiators, rather than sigh, increase their positive affect by expressing an emotionally positive response when they obtain the subject's agreement to surrender. When the police negotiator engages in a positive emotion message to the subject (e.g., "Great! You made a good decision here!"), the possibility exists for the positive emotion of the police negotiator to be matched by the subject, providing that extra emotional support to put the gun down and come out to end the standoff.

TRACKING EMOTIONAL DISTRESS CONCERNS

In tracking the emotional distress of the subject, the S.A.F.E. model suggests that police negotiators observe (and confirm) other possible behavioral patterns that may be present vis-à-vis the emotional distressed state. Sadness can be an indicator of depression and possible suicide. Therefore, police negotiators can look closely at possible suicide intentions of the subject (McMains & Mullins, 2006). Fear can be an indicator of unpredictable behavior, both with subjects and hostages. It may be more likely, for instance, for hostage takers, who are experiencing heightened levels of fear, to unexpectedly walk out the door with their gun to surrender. This unpredictable and highly dangerous act can result in the subject being shot. Similarly, during a tactical rescue attempt, hostages who are experiencing terror can run directly into the line of fire and get themselves killed while trying to escape.

The S.A.F.E. model suggests that subjects who are operating in a "disgust" emotion distressed frame may focus that disgust on themselves. This sense of self-disgust may be indicative of substantive abuse problems. The metaphors typically used with substance abuse, for instance, are essentially disgust metaphors, including "getting rid of the poison in my body," and "getting and staying clean." Sometimes, self-disgust may also be associated with other forms of abuse as well (e.g., sexual abuse).

Anger is typically a short-lived emotion. When subjects are operating in an anger-focused emotionally distressed state, explosive, violent actions can be unexpectedly taken. Expressed anger can be explosive and unpredictable. The subject may "lash" out at the first target in his or her field of vision. Walls may be punched, furniture kicked, hostages assaulted, or tactical officers may be shot at. Once anger is unleashed, because it is short-lived, the subject may regret his or her aggressive behavior. However, the damage may already be done.

Finally, shame is a long-lasting emotionally distressed state. Shame can take the form of overt shame, where the painful feeling is directly experienced but likely misnamed (e.g., "I feel miserable"), or the form of bypassed shame, where the shame is "bypassed" by dysfunctional thinking about "what I should have done or not done" (Retzinger, 1993). The S.A.F.E. model suggests that subjects who are experiencing dysfunctional levels of shame may have had previous "shaming" experiences, such as sexual or physical abuse. Under these conditions, shame often fuses with anger and produces a sense of "humiliated fury" in individuals (Retzinger, 1993). This humiliated fury can be directed internally with suicide or externally, with aggression and violence against others (e.g., suicide by cop).

STRATEGIES FOR NEGOTIATING EMOTIONAL DISTRESS

Crisis intervention skills (Roberts, 1991) provide a foundation for police negotiators to sensitively and appropriately respond to the subject's level of emotional distress (McMains & Mullins, 2006). However, while the use of crisis intervention techniques and active listening skills as articulated in the traditional expressive model are designed to increase "understanding," they do not directly address the *strategic* use of crisis intervention skills to influence the subject to surrender. That is, there is a lack of strategic negotiation of the subject's emotional distress in current crisis negotiation practices. The common view is that police negotiators should express understanding through the use of active listening skills toward the subject; by doing this, they will be better able to influence the subject to surrender.

This is clearly articulated by G.W. Noesner and M. Webster (1997) in their discussion of the change process involved in negotiating with a subject in a hostage/crisis situation: "The application of active listening skills helps to create an empathic relationship between the negotiators and the subject. Demonstrating this empathy tends to build rapport and, in time, change the subject's behavior" (p. 19). However, this approach does not articulate how this process can actually influence the subject to surrender, other than the assertion that active listening skills lead to influence. Further, this approach implies that active listening skills can act as "magic bullets" that bring relief to the hostage taker. From a different perspective, the S.A.F.E. model is consistent with B.R. Burleson and D.J. Goldsmith's (1998) view of supportive communication: "the search for verbal magic bullets is misguided: Any effect an act or message has on another's distress does not come about directly, but only through the effect it has on the other's reappraisal of his or her situation" (p. 259).

The S.A.F.E. model, with its focus on the emotional meaning, action tendencies, and appraisal processes around emotional distress provides the police negotiator a set of tools to strategically listen and influence the hostage taker toward a peaceful resolution. The S.A.F.E. strategies presented below are grounded in research on supportive communication (e.g., Burleson & Goldsmith, 1998) and other emotion-related research (e.g., Andersen & Guerrero, 1998; Lazarus, 1991).

The S.A.F.E. model emphasizes that when a subject is experiencing emotional distress, the police negotiator needs to respond to the subject's subjective emotional experience through supportive communication. There are three key features of supportive communication proposed in the S.A.F.E. model concerning emotional distress that help lessen the intensity of negative emotions and then help influence the subject toward more peaceful solutions to his or her current situation. The first involves the police negotiator focusing on the core feeling state of the subject (Hammer, 2005b). As Burleson and Goldsmith (1998) state, "There is evidence that, across a wide variety of situations, focusing on the feelings of the distressed other is consistently evaluated as helpful" (p. 248). Once the police negotiation team identifies the predominant S.A.F.E. frame of the subject as emotional distress, the police negotiator needs to correctly understand the core emotional experience or state of the subject (e.g., sadness and/or fear). Crisis intervention skills generally and active listening techniques more specifically can play a useful role in helping the police negotiator identify the core emotional reality of the subject (Hammer, 2005b).

The second feature of supportive communication, evidenced by research across a wide range of situations, is for the police negotiator to focus the subject on providing a description or explanation of his or her problem or situation. The police negotiator should encourage the subject in "telling his or her story" while avoiding evaluating the subject's actions or feelings (Burleson & Goldsmith, 1998). Again, active listening skills such as open-ended questions, paraphrasing, emotional labeling, and offering an explanation of the subject's thoughts, actions, and/or feelings have been identified as particularly supportive and effective in communicating understanding of the subject and his or her emotional experience (Burleson & Goldsmith, 1998; Elliott, 1985; Hill et al., 1988).

The third important feature of supportive communication with the subject focuses on the action tendencies of the subject's emotional state. The S.A.F.E. approach suggests that the police negotiator, after encouraging the subject to tell his or her "story" and how he or she feels, can then respond to the action tendency of the primary emotion the subject is experiencing. For example, the police negotiator can respond to the subject's emotion of intense "sadness" by emphasizing that the subject is not alone, he or she does not have to carry this loss by himself or herself, and *there is help available*. The action tendency of sadness is to seek help. By focusing on framing the negotiator's response to this action tendency, the negotiator gains influence and, in effect, offers a solution to the emotional distress the subject is experiencing. For subjects whose emotional distress state is fear, the negotiator can respond by emphasizing everything that the police and others are doing to reduce uncertainty and threat. In this case, the police negotiator can frame his or her responses to the subject by emphasizing a plan for resolution and safety. For hostage takers who have a primary emotional state of disgust, the police negotiator can emphasize what the subject can do to wash away his or her problems and start "clean" again.

For perpetrators who are in the throes of intense anger, the police negotiator can (1) refocus the attention of the subject away from the target of his or her anger or (2) help the subject reappraise the situation. Both of these strategies speak directly to the action tendency of anger to "attack the offending party." Finally, for the emotional distressed state of shame, the core action tendency is to hide, disappear, or die. In these cases, police negotiators can respond to this action tendency by acknowledging how difficult the situation is for the subject and how devastated he or she feels. The police negotiator can further emphasize that the subject is not alone and that people will understand. In other words, the police negotiator should focus on countering the sense the subject feels about being "cut off" from others by reinforcing that there are people who do understand how he or she feels and his or her situation.

Overall, focusing on the emotional experience of someone who is distressed is more helpful and supportive than avoiding, denying, or minimizing the depth or intensity of the feeling state (e.g., "You're situation is not as bad as it seems") of the subject. Supportive communication communicates understanding and functions to help an individual reappraise his or her situation, enabling more creative problem solving to emerge that can lead to a peaceful resolution rather than suicide or violent aggression against others. A core aspect of influencing the subject during this reappraisal process is for the police negotiator to frame his or her responses to the subject in terms of the action tendencies of the subject's core emotional distressed state.

S.A.F.E. MODEL SUMMARY

The S.A.F.E. model is not construed within more instrumental approaches to conflict or crisis negotiation. In this regard, the S.A.F.E. model is not designed to be an a priori prescriptive that considers the only viable path to resolving conflict as dependent upon a singular focus on the substantive areas of disagreement. More pointedly, the S.A.F.E. model is not based on the assumption that substantive goal management is at the core of crisis incident resolution. Rather, the S.A.F.E. model is based on the premise that the degree of conflict de-escalation or escalation (and therefore, peaceful resolution vs. violent outcomes) is grounded in the degree to which those S.A.F.E. frames that are salient to the interactants are addressed: the degree to which substantive demands are negotiated or ignored, attunement (relational closeness) enhanced or diminished, face honored or threatened, and/or emotional distress empathically transformed or intensified.

Also, the S.A.F.E. approach posits that contending parties establish stable interpretive frames (substantive demand, attunement, face, or emotional distress) through which they attach meaning and respond to self and other's actions. During crisis and conflict, these interpretive frames are oftentimes "held onto" with great vigor as they anchor a person's sense of control in highly stressful, volatile crisis situations.

Hostage takers can move into and out of these interpretive frames, however, during the course of an incident. One way in which subjects are more likely to move from one interpretive frame to another (to reframe their situation) is based on the degree to which the police negotiator is able to match or recognize and operate within the dominant frame of the hostage taker. The S.A.F.E. model argues that conflict de-escalates to the degree the police negotiator's framing "matches" the dominant frame in use by the hostage taker. Communicating within the same frame enables the parties to strive to create a sense of shared reality and thereby experience "progress" toward resolving/addressing the salient issues within the particular interpretive frame.

When this sense of progress develops, subjects feel understood and thus are more readily able to move toward agreement within that issue frame. For example, a hostage taker who is predominately concerned with face issues will be more willing to shift to a substantive demand frame (discuss procedures for surrender) if he or she experiences a sense of validation from the negotiator (face-honoring acts).

On the other hand, the S.A.F.E. model contends that escalation arises when the subject and the police negotiator (or TPIs) operate in divergent interpretive frames. When this occurs, the hostage taker (and negotiator) will likely feel misunderstood, manipulated, etc., which creates a sense of lack of progress that inhibits movement toward agreement on salient issues within the frame and less likelihood toward shifting to another frame.

Further, the S.A.F.E. model suggests that conflict escalates if parties attempt to shift interpretive frames prematurely when a sense of progress in addressing the concerns salient to that frame does not sufficiently emerge. In contrast, conflict de-escalates to the degree the parties shift interpretive frames (in a matched, synchronous manner) after a sense of negotiated progress is achieved within a frame. That is, police negotiators can effectively shift interpretive frames with a hostage taker after achieving a degree of resolution toward the salient issues within the discourse, interpretive frame.

As negotiation and bargaining research has demonstrated, successful conflict resolution will not be realized absent the management of relational and identity issues (Donohue, Lyles, & Rogan, 1989). Because hostage events are inherently stressful and potentially violent, the interpretive frames of attunement, face, and emotional distress often are more predominant as the negotiation progresses, while the substantive demand frame may emerge later in the negotiation after progress has been made between the subject and the police negotiator in these other frames. The S.A.F.E. model therefore posits that escalation of conflict is more likely to occur when attention is focused prematurely on substantive demands with lack of sufficient attention to the issues important to the hostage taker within the attunement, face, and/or emotional distress frames.

CONCLUSION

Since its initial inception in the New York City Police Department in 1972 (Boltz & Hershey, 1979; Hammer & Weaver, 1998), crisis/hostage negotiation has evolved into a integral facet of police procedure. This maturation has been accompanied by increased conceptual clarity and sophistication in how crisis/hostage situations are defined and the preferred methods for resolving incidents. Specifically, the traditional instrumental and expressive approaches to crisis negotiation each reflect the evolving philosophy of how negotiators should ply their trade. Yet, each model suffers from various limitations in theoretical comprehensiveness as well as in application. Most notably, these models are limited in terms of the overemphasis on a limited set of psychological traits of the suspect and the bifurcation of a suspect's motivation as either instrumental or expressive. Comparatively, the S.A.F.E. model extends these existing frameworks by focusing on the framing function of negotiator and suspect communication as it allows for the concomitant occurrence of instrumental and expressive needs of the parties involved.

The S.A.F.E. model as presented in this chapter has, by necessity, focused on the subject's behavior and what the police negotiator needs to know in order to effectively track and then respond to the subject during violent confrontations. This explanation of the S.A.F.E. model is, therefore, proffered from the perspective of the police negotiator (and other crisis intervenors) who must confront violent subjects.

While the S.A.F.E. framework is presented in this format, the model lends equal weight and interactional influence to the behavior of the police negotiator and the subject as they communicate with one another. Indeed, the S.A.F.E. framework could have just as easily been presented from the perspective of the subject as well. Therefore, it is important to note that at a meta level, the S.A.F.E. model provides equal value to assessment and negotiation strategies between contending parties. In short, the S.A.F.E. model equally applies the four frames to the police negotiator as well as to the subject, and in other presentations, for different audiences, a more "interactively" framed description of the S.A.F.E. model would be appropriate.

However, this book, as stated before, is directed to those individuals entrusted by society to respond to violent confrontations, namely, the police tactical and negotiation teams. Therefore, the explanation of the S.A.F.E. model is presented from their vantage point. In conclusion, the S.A.F.E. model is an integrative approach for discerning the functional implications of communicator discourse around four basic conflict issues, including substantive demands, attunement, face, and emotional distress.

PART III

Analysis of Four Critical Incidents and Summary

CHAPTER 7

The Alpha Incident: To Pay for One's Sins

BACKGROUND

The perpetrator, "Al," is a martial arts enthusiast in his early 40s. Armed with a rifle, he takes over a television studio in the downtown area of a medium-sized city in the United States.[8] The incident lasts a total of seven hours. After taking seven employees hostage, Al then conducts a television interview with one of the hostages, claiming his actions are designed to call attention to the plight of the "poor, blacks, and prisoners." He then informs the media that he had previously shot his girlfriend, Amy, and also had set explosives in another building (which he identified during the negotiation) in the downtown area. Ninety minutes later, Al provides a key to his apartment to one of the hostages, after which he then releases all seven hostages. During this time, he states he would like to "wage a gun battle with the police." Using the key provided by Al, police subsequently find Amy's body in his apartment along with a large arsenal of guns. Later, the police bomb squad locates the explosives and defuses them. About five hours later, while negotiating with the police negotiation unit, Al kills himself, ending the siege with suicide.

Table 1.1 (Chapter 1) identifies this incident in terms of a single male who had a fatal altercation with his girlfriend earlier (a domestic incident). He held hostages and subsequently released them. The event lasted seven hours and resulted in self-inflicted suicide. In this chapter, an initial topical analysis is presented, followed by a detailed episodic analysis of the communicative dynamics between Al and the hostage negotiator. The chapter concludes with an overall summary statement of the S.A.F.E. frame dynamics operative in this event.

TOPICAL EPISODE ANALYSIS

The discourse in this incident is comprised of 13 interactional episodes defined by conversation topic. Table 7.1 summarizes these episodes. The audiotaped negotiation begins with a "tabula rasa" topic of locating two acquaintances (episode 1, *location of two acquaintances*). Specifically, Al requests the help of the PN in finding two police officers whom Al had known in the past. While this topic reflects a request from Al for assistance from the PN, the PN was not able to locate these two individuals and informs Al of this fact. After informing Al of his efforts to help, the PN asks Al, "Where do we stand now? What do ya...where do we go from here?" [L8]. This question functions as an invitation for Al to continue the conversation on this topic or move the conversation to another subject. That is, the question can be interpreted by Al to continue with the more instrumental discussion of locating these two individuals or it also provides a platform for Al to move the conversation to a topic of his own choosing.

Episode 2 (*suicide*) begins as Al redirects the conversation to the topic of his impending suicide, clearly a more personal focus. Episode 3 (*group membership*) is initiated by the PN when he introduces a more general subject, namely, the kinds of groups Al has joined. After discussing this topic, Al again shifts the conversation back to his own situation, talking about his past use of drugs (episode 4).

In episode 5 (*reasons for drug addiction*), the PN shifts the topic by asking Al the reason for his taking—and becoming "hooked"—on drugs. In episode 6 (*location of two acquaintances*), Al again moves the topic back to the initial subject, the whereabouts of his two acquaintances; in this case, stating to the PN that he (Al) does not believe either one is really going to "come here." At this point, the PN moves the conversation to the more general topic of the kinds of activities, including karate and boxing, that Al enjoys (episode 7, *group activities*).

In episodes 8 (*Al's dog*) and 9 (*suicide*), Al shifts the conversation again to his own situation, specifically, his desire to have his dog with him and then his desire to commit suicide. In episode 10 (*chaos as a solution*), Al shifts the conversation to a more abstract, less personal topic: the need to create chaos in society in order to change society. However, he makes the point at the end of this discussion that, while chaos "uses up the system [L183]...my life will be used [up] but it [chaos] will continue on, it will be used up. And if there's a hereafter, I'll be waiting" [L185], thus moving the discussion "point" to the more personal focus of his ending his own life.

The PN then responds by shifting the topic back to the more general topic of *people Al knows* (episode 11). In episode 12 (*Al's dog*), the PN moves the conversation to discussing Al's dog, focusing on what can be done with the dog (insofar as the police are not going to risk someone to bring the dog to Al). In the final episode (13, *suicide*), Al takes the lead in shifting the

Table 7.1 Topical Episodes in the Alpha Incident

Episode #	Line #	Topic Shift by	Topic Description
1	1–8	N/A	*Location of two acquaintances* Al requests police negotiator (PN) to locate two individuals whom Al had known in the past. The PN responds by updating Al on the police's efforts to try to find these people.
2	9–17	Al	*Suicide* Al shifts the conversation to his intention to kill himself.
3	18–40	PN	*Group membership* Discussion with PN about the various groups to which Al belongs.
4	41–67	Al	*Past drug use* Al discusses his past use of drugs.
5	68–78	PN	*Reasons for drug addiction* PN questions Al concerning the reasons for his use of drugs in the past.
6	79–85	Al	*Location of two acquaintances* Al returns conversation to locating the two individuals requested earlier.
7	86–142	PN	*Group activities (karate and boxing)* PN changes topic to activities Al engages in, including karate and boxing and his time served in the Marines.
8	143–159	Al	*Al's dog* Al changes topic of discussion to him walking his dog and his attachment to the dog.
9	160–174	Al	*Suicide* Al moves the topic to his goal of committing suicide.
10	175–185	Al	*Chaos as a solution* Al changes the conversation to discussing creating chaos in society in order to change society.
11	186–189	PN	*People Al knows* PN shifts conversation by asking Al if there are people here he deals with all the time.
12	190–228	PN	*Al's dog* PN shifts conversation back to Al's dog and what can be done with the dog.
13	229–269	Al	*Suicide* Al shifts conversation back to killing himself.

conversation back to his desire to kill himself and the lack of trust (attunement) he feels toward the PN.

EPISODIC S.A.F.E. ANALYSIS

The first episode (*location of two acquaintances*) begins with the PN responding to a previously (unrecorded) request from Al to locate two individuals so Al could talk with them. This initial episode is enacted largely within a substantive demand frame between Al and the PN. That is, Al's question concerning the whereabouts of these two police officers is framed in terms of the more instrumental sense of "have you located them? where are they?" rather than an attunement frame of "can you help me?" The PN similarly responds to this request largely in instrumental or substantive terms, that is, providing information on the police's inability to locate the two individuals. Thus, information is exchanged around a peripheral substantive demand made by Al. At this point, there is no indication of attunement conflict between Al and the PN concerning this demand (e.g., a power struggle in finding and bringing these two individuals to the scene). Rather, the interaction is framed by both parties in terms of information exchange around one of the few substantive, although peripheral, demands expressed by Al.

After providing this information, the PN asks, "where do we stand now?" [L8]. This open-ended question can function either to continue the more instrumentally focused discussion around locating the two individuals or it can function as a frame transition device, permitting Al to shift S.A.F.E. frames. To this question, Al responds in terms of what he perceives his face goal is, namely, to present a more positive self-image to the police negotiator, through the face-saving act of committing suicide. In shifting to a face frame in episode 2 (*suicide*), Al responds to the PN's question, with "I have . . . I have to go out . . . I have to terminate myself. I induce no other way out" [L9]. Subsequent dialogue (as shown in the following list) in episode 2 reflects a pattern of face interaction that consistently emerges throughout the negotiation.

Alpha Incident: Episode 2 (suicide): Lines 10–16

L10	PN	Well, as I said before I think you're selling yourself short on that.
L11	Al	Nobody sells themselves short if they have to pick between the two.
L12	PN	But you're making assumptions that you only have a few choices and I don't think that's necessarily the case.
L13	Al	Well it isn't fair. I have to join Amy.
L14	PN	Well as I said before . . . I'm still trying to check on that situation too.
L15	Al	No she's gone I have to join her.
L16	PN	Well we don't know that for a fact yet, Al . . . you're making an assumption.

Al's self-face attack statement of "I have to terminate myself" is followed up by the PN with a "restore other face" statement ("I think you're selling yourself short on that"). Al's response in line 11 is again a self-face attack ("nobody sells themselves short if they have to pick between the two"), and the PN again responds with a restore other face statement ("But you're making assumptions that you only have a few choices, and I don't think that's necessarily the case"). In line 13, Al says, "I have to join Amy." At this point, the PN does not directly respond to this clear suicide statement. Rather, he comments, "I'm still trying to check on that situation, too" at which time Al responds, "No she's gone I have to join her." The PN again sidesteps this statement and says, "Well, we don't know that for a fact yet." Al, now clearly frustrated, asserts, "No, I know she's gone." [L17].

This discourse reflects Al's fundamental focus on self-identity issues and the importance of acknowledging his act of murder, while the PN attempts to "build up" Al's self-esteem in order to shift the dialogue to a more substantive platform (e.g., how to work this out). At the same time, there is an emotional "undercurrent" present for Al around his sense of sadness and shame. Al feels a strong sense of shame, reflected in his efforts at emotionally distancing himself from the fact that he just killed Amy. Al says, for example, "No she's gone I have to join her" rather than the more emotionally honest sentiment of "*my God, I killed my Amy. I can't live with myself anymore*." The PN responds to Al's emotionally distancing efforts by similarly separating Al from his action by suggesting to Al that he has a lot to live for. However, this approach avoids a deeper dialogue with Al about his feelings of shame, responsibility, and his suicidal intent. The result is that Al perceives the PN as disingenuous, thus establishing a secondary, though important, trajectory of increasing relational distance (attunement frame).

The PN responds to Al's last assertion by abruptly changing the topic in episode 3 (*group membership*) when he says, "Then again, the people that you're trying to help, they need you" [L18]. This next interchange (in the following two lists) reflects both face and emotional distress disjuncture. That is, Al and the PN are avoiding deeper discussion of Al's face needs and emotional distress, resulting in an increasing relational distance between them.

Alpha Incident: Episode 3 (group membership): Lines 18–24

L18	PN	Then again the people that you're trying to help, they need you.
L19	Al	They don't need me!
L20	PN	Who have they got?
L21	Al	They'll...they'll do it for themselves now
L22	PN	Who's going to do it for them?
L23	Al	They will do it.
L24	PN	They're just a...a big group of people with no leadership at all. You're the only hope that they've got.

Alpha Incident: Episode 3 (group membership): Lines 32–39

L32	PN	Do you belong to a...a group? Or do you have an organization of your own?
L33	Al	You'll find that out...I've messed things up.
L34	PN	Well, I'd just like to know...It's...you know again...I'm trying to point out to you that you're a strong person...You're an extremely strong person...and you've got a lotta...a lot of room to move and you've=
L35	Al	[I've]
L36	PN	=got a lot of things for people that you have a strong feeling for.
L37	Al	I've fouled it up.
L38	PN	Nothing...there's nothing that can't be corrected...nothing....
L39	Al	[I did something that cannot be corrected.]

Lines 18–24 reflect more overt tension between Al and the PN, with the PN attempting to tell Al that people need him and Al forcefully asserting that people do not need him! This sense of increased relational distance is reflected in Al's response to the PN question of "Do you belong to a group?" Al comments with both a strong relationally distancing message ("You'll find that out") and a return to self-face attack ("I've messed things up"). Again, the PN attempts to restore other face [L34], which is consistently rejected by Al when he says, "I've fouled it up" [L37], and again, "I did something that cannot be corrected" [L39]. The dynamics of Al's face concern (I am no good) and the PN's response (no, you are a good person) reflect this emerging pattern of face and emotional distress disjuncture, resulting in increasing contentiousness between the two parties.

Episode 4 (*past drug use*) is initiated by Al when he mentions that using drugs previously "messed him up." In this episode, the PN asks Al a number of questions about his drug use. These questions include "Do you think drugs are the whole problem?" [L44] and "Did you ever take anything else?" [L46], at which point the following dialogue takes place:

Alpha Incident: Episode 4 (past drug use): Lines 47–59

L47	Al	I've took acid in '68 and couldn't do anything else I was hallucinating so bad. I took angel dust in San Francisco unbeknownst to myself twice...people...sneaked it on me.
L48	PN	How'd that affect ya?
L49	Al	Bad...very bad.
L50	PN	Still get flashbacks from that?
L51	Al	I don't think so. I...you know it's...I know you people wanna write me off as crazy but=
L52	PN	[you know]
L53	Al	=I'm not that crazy, I may be slightly warped, who knows. Everybody's warped to a degree, but I am not that crazy.

L54	PN	But those are the exact things...that are...really your strong suit. If you could deal with...ya know convince people that you've had some bad trips with acid and angel dust...The far reaching effects of that still aren't known. But it...the flashbacks and the problems that occur from that are horrendous. Now=
L55	Al	What's that got to do with anything. I don't understand what you mean.
L56	PN	[but that's=] you know if that's having an effect on you now hopefully they can deal with that and any problems you've had up to this point you can attribute directly to that. Ya know so you write that off...it's not a problem.
L57	Al	Are you...are you trying to tell me the bullshit that I should try to say that the things that happened to Amy can be attributed to drugs! It's bullshit. I will not...I will not cop that. I pay for that.
L58	PN	Do you know that for a fact?
L59	Al	I will pay for it. I know for a fact my hand will pay for that.

This episode concludes with marked escalation brought about by the disjuncture between Al's focus on face concerns and the overt introduction of a substantive frame by the PN. As this episode begins, the questions being asked by the PN are interpreted by Al as genuine interest in understanding his previous life experiences around the use of drugs. However, when Al vehemently denies he is "crazy," the PN responds with "that are...really your strong suit...convince people that you've had some bad trips...." At this point, Al is utterly confused [L55]. The PN then clarifies what he means, suggesting that because Al had used drugs in the past, he could use this in order to reduce any sentence he might receive for killing Amy [L54, 56]. This abrupt introduction of a substantive frame by the PN (which is designed to give Al some hope that he can bargain during trial) is interpreted by Al as lack of genuine interest in Al's face needs. Because of this, Al ex plodes [L57] and renews his commitment to kill himself in order to pay for what he did to Amy. Further, Al continues to euphemistically refer to his murder of Amy using emotionally distancing discourse, such as "are you... are you trying to tell me the bullshit that I should try to say that *the things that happened to Amy* can be attributed to drugs! It's bullshit. I will not... I will not cop that. I pay for that." Again, the underlying sentiment for Al is, "*I did something terribly wrong! I killed Amy! Trying to cop a plea bargain in court for killing my girlfriend does not make me feel better! It makes me feel even less worthwhile—and ashamed.*" This emotion of shame, within the frame of emotional distress, is not acknowledged by the PN. As S.M. Retzinger (1993) cogently finds, when not acknowledged, the emotional experience of shame generates its own fuel toward fulfilling its action tendency, namely, to disappear or die (in this case, through suicide).

Episode 4 (*past drug use*) ends with Al focusing on how he cannot sleep or live with the fact that he killed Amy. The PN reverts to the earlier strategy of responding to Al's self-face attack statements with efforts at restoring Al's face rather than acknowledging (validating) Al's view of himself. Al concludes this episode by stating, "I'm gonna have to pay for that [killing Amy]. Such a good person" [L67]. This episode again reflects the face and emotion pattern dynamics discussed previously.

The PN, perhaps sensing that the negotiation is becoming more positional and contentious, shifts the topic in episode 5 (*reasons for drug addiction*) back to Al's previous drug use and asks him, "What were you trying to raise money for?" [L68]. Episode 5 is relatively short in duration, with the PN attempting to engage Al in talking about his earlier experiences in San Francisco. However, Al is not particularly interested in discussing this topic in detail and provides perfunctory, short-answer responses, as reflected in this episode-ending dialogue:

Alpha Incident: Episode 5 (reasons for drug addiction): Lines 74–78

L74	PN	When were you last in San Francisco?
L75	Al	Seventy-three and seventy-four.
L76	PN	You haven't been back since?
L77	Al	No.
L78	PN	Do you still have contacts out there?

Episode 6 (*location of two acquaintances*) begins abruptly when Al simply changes the topic, refusing to answer the PN's question "do you still have contacts out there?" Rather, Al laughs, then sighs and says, "What, [the police acquaintances] are not comin' in, though, huh?" [L79]. The brief dialogue in episode 6, as well as the more extended discussion of various group activities Al is involved in (episode 7) and the kind of dog Al has (episode 8), reflects a period of small talk around general topics that are not relevant to either the situation or Al's face or emotional frame needs. In effect, this discourse functions only as small talk. Because attunement was not a predominant frame for Al at this time, the more social conversation present in episodes 7 and 8 are merely conversational "fillers" rather than meaningful dialogue around issues of relationship building and trust. At the end of episode 8, however, Al abruptly moves the conversation back to his intention to commit suicide when he comments that he "wanted to take him (the dog) with me, but I just...I couldn't do it" [L159].

Episodes 9 (*suicide*), 10 (*chaos as a solution*), and 11 (*people Al knows*), while focusing on different topics, function as underlying disjuncture between Al's primary face and emotion frames and the police negotiator's efforts at finding a "substantive" opening within which to redirect the conversation to the instrumental platform. In episode 9, Al again comments that he has failed, while the PN responds as he did in past episodes, with a face restoration statement that, unfortunately, does not provide a functional acknowledgment of the hopelessness and shame being experienced by Al. For example, Al comments, "I've accomplished absolutely nothing" [L167], and the PN responds with "well, as I say, I am sure that at this moment there are people all over the city here that are looking up to...to you..." [L168]. As in previous episodes, this interchange simply reinforces the disconnection between Al and the PN concerning the need to attend directly to Al's feelings of shame (emotional distress) and sense of inadequacy (face frame).

While the topic of chaos (episode 10) at a society level is a more abstract, less personal topic, the underlying frame for Al continues to be face. In this interaction, Al talks about the need for chaos in society in order to get society to change. Yet Al's discussion of the need for chaos in society is grounded in his own face frame, as he concludes by saying, "my life will be used [up]....And if there's a hereafter, I'll be waiting" [L185]. That is, for Al, the more abstract discussion of chaos in society is, in reality, a personal discussion of Al's own sense of failure (face frame). Similarly, in episode 11 (*people Al knows*), the situation is continuing to escalate, reflecting discontinuity between the face frame of Al and the difficulty in addressing this frame directly by the PN, as the following dialogue illustrates:

Alpha Incident: Episode 11 (people Al knows): Lines 186–189

L186 PN	Are there people...here...that you deal with all the time...that know what your goals are...and...
L187 Al	I would be a fool to answer that and you knew that.
L188 PN	Well...I'm just...I'm really trying to shed some light on the whole thing and where you're coming from...and...what we're going to do here. So that's uh...
L189 Al	[There...isn't much...time left for me (pause)

By episode 12 (*Al's dog*), the PN asks Al what they can do about the dog. Al and the PN then discuss who could possibly bring the dog to Al. While Al suggests a number of people whom he trusts to bring his dog to him, the PN reminds Al that "Again, all of those people...I am sure all of them would bring the dog to you...as long as you didn't have the weapons" [L208]. Al quickly responds by saying, "I told you I intend to terminate myself" [L209]. Somewhat later, a similar dialogue ensues.

Alpha Incident: Episode 12 (Al's dog): Lines 218–222

L218 PN	What...what would the problem be with giving up the weapons and then letting them bring the dog in?
L219 Al	(laughs) Are you...do you think I am totally crazy? Giving up the weapons? I have nothing...I can't even terminate myself!
L220 PN	I still think that we should look at this as where we're gonna go with the future...not where we're gonna end...there's a lot to the future.
L221 Al	I'm going into the dirt...I would like my dog to go with me.
L222 PN	That kind of a position...well...nobody knows who you are.

These interchanges again reflect the fundamental face frame within which Al is operating, the increasingly less effective efforts of the PN in attempting to give Al some reasons for living (face restoration rather than either acknowledging Al's view of himself or acknowledging Al's emotional distress state), and the effort of the PN to use the dog as an "instrumental" demand by Al with which some bargaining can now take place (e.g., give up your weapons and I will let you have your dog).

The final episode (13, *suicide*) begins with the same interactional dynamic within the face frame, reflecting increased frustration on the part of Al, who declares, "I could rip this place apart" [L229]. The PN responds, "But there again you're hurting people" [L230], followed by Al declaring, "Well, if they want to come in and try to take me, that's fine...I'm gonna do myself in...so that's unnecessary. But if they want to battle...what the hell. A warrior's way to go is just as fine a way as any other way to go" [L231]. Al is clearly declaring his desire to die, either by his own hand or by "victim precipitated homicide" in which the police are goaded into attacking Al so that he can go out in a "blaze of glory."

The PN responds to this declaration by saying, "I think you're being too hard on yourself, Al" [L232], after which the following now too familiar pattern emerges:

Alpha Incident: Episode 13 (suicide): Lines 233–239

L233 Al	No, I wasted it.
L234 PN	I think you need to turn it around, start thinking the other direction... where you go from here and what you can do for people.
L235 Al	I can't do anything for anyone now.
L236 PN	Why not?
L237 Al	It's all over...I told you I lost my viability.
L238 PN	I think you just made yourself stronger...
L239 Al	[I just flipped out...] No I flipped out...that's it...that's the madman...that's a deranged person...my viability went down the tubes.

As Al increasingly declares his intention for suicide, he also now directly addresses the lack of relational trust (low attunement) between himself and the PN in the very next interchange:

Alpha Incident: Episode 13 (suicide): Lines 240–253

L240 PN	Well...I think if you talked to a lot of other people in this world that you would find that that's not the case.
L241 Al	Well...ya know...I...I know this is your job to try to con me but...it just=
L242 PN	[No I'm not trying to con you!]
L243 Al	=It just doesn't work.

L244 PN	[wait] now let's get that straight right now...
L245 Al	Well you tried to con on Amy not being dead. I know she's dead.
L246 PN	I'm not trying to con you...I'm telling you facts that I have.
L247 Al	Well, they gave you false information.
L248 PN	I can't be assured of anything...anything that you ask me I'll try and accomplish....
L249 Al	[well see that's] what I mean, nobody can be assured of...
L250 PN	[You've got] to trust...to trust me.
L251 Al	I can't trust anybody right now.
L252 PN	[for me to con] you would be stupid.
L253 Al	All I can do is trust myself.

During this segment, Al is forcefully confronting the PN around attunement concerns and at the same time asserting his primary face concern to restore some sense of honor through suicide coupled with his sense of hopelessness and shame in killing Amy. Al is essentially communicating to the PN that "*you no longer have influence with me. I am alone in this situation and that any help would be fruitless for me.*" Both Al and the PN are talking "past" one another.

Shortly thereafter, Al directly asks the PN, "What do you think...you think I should just shoot myself, or you guys wanna come in and try to take me?" [L263]. With this question, he reduces his focus in interacting with the PN to the existential question of how he is to die. The face goal of suicide is now all consuming for Al. The PN continues his attempts at face restoration (but not coupled with acknowledgment of Al's self-image he is asserting) and looking for openings to instrumentally "bargain" with Al. For example, the last comment made by the PN to Al is, "You have the whole system available to you...it's up to you now to use it. The whole system is waiting ...and you can work that system any way you want...to your advantage" [L269]. Unfortunately, Al, operating so centrally in a face frame and experiencing an unbearable sense of shame and remorse, has no desire or focus on "working the criminal justice system to his advantage." He is not interested in working out a substantive "deal" concerning his crimes.

In short, the substantive frame (for working out a deal) from which the PN was attempting to assert throughout the interaction was consistently rejected by Al as largely irrelevant. For Al, face and, secondarily, emotional distress were the predominant frames within which he experienced his interactions with the PN. Because of the disconnection between Al and the PN in terms of divergent frames, Al's frustration increased, his sense of the inevitable solidified, and attunement (trust) diminished. Al's emotional distress fueled his sense of failure, shame, and desire to end it all. At this point in time, Al took his weapon and killed himself.

OVERALL S.A.F.E. FRAME ANALYSIS

As this incident begins, Al's arrival at the television station is largely a "spur-of-the-moment" act in response to his shooting his girlfriend, Amy. While he initially takes hostages, he relatively quickly releases all of the captives. Why did Al decide to go to a television studio? In his impromptu television interview, Al states that he is taking over the station on behalf of the "poor people." However, this "goal" of "helping the poor, blacks, and prisoners" functions largely as a self-face restoration act on the part of Al (face frame). He arrives at the television studio also experiencing a great deal of emotional distress, particularly profound shame as a result of his killing of Amy. As such, *what "drives" Al throughout this incident are strong face needs coupled with heightened emotional distress.* When Al claims he is bringing to the attention of people everywhere the plight of the poor people in America, he is sadly attempting to present himself to others in a "positive light," as a compassionate individual. Therefore, his very first act of communication was indicative of a fundamental face frame through which he was currently experiencing his situation.

The PN operates within the substantive demand frame throughout this incident and does not acknowledge Al's face needs. Overall, the communication dynamics between Al and the PN reflect a disconnection between two core S.A.F.E. frames. One core S.A.F.E. frame for Al is that of face, specifically his desire to commit suicide—an act that, from Al's perspective, provides him an acceptable face-saving/restoring final act. For Al, his main goal is to end his life, either in a shoot-out with the police or by killing himself.

The introduction by Al of this face frame in the negotiation is largely avoided by the PN, whose efforts primarily focus on initiating a substantive demand frame through bargaining, in order to persuade Al to surrender.

A secondary S.A.F.E. frame disjuncture takes place around Al's inability to cope with the degree of emotional distress he is experiencing, specifically his feelings of shame as a result of killing Amy. For Al, this heightened level of emotional distress provides the "fuel" for maintaining his commitment to kill himself to atone for what he "did to Amy." Unfortunately, the PN did not engage Al around these core emotions. Therefore, the situation continues to escalate as a result of divergent S.A.F.E. frames between Al and the PN. This escalation continues to the point that Al completes the suicide act to which he consistently expressed his commitment throughout the negotiation.

Face issues, experienced as a result of his killing of Amy, coupled with an inability to cope with the staggering feelings of shame, were important frames for Al in this incident. He experienced his discourse (interaction) with the PN primarily through the lens of face needs and his sense of an unbearable weight of negative feelings of shame. In contrast, the dominant frame for the PN was substantive demands, such that the PN was attempting to resolve the situation by focusing on generating substantive demands in order to initiate a process of tit-for-tat bargaining with Al. For the PN, he primarily experienced his discourse (interaction) with Al in terms of substantive demands or issues with which he could influence Al into surrendering. Because the PN did not enter deeply in the "emotional world" of Al, little progress was experienced by Al within this S.A.F.E. frame. Because of the consistent disjuncture in frames between Al and the PN, attunement remained very low throughout the incident, with relational distance increasing as the event unfolded.

Core Interactional Pattern

The core interactional pattern that emerged between the PN and Al that escalates the situation can be summarized as follows:

1. Al purposively shifts the topic of conversation to his sense of failure and his overwhelmingly negative self-image through statements such as "I've really fouled things up" (face frame). The dynamics of Al's face concern (I am no good) and the PN's response (no, you are a good person) reflect this emerging pattern of face needs disjuncture, resulting in increasing contentiousness between the two parties.
2. The PN sees no way to "negotiate" except through bargaining (substantive demand frame) with Al when Al makes such statements. Therefore, the PN does not acknowledge Al's face needs (i.e., does not express his understanding of how Al sees himself in this tragic situation).
3. Rather, the PN attempts to offer Al an alternative way to see himself and think about his situation through face-honoring statements (e.g., "I still think that we should look at this as where we're gonna go with the future") followed by efforts to shift Al into a substantive demand frame so a "deal can be worked out."
4. Al continues to feel misunderstood and manipulated (face needs not acknowledged) and restates his "I'm no good" face message. The PN does not validate Al's face needs and continues to respond with "you are a good person" (face-honoring response) with an attempt to shift Al into a substantive demand frame.

Overall, this incident reflects significant S.A.F.E. frame disjuncture between Al and the PN that is consistent throughout the negotiation. This divergence in frames escalates the situation to the point where Al, a man who murdered his girlfriend, no longer feels there is anything more to talk about with the PN. The event ends with Al committing suicide.

CHAPTER 8

The Bravo Incident: The End of the Line

BACKGROUND

This incident begins with "Bill" and his girlfriend, "Bonnie," attempting to rob a bank. Both Bill and Bonnie earlier committed a crime that included the shooting of a police officer. The bank robbery took place in a small city in the United States. While they were robbing the bank, a deputy pulled up to the bank and immediately requested additional assistance, resulting in the police surrounding the bank and 11 hostages being held inside the bank.

Bill was currently on parole, having been released from prison. He knew he would be returning to prison for bank robbery. Bonnie was aware that she would likely serve some time in prison as a coconspirator. During the course of negotiation, Bill releases 10 hostages initially; then, near the end of the negotiation, he releases the final hostage, "Betty," the assistant bank manager and indicates he and Bonnie will come out in 20 minutes. Fifteen minutes later, two gunshots are heard. The tactical team then inserted tear gas and entered the bank where they found both Bonnie and Bill dead from self-inflicted gunshot wounds. Both Bill and Bonnie participate in the negotiation, as well as five third-party intermediaries (TPIs) and the police negotiator. These TPIs were (1) Barb, a friend of Bonnie, (2) Butch, a friend of Bill, (3) Bud, a friend of Bill, (4) Beth, a friend of Bonnie, and (5) Bob, a newspaper reporter. In addition, the remaining hostage (Betty, the assistant bank manager) also talks with the police negotiator during the course of the event.

Table 1.1 (Chapter 1) identifies this incident in terms of a male and female who attempted to rob a bank (criminal incident). Previous violent acts included the shooting of a police officer earlier. Several hostages were held and subsequently released. The event lasted 5.5 hours and resulted in a double suicide. In this chapter, an initial topical analysis is presented, followed by a detailed episodic analysis of the communicative dynamics between Bill and Bonnie and the police negotiator, as well as several third-party intermediaries. The chapter concludes with an overall analysis of the S.A.F.E. frame dynamics present in this incident.

TOPICAL EPISODE ANALYSIS

The incident consists of 47 distinct interactional episodes defined by conversation topic. Table 8.1 summarizes these episodes. As the audiotaped negotiation begins, Bill, Bonnie, and Betty (the remaining hostage) are in the bank they were attempting to rob. The bank is surrounded by the police. The audiotaped negotiation begins with Bill telling the police negotiator that he is not ready to "get locked up yet" [L4]. Immediately following this brief exchange, Bill jokingly asks the PN, "Why, why don't you roll me up a couple of joints—got out of that dope you got off my old lady and send 'em over?" [L9]. The PN then responds good-naturedly that the deputy must have the marijuana to which Bill laughs and says, "well, don't let him smoke it cause it's some good stuff" [L15].

Shortly thereafter, the PN allows Barb, a friend of Bonnie, to get on the line with Bill. Barb initially talks with Bill (episode 3) and then talks more extensively with Bonnie (episodes 4–7). These conversations with Barb reflect a general focus on both hostage takers' fear of the police swarming the building, their fear of going to prison, and their desire to end it all through suicide.

During episodes 8–10, the PN returns to the line, talking directly with Bill about getting a lawyer when they surrender and whether they will be charged federally or by the state prosecutor.

Following this discussion, Butch, a friend of Bill's, comes on the line and talks at length with Bill about a variety of topics, including surrendering, lawyers, Bill's desire to kill himself, past criminal experiences, and reasons for committing the bank robbery (episodes 11–17).

In episode 18, the PN returns and continues the conversation along the same lines, talking about Bill's request to talk to a federal attorney, release of the hostage, surrendering, and Bill's restatement of his and Bonnie's desire to kill themselves (episodes 18–20).

In episodes 21–23 and 25–28, another outside, third party begins talking with Bill. Bud, a friend of Bill, comes on the line and engages in a lengthy conversation with Bill, sharing his own personal difficulties in life and encouraging Bill and Bonnie to surrender rather than commit suicide. Bud also inquires about what will happen when a deadline set earlier by Bill (3:00 P.M.) arrives. In episode 24, the police negotiator briefly talks to Bill about suicide.

In episode 29, the PN talks briefly with Bill, again emphasizing that surrender is their only viable option, while Bill continues to restate their goal of suicide. In episode 30, the PN talks with the hostage (Betty), reassuring

Table 8.1 Topical Episodes in the Bravo Incident

Episode #	Line #	Topic Shift by	Topic Description
1	0001–0008	N/A	*Anxiety regarding incarceration* Bill expresses his underlying resistance to "being locked up."
2	0009–0026	Bill	*Marijuana* Bill begins a lighthearted conversation with the police negotiator (PN) about having the police bring him some of the marijuana Bonnie had, which the police now have in their possession.
3	0027–0096	Bill	*Fear of prison and police* Barb talks with Bill, attempting to convince Bill that if they surrender, they will be better off. Bill expresses his fear of prison and general feelings of hopelessness (e.g., "A whole army of good lawyers couldn't help me"). Bill also expresses fear of police storming the bank.
4	0097–0128	Bill	*Bonnie's suicidal state* Barb talks with Bonnie and tries to convince Bonnie she should simply "walk out." Bonnie expresses her fear of prison and her preference to kill herself rather than surrender.
5	0129–0166	Bonnie	*Reasoning behind bank robbery* Bonnie tells Barb they needed money, did not think they would get caught, and they had to leave town as reasons for attempting to rob the bank.
6	0167–0182	Barb	*Condition of hostage* Barb checks on the condition of the hostage (Betty) while continuing to talk with Bonnie.
7	0183–0235	Barb	*Surrender* Barb now gets back on the line with Bill and attempts to convince him that the earlier they give up, the better. Barb offers to help, but Bill restates that he does not see any options.

Episode #	Line #	Topic Shift by	Topic Description
8	0236–0304	PN	*Lawyers* Police negotiator gets back on the line with Bill and discusses the usefulness of court-appointed lawyers and whether Bill and Bonnie will be charged federally or by the state prosecutor.
9	0305–0319	Bill	*Bonnie's fear of prison* Bill confides to PN that Bonnie wants Bill to kill her because she is afraid of going to prison.
10	0320–0369	PN	*Surrendering* Police negotiator changes topic back to surrendering as the best thing to do right now.
11	0370–0437	Butch	*Surrendering* Butch, a friend of Bill, now gets on the line with Bill and asks Bill when he is coming out. Butch talks about why surrendering is the best thing to do in the circumstances.
12	0438–0485	Butch	*Bill committing suicide* Bill and Butch talk about suicide. Butch appeals to Bill's sense of obligation to his son. Butch tries to convince Bill to release the hostage and convince Bill that other people care about him and Bonnie.
13	0486–0570	Butch	*Lawyers and former convictions* Butch continues talking to Bill about surrendering and the value of a lawyer. Both talk about past criminal experiences.
14	0571–0630	Bill	*Butch discourages suicide* Butch attempts to convince Bill that killing Bonnie and then himself is not a good solution to their problems.
15	0631–0640	Butch	*Reason for bank robbery* Butch asks Bill why they tried to rob a bank. There is discussion about Bill's need for more money and he saw no other way.
16	0641–0683	Butch	*Surrendering* Butch again asks Bill when they are coming out. Bill is noncommittal.

Table 8.1 (continued)

Episode #	Line #	Topic Shift by	Topic Description
17	0684–0710	Bill	*Bill asks to talk to federal attorney* Bill asks Butch to get the police to have a federal lawyer call Bill. A discussion ensues concerning which phone line to leave open for the federal attorney to call Bill.
18	0711–0747	PN	*Releasing the hostage* The police negotiator gets back on the line with Bill. The PN asks Bill to release the hostage and promises that the police will not storm the bank.
19	0748–0758	PN	*Legal process—being federally charged* The police negotiator talks with Bill about the process of being federally charged and assures Bill that this will happen if he surrenders now and does not hurt anybody.
20	0759–0790	Bill	*Suicide* Bill switches the conversation to suicide and killing Bonnie. The police negotiator repeats that suicide is "dumb."
21	0791–0809	Bud	*Difficulties in life* "Bud," another friend of Bill, gets on the phone with Bill and describes difficulties he has had in life.
22	0810–0840	Bill	*How Bud heard about the bank robbery* Casual conversation occurs between Bud and Bill about the bank robbery; Bud describes how he heard about it. Bill describes how Bonnie shot at the police.
23	0841–0879	Bud	*Commiserate together* Bud tells Bill of a difficulty he had the other night and suggests that he bring a beer or two to Bill so the two of them can rap (talk).
24	0880–0931	PN	*Suicide* The police negotiator gets back on the line with Bill. The PN attempts to convince Bill going to jail will not be that bad; Bill talks about killing himself. Bill keeps repeating that he is "tired."

Episode #	Line #	Topic Shift by	Topic Description
25	0932–1001	Bud	*Bill's sense of hopelessness* Bud gets back on the line with Bill. Bud again says he understands because he (Bud) was suicidal last weekend. Bill explains why he feels he has no options.
26	1002–1029	Bud	*3:00 P.M. deadline* Bud continues talking with Bill, attempting to find out what Bill and Bonnie are planning when 3:00 P.M. arrives (a time Bill indicated earlier he would release the hostage and then "something is going to happen").
27	1030–1062	Bill	*Problems are not so bad* Bud again compares his situation to Bill's and tells Bill that his options are not that bad. Bud downplays the amount of trouble Bill and Bonnie face with the authorities.
28	1063–1071	Bud	*Being surrounded* Bud says it would be nice if the police would leave, at which point Bill expresses his fears about being surrounded by the police.
29	1072–1157	PN	*Surrender vs. suicide* The police negotiator gets back on the phone with Bill. Bill expresses concern about the police swarming the building. The PN points out that surrendering is the only option. Bill again expresses his intention to kill himself.
30	1158–1197	PN	*Release of hostage* Betty, the assistant manager/hostage, talks with the police negotiator. The PN discusses with Betty how she should leave the bank when released.
31	1196–1228	PN	*Bonnie's fear of prison* Bonnie gets on the line with the police negotiator. The PN attempts to tell Bonnie that prison is not so bad; Bonnie states she would rather die than go to jail.
32	1229–1283	Bill	*Bill's fear of being shot* Bill gets on the line to talk with the PN. Bill expresses concern over being shot by the police. Bill and the PN discuss what is happening on the "outside."

Table 8.1 (continued)

Episode #	Line #	Topic Shift by	Topic Description
33	1284–1315	PN	*Attempt to call mother* Bill tries to call his mother using another telephone in the bank. He is unable to locate her. The PN attempts to have the telephone operator "break in" the line so the he can continue to talk to Bill.
34	1316–1339	PN	*Agreements reached* The PN restates to Bill that they have an agreement: after Bill is able to talk to his mother, at 3:00 P.M., Bill will release the hostage. Bill states at 3:00 P.M., they will either commit suicide or come out.
35	1340–1457	Beth	*Suicide* "Beth," a friend of Bonnie, talks to Bonnie on the phone. Beth tells Bonnie how much she will be missed and how people love her. Bonnie restates she has nothing to live for.
36	1458–1478	Bonnie	*How Beth heard about the bank robbery* Beth and Bonnie talk about how Beth heard about the bank robbery.
37	1479–1542	Beth	*Suicide* Beth again brings up her concern for Bonnie and pleads with Bonnie to come out and not kill herself.
38	1543–1629	Bill	*Request for cigarettes* The PN gets on the phone with Bill. Bill reiterates that the hostage will be freed at 3:00 P.M. Bill requests some cigarettes.
39	1630–1684	PN	*Getting the cigarettes* The PN attempts to convince Bill that Bonnie is "crazy" and they should surrender. Bill and the PN discuss how the cigarettes are going to be delivered. Bill receives the cigarettes.
40	1685–1710	Bill	*Waiting to talk to Bill's mother* Bill and the PN talk about waiting for Bill's mother to arrive home so Bill can talk to her. Bill waiting to hear from his mother.
41	1711–1718	Bill	*Tactical team too close* Bill asks the PN to have the tactical team move farther away from the bank building.

Episode #	Line #	Topic Shift by	Topic Description
42	1719–1825	PN	*When releasing hostage* The PN discusses with Bill when he is going to release the hostage. Bill still has not talked to his mother.
43	1826–1883	PN	*Hostage instructions* The PN talks to the hostage and gives her instructions on how to leave the bank once she is released and what direction to run.
44	1884–1913	Bill	*Talks to mother* Bill talks to his mother; the PN and Bill confirm that the hostage will be released now that Bill talked to his mother.
45	1914–2054	PN	*Arrangements for hostage release* Bill requests more cigarettes and agrees to release the hostage. Bill requests 20 minutes to be alone with Bonnie after the hostage is released. The PN discusses the logistics for getting more cigarettes to Bill and how the hostage is to be released. Cigarettes are delivered and the hostage is released. Bill and Bonnie are given 20 minutes.
46	2055–2088	Bob	*20 minutes alone* A phone call is received by the PN from Bob (newspaper reporter), who reports Bill just called him and asked the reporter to tell the police to leave Bill and Bonnie alone for 20 minutes and to not charge the building because they "don't want anybody else to get hurt but me and Bonnie."
47	2089–2117	PN	*To be buried together* The PN and Bill talk during the 20-minute time period. Bill talks about suicide and the PN tries to get him to dismiss the idea as irrational. Bill and the PN talk about what Bill said to the reporter. Bill confides he asked to reporter to make sure "me and Bonnie get buried together."

her that when she is released, she should leave the building quickly and run toward the authorities.

In episode 31, the PN talks directly with Bonnie, attempting to convince her that prison is "not so bad." Bonnie responds by saying she would rather die than go to jail. In episode 32, Bill and the PN again talk, with Bill expressing his fear of being shot by the police. In episode 33, Bill attempts to call his mother (using another telephone in the bank), but is unable to locate her. By episode 34, the PN and Bill again reconnect, with the PN reinforcing that they have an agreement: namely, that after Bill talks to his mother, at 3:00 P.M., the hostage will be released. Bill's response is that they will release the hostage and then either commit suicide or come out.

Episodes 35–37 involve a conversation between Bonnie and her friend Beth. This conversation is quite emotional, with Beth telling Bonnie how much she will be missed if she kills herself and how devastated other people who love Bonnie will be if she ends her life. Beth relates the difficulties she felt when her father committed suicide when she was young.

In episodes 38–42, the PN comes back on the line with Bill. Bill requests some cigarettes and the PN arranges for the cigarettes to be placed near the bank door. Other topics discussed include why Bill is not yet able to talk to his mother (he is waiting for her to arrive home from work), Bill's concern that the tactical team is too close, and when the hostage will be released.

In episode 43, the PN talks again with the hostage, giving her instructions on which direction to run once she is released. Shortly thereafter, Bill is able to contact his mother, whereupon the PN reconnects with Bill to confirm that the hostage should now be released as Bill has talked with his mother (episode 44).

Episode 45 involves direct conversation between the PN and Bill, initially confirming arrangements for the release of the hostage (which is subsequently done) and allowing Bill and Bonnie 20 minutes alone before they give themselves up. During this time (episode 46), Bill calls a newspaper reporter (Bob) and requests the reporter call the PN directly and tell the police to wait 20 minutes and not charge the building because they "don't want anybody else to get hurt but me and Bonnie" [L2060]. In the final episode (47), the PN and Bill again talk. The PN tries to talk Bill out of killing himself and Bonnie. Bill confides that he asked the reporter to make sure "me and Bonnie get buried together" [L2112]. Shortly thereafter, two gunshots are heard.

EPISODIC S.A.F.E. ANALYSIS

Due to the large number of episodes present in this extended negotiation, the S.A.F.E. analysis is presented in terms of the primary interactions that take place between the various parties. Initially, episodes 1–2 involve preliminary interactions between the PN and Bill. As the audiotape negotiations begin, Bill asserts that he is simply not ready to get "locked up yet" [L4]. At this point, he expresses one of his substantive demands: to avoid going to prison. However, the PN does not follow up this statement to further explore the fear or concern that may underlie Bill's desire to avoid jail time.

In episode 2, Bill and the PN engage in what is to be the only lighthearted bantering between them. This brief interaction is initially grounded in an attunement frame, where a beginning effort is made by both parties to lessen the relational distance between them. As mentioned earlier, Bill asks the PN to "roll me up a couple of joints—got out of that dope you got off my old lady and send 'em over" [L9]. Soon thereafter, after initially expressing his surprise that the police have the marijuana, the PN says, "must have been some deputy that arrested them must have that [the marijuana]" [L14], to which Bill laughingly comments, "Well, don't let him smoke it cause it's some good stuff" [L15]. After a pause, the PN, not sure where to go with this conversation, says, "well, anyway" [L20], to which Bill immediately responds, "I'll come out when I get ready. I'm just sitting here, we're having a little bullshit session" [L21].

This last comment by Bill functions to relationally distance himself from the PN, letting the PN know that this "good buddy" talk is just that: "a little bullshit session" to pass the time. Therefore, this small talk did not interactively function as a relationship-building move. Perhaps recognizing the futility of relationship development (attunement) at this point, the PN brings Barb, a friend of Bonnie, on the line.

Episode 3 involves conversation between Barb and Bill and is largely framed in instrumental (substantive demand) terms by both parties. While both parties function within this shared frame, Bill is unwilling to accept Barb's demand that he and Bonnie give themselves up. Because both parties are framing their interaction instrumentally, attunement, face, or emotion issues are not centrally addressed. The following list presents a straightforward request by Barb for Bill to come out. Bill responds by rejecting this request by simply concluding, "I ain't ready yet" [L36].

Bravo Incident: Episode 3 (fear of prison and police): Lines 28–38

L28	Bill	Hey, girl, what are you doin?
L29	Barb	I'm fine. How are you?
L30	Bill	Well, pretty good.
L31	Barb	You doing ok?
L32	Bill	Ya, I'm smoking cigarettes and drinking coffee.
L33	Barb	Why don't you come on out before it gets worse, Bill.
L34	Bill	I'll come out before it gets worse.
L35	Barb	No, come on and do it now, let's just get it over with. You know.
L36	Bill	I ain't ready yet, Barb.
L37	Barb	Why?
L38	Bill	Aw, I just ain't.

Recognizing that this more instrumental approach simply yielded positional adherence in Bill, Barb attempts to soften her substantive demand to Bill by alluding to her relational concern for the well-being of Bill and Bonnie as follows:

Bravo Incident: Episode 3 (fear of prison and police): Lines 41–52

L41	Barb	Well, don't worry about me, you know.
L42	Bill	Uh huh. Well, I do. I like you pretty good, girl.
L43	Barb	[laughs] Yeah, and I'm worried about you right now. Why don't you come on out before somebody gets hurt. We don't want anybody hurt today.
L44	Bill	Momma, I'm ain't gonna hurt nobody.
L45	Barb	Well, I know that but it's just easier if you just come out now and you know, just kind of
L46	Bill	[laughs]
L47	Barb	= throw it in the wind, you know. You're just making it worse on yourself.
L48	Bill	Uh hon, I couldn't get it no worse on me, little darling.
L49	Barb	Yes you could, if you just volunteer to come out, Bill, it would be better.
L50	Bill	Mm, hm.
L51	Barb	Honest it will.
L52	Bill	Yeah.

Within this "softened" substantive demand frame of Barb, Bill also "softens" his antagonistic stance toward Barb, yet continues to assert his resistance to coming out. Further, Bill responds with a self-face attack message, "Uh hon, I couldn't get it no worse on me, little darling" [L48], suggesting his sense of failure in this situation. Barb's response to this self-face attack statement by Bill is again instrumentally framed when she says, "Yes you could, if you just volunteer to come out, Bill, it would be better" [L49]. Bill's responses of "mm, hm" [L50] and "yeah" [L52] represent a disjuncture between the instrumentally focused frame of Barb and Bill's tentative introduction of a face need. While Barb asserts her demand that he simply "come out," she does not attempt to offer either some way of "getting a better deal if he comes out now" (bargaining) or problem solving underlying interests (e.g., safety). Consequently, while she is operating in a substantive demand frame, it is a hollow negotiation effort insofar as no real substantive demand work is undertaken to enable Bill to reframe his situation and find a substantive-based reason to surrender.

This pattern of a substantive demand frame for Barb, countered with Bill reasserting his own demands and tentatively attempting to shift the interactive frame to addressing his own face concerns, characterizes the disjuncture that increases as they continue to talk with one another. For example, Barb suggests Bill could get a good lawyer, to which he comments, "a whole, a whole army of good lawyers couldn't help me—when you get caught dead in the act" [L73]. Barb, remaining instrumental in her response to this face need statement, suggests, "well yeah that's kind of rough but if you give up easily it's gonna go a lot easier on you" [L75].

After assuring Barb that he would not harm Betty (the hostage) unless the police storm the building, Bill attempts to lighten the conversation by telling Barb that Bonnie is now playing with some balloons. Bill then again reiterates, "just, just tell them I ain't gonna let anybody get hurt, unless they rush this bank" [L90], to which Barb again responds, "Okay, well, they, they're not going to. But if you just come on out" [L91], at which point Bill now interrupts with "well, I'll come on out when I get ready, baby" [L92]. Clearly frustrated, Barb then says, "well, I know Bill, but don't be so stubborn this one time, do it for me" [L93]. At this point, the disjuncture between Barb and Bill reaches a point where Bill simply puts Bonnie on the line to talk to Barb.

Episodes 4–6 involve an extended conversation between Barb and Bonnie. Bonnie is experiencing extreme emotional distress, reflected in disjointed speech patterns, heavy breathing/sighing, and numerous outbursts of laughter that is not relevant to either the situation or the content of the discussion. Secondarily, Bonnie is also experiencing significant perceived threat to her self-image (a face frame). These related frames for Bonnie are expressed most directly in her fear of going to jail and her desire to commit suicide. In contrast, Barb remains largely within the substantive demand frame, continually refocusing the discourse to a request that Bonnie surrender. This disjuncture between the more substantive demand frame discourse of Barb and the more emotional distress frame concerns dominant for Bonnie leads to a sense of "talking past one another." The following list illustrates this disjuncture between Bonnie's fears and Barb's more instrumental goal of convincing Bonnie to come out.

Bravo Incident: Episode 4 (Bonnie's suicidal state): Lines 109–116

L109	Barb	No, they didn't tell me no lies, and everything's gonna be alright, you know. You'll make it a whole lot easier on yourself if, just, you know, throw things down and walk out.
L110	Bonnie	Oh, honey. Couple years, that ain't gonna do me no good.
L111	Barb	Well, a couple years isn't gonna be near as bad as you know, spending a, a lot of time in there.
L112	Bonnie	Oh honey, I'd much rather do it, do it right now. And get it over with instead of any time at all.
L113	Barb	Hey, don't do that, you got plenty of life ahead of you and you can
		[ ] [ ]
L114	Bonnie	[laughs] [oh shit]
		No man, you don't straighten this out like that. Once you got =
		[ ]
L115	Barb	Sure you
L116	Bonnie	= a record you always got a record.

Bonnie then proceeds to tell Barb that she feels her situation is hopeless insofar as she shot a police officer. As she describes this, her emotional distress is readily apparent in the disjointed description she provides as follows:

Bravo Incident: Episode 4 (Bonnie's suicidal state): Lines 123–128

L123	Barb	Don't be, ah you know, hurtin yourself or anything. It's not gonna do any good.
L124	Bonnie	Oh I know that. I know that, but walkin out right now can't do me no good either.
L125	Barb	It'd do you a lot more good than sittin in there and waitin and waitin, it just makes your chances that much worse.
L126	Bonnie	Honey, I been tah—shot at a cop, ya know? They ain't, they ain't [ ]
L127	Barb	But you threw down the gun, you didn't take a second shot—it hasn't—it musta show something.
L128	Bonnie	= yeah (laughs), that they had a gun in the back of my head. (laughs) that's why I turned down, you know

Barb, however, does not respond within the asserted emotional distress frame to Bonnie's heightened emotional upset. During the remaining discourse in this episode, Bonnie reassures Barb that Bill will not hurt the hostage. At the same time, Bonnie deflects Barb's repetitive efforts at requesting Bonnie to simply walk out the door. For example, Barb again states, "if you just come on out now it sure gonna make it a lot easier and I'll do everything I can to help you both" [L174], to which Bonnie sighs, "Oh honey, there ain't nothing you can do" [L175]. At this point Barb retorts, "Well, you never can tell" [L176], followed by Bonnie's comment, "What's done is done, you know" [L177]. After this interchange, Bonnie puts Bill back on the line.

By episode 7, Barb is even more directive toward Bill in attempting to convince him to surrender:

Bravo Incident: Episode 7 (surrender): Lines 186–196

L186	Barb	You ready?
L187	Bill	Ready for what?
L188	Barb	You ready to come out?
L189	Bill	Mm mm.
L190	Barb	You comin?
L191	Bill	(laughs) I ain't go'in out till I get ready, hun.
L192	Barb	When you gonna be ready?
L193	Bill	I don't know.
L194	Barb	You don't know [ ] gonna be going, be ready
		[ ]
L195	Bill	Maybe in ten—I don't know, maybe in ten minutes, maybe at midnight, I don't know
L196	Barb	Aw, come on, Bill. You're just makin it all, just hurtin yourself you know.

The following list presents dialogue between Barb and Bill in which Bill again expresses his fear of getting killed by the police if he should come out. This fear is indicative of the emotional distress Bill is experiencing at the time. Again, his disjointed explanation clearly illustrates the emotional distress he is under.

Bravo Incident: Episode 7 (surrender): Lines 197–201

L197	Bill	I know the longer, the longer we stay the more, the more, the more the longer we got to live you know and the more them uh reporters will be up here to, to see me if they blow me away without a without a good reason an a you know
L198	Barb	Bill, they're not gonna do that, they aren't. They're not here to blow you away. You done something wrong all they [ ]
L199	Bill	(laughs) Yeah really. Messed it up today, didn't I?
L200	Barb	Yeah you messed it up.
L201	Bill	Blowed it.

At this point, Bill is representing most directly a substantive demand concern or "underlying interest" (personal safety) to Barb. Unfortunately, her reassurance that he will not be harmed is not convincing for Bill. Further, Bill returns rather quickly to the more dominant face frame within which he is operating and his sense of failure, that he "blowed it" [L201].

Following this interchange, Barb continues to insist that Bill come out, while Bill becomes more adamant that he and Bonnie are going to stay inside the bank until they decide what they are going to do. Increasingly, in episode 7, Bill sighs, comments that there is nothing anyone can do, and he is "dead meat" if he comes out [L219]. By the end of this dialogue, both parties are simply repeating themselves, with an instrumentally contentious formula as follows:

Bravo Incident: Episode 7 (surrender): Lines 230–233

L230	Barb	Yeah, Bill but listen, come on out and I'll help you, honest to God I will.
L231	Bill	Aw, baby, there ain't nothing you can do to help [ ]
L232	Barb	Bill, there is.
L233	Bill	Girl. I'll come out when I get ready, just don't sweat it, okay?

At this point, Barb puts the PN back on the line (episodes 8–10). These episodes are a critical disjuncture between Bill and the PN. In these episodes, Bill offers two concrete demands related to his and Bonnie's fear of prison. Further, unlike previous episodes, both Bill and the PN are operating within the same frame, namely, the substantive demand frame. However, because there is no specific effort directed at meeting Bill's underlying interests of personal safety, the repetitive requests by the PN for Bill to simply "come out" fall on deaf ears inside the bank. Further, Bill repeatedly attempts to shift the conversation to his sense of failing (a face frame). However, both Barb and the PN reject this shift to a face frame discussion. Bill's perception of the hopelessness of the situation is, unfortunately, reinforced by the time episode 10 nears the end.

The following presents the initial discourse (episode 8) between the PN and Bill, in which substantive discussion around the availability of an attorney for Bill and Bonnie is explored.

Bravo Incident: Episode 8 (lawyers): Lines 239–246

L239 PN Hey listen, you know the, will get you lawyers. You don't even have to worry about springing for that. We'll get you
[ ]
L240 Bill Ya, I know about them court appointed lawyers, that last one I had sold me down the river for ten years.
[ ]
L241 PN Now Bill wait. Now let me tell you, these they had a public defender's office in [City A] and a
[ ]
L242 Bill Yea, but I ain't go'in to=
L243 PN [muffled]
L244 Bill =I ain't go'in to [City A], I'm go'in to [City B]
L245 PN No you go, well, if you get charged federally you go to [City A]. Because the court's in [City A] if you got charged federally.
L246 Bill Yeah, if.

At this point, the PN is specific and clear that an attorney can be provided to Bill and that he (and Bonnie) would be charged federally. However, Bill remains unconvinced that this could be successfully completed.

In the next set of dialogue, which follows, Bill now more actively explores with the PN these substantive issues:

Bravo Incident: Episode 8 (lawyers): Lines 249–272

L249 PN What do you want? What kind of guarantees do you want? I mean I'd like to get this thing over with. They got to get me back to [City C].
L250 Bill If I get anything, I want—it's got to be federal.
L251 PN You want to be charged federally.
L252 Bill You're God damn right.
L253 PN Alright.
L254 Bill I'll tell you what will happen. I'll come out
[ ]
L255 PN We'll get a United States attorney to charge you federally.
L256 Bill You have him call me.
L257 PN Have him call you?
L258 Bill Yeah.

L259 PN I know—I just spoke to him. I work for him.
L260 Bill Well, you have him call me and guarantee it.
L261 PN Well. I'll guarantee it. How's that?
L262 Bill I want
[ ]
L263 PN I haven't lied to you yet, have I. I said let the two officers go and let that girl go. And you know I could've kept them.
L264 Bill I know that.
L265 PN Alright so I haven't lied to you
[ ]
L266 Bill I—you have him call me
[ ]
L267 PN I haven't lied to you at any point throughout this. You know what time it is, it's 12:30.
L268 Bill Yeah, I know it.
L269 PN And it's on a Friday.
L270 Bill I know it.
L271 PN Ah, we—my boss is standing right here and ah
[ ]
L272 Bill Have him call me at 2213.

In this segment of episode 8, Bill makes a clear request to personally talk with the federal attorney. This request is made because of his fear of being shot by the police and the lack of attunement development between Bill and the PN. Bill wants the attorney to call him and guarantee that he (and Bonnie) will be charged federally. This substantive demand of Bill also reflects an underlying issue of relational mistrust between Bill and the PN. The PN, rather than attempting to demonstrate cooperative behavior with Bill (by indicating he will do everything in his power to get the federal attorney to call Bill to confirm this agreement), instead, attempts to reassure Bill that he can be trusted.

Unfortunately, it is clear that Bill does not trust the PN and dismisses the PN's efforts at relational assurance. Bill cuts the PN off, returning to his request: "have him call me at 2213" [L272]. This discourse disjuncture, largely located within the substantive demand frame (with underlying import around attunement issues), continues in an increasingly contentious manner.

Somewhat later in episode 8, the PN specifically communicates to Bill that he is likely not going to be able to arrange the phone call to the federal prosecutor. Bill responds to this news by commenting, "Well, I'm not gonna come out right now. I'm gonna sit here" [L286], indicating that the discussion around his demands of being charged federally is now over. For Bill, he believes that the PN is not going to meet his demand to talk to a federal prosecutor and perhaps also not charge him federally. While both Bill and the PN are operating within a substantive demand frame in episode 8, they do not interactionally "make progress" in addressing the substantive demands of either the PN or Bill. Further, the underlying relational mistrust, which could have been preliminarily addressed through cooperative action by the PN (e.g., permitting Bill an opportunity to talk to a federal prosecutor), was not lessened.

Following this interchange, patterns of frame mismatch between the PN and Bill, and between the third party and both Bill and Bonnie, escalate the conflict among the parties. Further, the inability to demonstrate instrumental issue progress when the PN and Bill were both operating largely within the substantive demand frame further solidified an escalatory pattern of interaction. Finally, the appeal to relational trust by the PN did not function to decrease attunement distance, as cooperative behavior between the PN and Bill was not undertaken concerning Bill's request to talk to a federal attorney.

Episode 9 is relatively short. In this exchange between Bill and the PN, Bill returns to a face frame that reflects the earlier pattern of the hostage takers' desire to kill themselves and the PN's efforts at countering this discussion with face statements that are more face threatening than face honoring:

Bravo Incident: Episode 9 (Bonnie's fear of prison): Lines 306–311

L306	PN	Why, what are you talk'in about?
L307	Bill	Ah, we're just talk'in. She still, she wants me to blow her up.
L308	PN	Well, you're not gonna do that, you got more sense than that, don't ya?
L309	Bill	I don't know.
L310	PN	Hell ya you got more sense than that. You don't want to shoot her. What do you want to shoot her for?
L311	Bill	Cause she wants me to.

By episode 10, the PN and Bill are back to the all-too-familiar disjuncture between the substantive demand frame asserted by the PN and the predominant face frame that characterizes Bill's response. The next list illustrates the parties' return to this more familiar, yet escalatory, interactional pattern.

Bravo Incident: Episode 10 (surrendering): Lines 346–359

L346	PN	So now it's time to, to face up.
L347	Bill	Uh huh.
L348	PN	So, uh, I want you to do it right now. I know you don't want to but you're not going to want to anymore tonight than you do right now.
L349	Bill	No, I will.
L350	PN	Huh?
L351	Bill	I will as soon as I get ready, I'll come out. And ain't nobody gonna get hurt.
L352	PN	No one's gonna get hurt, get you an attorney, we charge you federally; we can tell you all of these things if you just do it.

L353	Bill	I'll do it.
L354	PN	But if you don't, well, you know, Christ, this could go on; this could go on for weeks.
L355	Bill	No it can't, we'll get hungry 'fore then.
L356	PN	That's right.
L357	Bill	[laughs]
L358	PN	So ah, just hang in there and
		[ ]
L359	Bill	I ain't in no hurry.

While Bill continues to assure the PN that he will not hurt anyone, he also is saying that he is not willing to come out right now but may come out when he is ready. The more the PN insists that Bill surrender, the more Bill resists this request by asserting his own independence. Relationally, the parties are increasingly moving farther apart.

Episodes 11–17 involve an extended conversation between Bill and his friend "Butch." The interaction begins with Butch requesting that Bill give himself up, to which Bill, predictably, replies that he is not ready yet. The following list presents this pattern that continues throughout Butch's discussion with Bill.

Bravo Incident: Episode 11 (surrendering): Lines 375–379

L375	Butch	Ah, wantcha ta do me a favor.
L376	Bill	What's that?
L377	Butch	Stop all this nonsense hey =
		[ ]
L378	Bill	Huh.
L379	Butch	= listen the man's tell'in you the truth. If you wait, hey, nobody gets hurt, you won't get wasted, nobody gets hurt, do a little time and uh, hell, I'll even go with ya. How's that?

Throughout, Butch tells Bill, "hey, hey, this is, this is a bunch of nonsense, Bill, you got better sense than that, son" [L383], "hey, you're just makin' matters worse. If you come on out now it just gonna be a whole heck of a lot easier" [L385], and "Bill, if you don't come on out now, ah, things are really gonna get bad. And I don't wanna see that, and I don't really believe you wanna see that. Ah, you know, I know you. And ah, I just wish you would" [L509]. Throughout, Bill's interaction with Butch, he attempts to redirect the conversation to his desire to kill himself and Bonnie's request that Bill kill her. Throughout this interaction, Butch operates, similar to the PN, in a predominant, substantive demand frame, looking for opportunities to convince Bill to surrender. Yet, Bill now remains within the face frame and continues to attempt to talk to Butch about his and Bonnie's desire to commit suicide:

Bravo Incident: Episode 11 (surrendering): Lines 407–413

L407	Butch	It gets worse and worse and, and worse and minutes pass and it gets that much worse. So why don't ya throw that old thing out to ole little brother out here. You know, I wouldn't ask you if it wasn't right, Bill.
L408	Bill	I will when I get ready =
L409	Butch	[muffled]
L410	Bill	Bonnie want me, Bonnie wants me to blow her away and = [ ]
L411	Butch	Hey you got better sense.
L412	Bill	= do that well then I won't.
L413	Butch	You don't want to do that. You gonna do that then you oughta let Betty go.

In this interaction, characteristic throughout Bill's discourse with Butch, Bill introduces Bonnie's wish to have Bill kill her. Butch, however, similar to the PN's response to this topic, simply counters with, "you don't want to do that." Essentially, Bill is introducing the face issue of his and Bonnie's damaged self-image, coupled with heightened levels of emotional distress, reflected in their fear of going to a state (as opposed to a federal) prison. Unfortunately, this face concern and underlying emotion of fear are not attended to by Butch. The result is the familiar interactional pattern of, "I am going to kill myself," "No, you should not." At one point a bit later, Butch attempts to relationally connect to Bill, saying,

> Listen, really, it's a—you're just makin it that much worse on yourself. You think you done much worse than your mama has done? I know you said they don't care none about you but they do. Your whole family, your brother, sister, just think of the people that you're hurting. See, you're not really hurting your own self, you're hurtin friends and family who love you. The people who really do care about you. I mean, I know a lot of times it's been hard and ah, well, you know, you just think the world turns against you that, ah, I've thought that way myself, ah, many, many, many, many times. You've always got yourself, I'd much rather see you alive, than dead you know, really, seriously [L479],...Just think about it about five minutes and come on out. OK [L481].

This effort at building attunement is not successful, primarily because Bill is not experiencing this tense situation in terms of relational trust issues. Rather, Bill is making sense of the event through a face frame, a frame in which he feels like it's "the end of the line" for him and Bonnie. He is expressing a sense of failure and hopelessness coupled with a fear of going to a state penitentiary. This discord is expressed by Bill as he simply reiterates, "I ain't com'in out till I get ready" [L482].

At times, Bill expresses some ambiguity about giving himself up, yet at other times, he states that both he and Bonnie are committed to killing themselves. For example, when asked by Butch, why don't you come out now, "what is it that you gotta prove, what is it you gotta prove?" [L545], Bill responds, "I ain't trying to prove nothing. I just ain't want'in to get those handcuffs on me just right now, you know" [L546]. Later, however, when talking to Butch about how they were caught, Bill says, "Well we wasn't planning on getting caught but had decided if we did get caught that we couldn't go to jail" [L576], implying that if they were caught, they had already made a pact to commit suicide.

After Butch makes another plea for Bill to surrender, Bill indicates that "we'll do some—we'll do something by closing time, that's three o'clock. One way or another" [L652] and again says, "I promise you I'll do something by three" [L658]. Bill deliberately leaves open the possibility that they will either come out or commit suicide. Unfortunately, Butch does not address these face concerns and explore Bill's sense of ambivalence toward living or dying. Immediately following this self-imposed deadline, Bill reminds Butch to tell the PN to get the federal attorney (see the following list).

Bravo Incident: Episode 17 (Bill asks to talk to federal attorney): Lines 684–702

L684	Bill	Yeah, tell him to get that federal attorney to call me.	
L685	Butch	Well they can't call in the bank, you have to call over here.	
L686	Bill	Number 2213 is the line open, have him get that federal =	
			[ ]
L687	Butch		2213
			[ ]
L688	Bill		= attorney.
L689	Butch	2213.	
L690	Bill	Tell him to get that federal attorney to call me.	
L691	Butch	All right, I sure will.	
L692	Bill	Ok.	
L693	Butch	Uh huh, I'll be, ah, I'll be here, ok?	
L694	Bill	Ok.	
L695	Butch	All right. Hey Bill?	
L696	Bill	Huh.	
L697	Butch	You got this number here? 6347?	
L698	Bill	We'll just leave this line open.	
L699	Butch	Leave the line open.	
L700	Bill	Yeah.	
L701	Butch	Ok. What's that number that's over there in the bank? 2213?	
L702	Bill	Mm hm. Just tell him to have that federal attorney call me.	

In this last interaction with Butch, Bill again returns more strongly to his request to talk to the federal prosecutor. He is adamant that he talk to the lawyer and is making deliberate efforts to get Butch to talk to the PN about this request. For Bill, he just imposed a deadline of 3:00 P.M., in which he is now committing to either give up or killing Bonnie and then himself. In order for him to surrender, *given the predominant face frame within which he is operating, he is expressing a strong need for a face-restoring act for both Bonnie and himself.* Talking with the federal attorney and obtaining a guarantee that they would be tried in federal court, with a court-appointed attorney, is the primary face-restoration act he is attempting to create. Thus, while a conversation with the federal prosecutor functions, at one level, as a central, substantive demand; at another level, it functions as a face-restoration act. In this sense, having the federal attorney is not simply an instrumental request (which can be answered by the PN simply by reassuring Bill that he will be charged federally), but a face-saving mechanism with which Bill may consider giving himself (and Bonnie) up to the authorities. As the incident develops, the lack of follow-up on this substantive demand/face-saving act of talking directly with the federal attorney plays an important role in further escalating the situation and, inadvertently, reinforcing in Bill his increasing sense that nothing can really be done to help him or Bonnie if they surrender.

Episodes 18–20 involve interaction directly between the PN and Bill. Bill's substantive demand of speaking directly with the federal attorney is not pursued by the PN. Interaction at this point clearly reflects a lack of progress in addressing the more fundamental face needs expressed by Bill and a lack of attention to the substantive demand to talk with the attorney. The PN focuses even more directly on his desire to have Bill and Bonnie surrender and release the remaining hostage. In an effort to both bargain and pressure Bill into releasing Betty, the PN says, "Hey, I'll tell you what, what'd if I, I'd give you another promise...that is, you let her go and we won't rush that bank" [L716, 718]. Bill, however, responds by simply restating that he is not going to hurt her. The PN continues to pressure Bill toward surrender. The following list presents the increasingly contentious pattern of interaction between the PN and Bill, in which Bill asserts a stronger position of relational distance by emphasizing "if" he decides to surrender:

Bravo Incident: Episode 18 (releasing the hostage): Lines 739–747

L739 Bill Yeah, if I'm com'in out.
L740 PN Well, what are you gonna do if
[ ]
L741 Bill Well, if I don't come out I'll send Betty out.
L742 PN So you'll send her out at three for sure.
L743 Bill Yeah, if I don't come out.
L744 PN Huh?
L745 Bill Yeah, if I don't come out I'll send her out.
L746 PN All right. Well, ah =
[ ]
L747 Bill Let me have a little time to think.

In response, the PN summarizes the substantive agreements he believes he has with Bill, including being charged federally and having a court-appointed attorney represent Bill and Bonnie.

The next list illustrates the growing attunement distance between the PN and Bill, as Bill's underlying substantive demand of talking with the federal attorney is not addressed and his face needs remain unacknowledged.

Bravo Incident: Episodes 19–20 (legal process—being federally charged and suicide):

L754 PN = it's their full-time job, that's what they get paid to do. And ah, that's all free, you know, there's no charge for that. And then ah, if you're charged federally, you're gonna go to a federal penitentiary. Which is a lot better =
[ ]
L755 Bill You say'in if I'm charged federally.
L756 PN Ok, you are charged federally if that's what you want. I mean you know you're the one that's call'in the shot. You hurt somebody over there, well, you're probably gonna go to (city 4, state prison). That's for damn sure.
L757 Bill I ain't gonna hurt nobody.
L758 PN Because ah if you give up right now you'll probably get, you'll get charged federally that'll be the deal. But if you drag this thing on and on and on and hurt that woman or hurt anybody else =
[ ]
L759 Bill I'm not gonna hurt, the only person that I might hurt is me.
L760 PN Well, that's just that's just dumb.
L761 Bill Well.
L762 PN But if you ah like if you hurt Bonnie or you hurt tah Betty over there, you're gonna go to (city 4, state prison). You know because we won't have anything to do with it. You get charged with murder or whatever you do to 'em. And that's just dumb; they haven't done anything to you.
L763 Bill Yeah, well, if I do anything to Bonnie it's 'cause she wants it.
L764 PN Well, that's dumb.
L765 Bill Then I =
[ ]
L766 PN That's really dumb.
L767 Bill Do it to myself.
L768 PN You know ah you know you can end up in hell for doing something like that.
L769 Bill I'm gonna end up there anyhow.

At this point in episode 20, the PN is engaging in face-attack messages (e.g., "that's just dumb") and is attempting to pressure Bill to move into the substantive frame within which the PN believes a "deal" can be worked out. Unfortunately, Bill refuses to enter this frame, as his predominant frame is that of face concerns. A stalemate of frame disjuncture comes to a head at this point, resulting in little left for the PN and Bill to talk about.

Another friend of Bill, "Bud," is then put on the line to talk to Bill. Episodes 21, 22, 23, 25, 26, 27, and 28 involve extended conversation between Bud and Bill. Briefly, in episode 24, the PN returns to the telephone to talk to Bill. Beginning in episode 21, Bud attempts to reinforce his relationship (attunement) with Bill by suggesting that he (Bud) should come over to the bank so that he could talk face-to-face with Bill. Bud tells Bill that he did something stupid last Saturday night and uses this past situation as an attempt to relate to Bill's current situation. However, this effort does not result in increased relational closeness between Bill and Bud, largely because Bill knows the police are not going to permit Bud to come into the bank and he does not see the relevance of what Bud did last Saturday night with his dire, current situation. Thus, while a generally pleasant conversation takes place, with Bud offering to bring four cans of beer to Bill, episode 23 ends with Bill commenting, "well, they won't let you come in here anyway" [L852]. While both Bill and Bud are predominantly in the attunement frame, they are not able to engage in any substantial cooperative, reciprocal behavior due to the fact that Bud knows, and Bill knows, that Bud will not be able to simply enter the bank in order to continue talking with Bill. In this sense, Bud's efforts at "bonding" with Bill are ineffectual insofar as Bud is not able to demonstrate cooperative behavior either on his own or on behalf of the police surrounding the bank.

As a result, the PN comes back on the line in episode 24. Once back on the line, Bill again asserts more directly and forcefully that he may kill Bonnie and himself. The PN, again, does not enter the face frame within which Bill is operating. As Bill says, "Ah, we won't blow none of them people up out there. We ain't—anybody gets shot, it's gonna be me and her. So don't, don't sweat that" [L895]. The PN responds, "Well that's a, that's a pretty dumb thing to do you know" [L896]. At this point, attunement between the PN and Bill has deteriorated to the point where further conversation appears difficult for both parties. Bill concludes talking with the PN by sighing and stating that he is very tired (see the following list). Again, the PN does not enter the face frame with Bill by, for example, asking Bill what he means when he says he is tired or he wants to kill himself and Bonnie.

Bravo Incident: Episode 24 (suicide): Lines 919–930

L919	Bill	= I'm tired
L920	PN	= I can't conceive killin myself.
L921	Bill	[Sighs]
L922	PN	You know.
L923	Bill	I'm just tired.
L924	PN	Everyone's got problems.

L925	Bill	Just tired.
L926	PN	Ah yeah well I'd be a little tired too, you know you're draggin this thing on here, here's the middle of the afternoon. Quarter after one.
L927	Bill	Yeah [ ].
L928	PN	Well anyway you just wanna wait till three huh?
L929	Bill	Yeah.
L930	PN	Well I don't know what else to tell you. Just a minute, your buddy wants to talk to you.

This discourse clearly reflects the divergent frames that are now established between the PN (substantive demand) and Bill (face frame) and the disconnection that results. Bill sees no way out from this situation and is experiencing talking with the PN as less and less productive. The episode ends literally with the PN acknowledging that he does not know what else to tell Bill.

Episodes 25–28 take place with Bud again talking to Bill. At different times, Bud attempts, unsuccessfully, to tell Bill about what happened to him last Saturday night by making a topic shift transition that lacks any transitional markers. Each time Bud tries to tell Bill what happened to him on Saturday night, Bill interrupts and shifts the conversation to his own situation (a face frame). For example, soon after getting back on the line, Bud says, "Ah but tah, for sure, would you ah, let me walk in and out of there with no problems just so I can come talk to ya?" [L934]. Bill responds, as he did earlier, saying, "No man, it'd be better, just stay over there, Bud, you know" [L935]. Bud then immediately attempts to change the topic of the conversation by saying, "No, now Bill, I'd like to tell you, you know, what I went through last Saturday night" [L936], at which point Bill interrupts Bud with "Hey, brother" [L937], "when they, when = [L941], " = when they bust me man, there ain't gonna be no, ah, twenty fuck'in years" [L943]. This pattern repeats itself when Bud again says, "Well shit. I'd like to really come over and see ya cause I think I could tell you my problems and you could tell me yours" [L1030], to which Bill immediately rejects this discussion, by saying, "I ain't got no problems other than I'm face'in a whole bunch of time" [L1031]. Yet again, following a conversation about drinking coffee and smoking pot, Bud simply attempts to shift the topic to what happened to him on Saturday night, when he says, "You sound, you're sounding about as down as I was Saturday" [L1050]. Bill responds by again interrupting Bud and commenting, "Yeah" [L1051] followed immediately with "tired" [L1053], resulting in Bud not being able to elaborate on his own story.

Across these episodes, Bud largely communicates in a substantive demand frame, attempting to convince Bill that he should surrender because he will not likely get much of a prison sentence. At other times, Bud attempts to relate to Bill within an attunement frame, by focusing on the fact that they are friends and Bud can support Bill. In both cases, Bill is operating within a stable face frame and, therefore, frame incongruence continues and the situation, slowly, escalates. The next three lists illustrate the disjuncture in substantive frame discourse elaborated by Bud in his effort to convince Bill to surrender and by Bill's rejection of Bud's recommendations.

Bravo Incident: Episode 25 (Bill's sense of hopelessness): Lines 943–961

L943	Bill	= when they bust me man there ain't gonna be no [ ]. twenty fucking years.
L944	Bud	What are you talking about ya, ain't done nothin yet
L945	Bill	Hey I've done got a conviction in (City A) now, and I've got three more charges pending in ah in (City B) =
L946	Bud	Bill all you've =
		[ ]
L947	Bill	= I've got all of this shi– =
		[ ]
L948	Bud	= done here is discharged a weapon in the city limits there that's no big deal.
L949	Bill	Attempted bank robbery.
L950	Bud	Well you got any money on ya?
L951	Bill	Huh?
L952	Bud	Attempted bank robbery.
L953	Bill	Yeah. [ ]. [Laughs].
L954	Bud	Well, well, ok.
L955	Bill	I'm gonna light a cigarette with a hundred dollar bill and see what it feels like. [Laughs]
L956	Bud	[Laughs] Wish you'd come over here and light mine. Get—see how you are. [ ] the shit. Why, why don't you, hey man everything's cool why don't you just come on out of there.
L957	Bill	Hey man I ain't go'in to no Goddamn state joint. Huh.
L958	Bud	What do ya mean state joint, you ain't go'n nowhere =
		[ ]
L959	Bill	Aw
L960	Bud	= you haven't really done nothin.
L961	Bill	Bullshit.

Bravo Incident: Episode 25 (Bill's sense of hopelessness): Lines 968–983

L968	Bud	Ok. you—what did you do ask for a car or something to get outa here or what?
L969	Bill	Yup.
L970	Bud	Did they give you one?
L971	Bill	Oh no.
L972	Bud	Huh?
L973	Bill	They ain't gonna play no game.
L974	Bud	I'll give you mine.

L975	Bill	Oh yeah but I couldn't get to it.
L976	Bud	I'll have 'em bring it up here if you want it.
L977	Bill	Yeah but I couldn't get to it.
L978	Bud	Ah, what do ya mean, them shootin ya?
L979	Bill	Yeah.
L980	Bud	They ain't gonna shoot ya ain't done nothin.
L981	Bill	Bullshit. I walk out of here with a hostage and you watch 'em blow my shit away.
L982	Bud	Hey, well you know I went to cop school just like anybody else dude and they are not supposed to fire back unless you endanger their life and that's what firing at them and I know you're not gonna do that.
L983	Bill	Yeah but they ain't gonna let me outta here without a hostage.

Bravo Incident: Episode 26 (3:00 P.M. deadline): Lines 1004–1014

L1004	Bud	Well you know just between me and you, since you know these guys, you kinda leavin, what is go'n on?
L1005	Bill	I just told them I'd let them know somethin at three o'clock.
L1006	Bud	Why don't you let me know before three, I gotta get, go get some more beer.
L1007	Bill	Well I'll just turn Betty loose.
L1008	Bud	Huh?
L1009	Bill	I'll let uh th– the lady here at the bank loose.
L1010	Bud	What is that the bank manager or something?
L1011	Bill	Yeah.
L1012	Bud	Ok. Well then maybe you guys are gonna do somethin stupid.
L1013	Bill	Yeah, probably.
L1014	Bud	Shit.

In each of these instances, Bud attempts to minimize the crimes Bill committed. However, Bill is having none of that and consistently rejects Bud's interpretation of Bill and Bonnie's legal problems.

Thus Bud interacts with Bill largely within a substantive demand frame, attempting to persuade Bill to surrender either by trying to relate what happened to him last Saturday night or, more directly, by "bargaining" with Bill by minimizing the charges Bill will face. Bill, however, remains largely within a face frame, focused on his decision to kill himself and Bonnie in the context of his low self-image and fear of returning to prison. This disjuncture, similar to that between the PN and Bill, leads Bill to more directly inform Bud of his solidifying intention to commit suicide.

Bravo Incident: Episode 27 (problems are not so bad): Lines 1032–1037

L1032	Bud	Well ya ain't facin nothin man
L1033	Bill	Well I got done got two years convictions, and then jumping bond that's another five years, and then ah, ah, facing a robbery charge down there in (City B), facin a damn shootin down there in (City B). I shot a dup down there.
L1034	Bud	Well I've shot guys before. Matter of fact back well, I got shot in the face real good once.
L1035	Bill	Yeah.
L1036	Bud	No big deal, them guys you know, matter of fact the guy that shot me got away with it. I mean even went to court and they let him loose.
L1037	Bill	Yeah but they you know I've got all that shit plus this. Aw.

There is now a clear, patterned mismatch in S.A.F.E. frames between the PN and the TPIs and Bill and Bonnie. The police negotiator, as well as the TPIs who have all talked to either Bill or Bonnie, remains grounded in substantive demand frames (with some attunement frame work by some of the TPIs). However, these frames are not central for Bill or Bonnie, who are operating in a face frame and an emotional distress frame, respectively.

By episode 29, the PN gets back on the line and first informs Bill that Bud is not going to be able to enter the bank. As in past interactions, the PN continues to request that Bill give himself up and release the hostage. Bill counters by saying that he is going to release the hostage at 3:00 P.M. Bill also restates that he is not going to harm anyone. For example, the PN comments, "I'll tell you what, we won't do anything till three o'clock if you let her go" [L1125], to which Bill responds, "I'll let her go at three o'clock" [L1126].

During this episode, the PN tells Bill he is not going to get shot if he surrenders, and if Bill follows directions on how to surrender, everything will work out well. After reviewing some of the steps Bill can take (e.g., throwing out his gun through the window), the following dialogue takes place:

Bravo Incident: Episode 29 (surrender vs. suicide): Lines 1145–1154

L1145	PN	= nobody's gonna shoot ya, no ones gonna do anything to ya at all.
L1146	Bill	I told you at three o'clock and let you =
		[ ]
L1147	PN	three o'clock
		[ ]
L1148	Bill	= let her go.
L1149	PN	Alright. Then what's gonna happen after you let her go?
L1150	Bill	Mm I don't know. Whatever Bonnie decides she wants done.
L1151	PN	Whatever Bonnie huh?
L1152	Bill	She wants blowed up well that's what we'll do.
L1153	PN	Then you're gonna blow her up, then what, are you gonna blow yourself up too?
L1154	Bill	Yeah.

Bill again restates that by 3:00 P.M., the hostage will be released and Bonnie will make the final decision on whether they will kill themselves or give up.

In episode 30, Betty, the hostage, talks with the PN. This discussion takes place within the substantive demand frame, with the PN providing instructions to Betty on where she should go once she is released.

In episode 31, the PN talks with Bonnie:

Bravo Incident: Episode 31 (Bonnie's fear of prison): Lines 1211–1220

L1211	PN	= everything you're from Bill is the state prison. Which is, ah some [unclear] and pretty mean. But federal prisons are a whole lot better.
L1212	Bonnie	Yeah but I'm still locked up.
L1213	PN	Yeah but see you know you get into things, so what do you want to do you say just because = [ ]
L1214	Bonnie	How am I gonna get into anything if I'm locked up in jail? [Laughs]
L1215	PN	= so what I'm trying to say to you is, is you, is you, is you wanna end it alright here? Right? [ ]
L1216	Bonnie	I'd I'd rather die than go to jail, yeah.
L1217	PN	Boy, I tell you, you must not think much of your life.
L1218	Bonnie	I don't think much of jail. [Laughs]
L1219	PN	Huh.
L1220	Bonnie	You know.

In episodes 32–34, Bill now gets on the line with the PN. In episode 32, the now familiar pattern of interaction again takes place between the PN and Bill, with the PN elaborating on how Bill should throw out his gun, whereupon the PN would come to the bank door so that they could walk out together into the street. The PN reassures Bill that the police will not shoot Bill or Bonnie, especially if the PN is walking with them. Unfortunately, Bill remains unconvinced.

In episode 33, the PN contacts a telephone operator to cut in on the line, as Bill is making a phone call to his mother. However, his mother had just left work and, therefore, Bill is not able to reach her.

In episode 34, the PN and Bill again confirm their agreement concerning the release of the hostage at 3:00 P.M., as the following dialogue suggests:

Bravo Incident: Episode 34 (agreements reached): Lines 1321–1330

L1321	PN	So ah, is anything new?
L1322	Bill	I'm just waitin on that call and I'll talk to her and then we'll do something. It'll be about three o'clock then.
L1323	PN	Alright. You're still planning on what we talked about before.

L1324 Bill Yeah. I'm gonna let Betty out.
L1325 PN Alright that'll be good.
L1326 Bill Ok. I won't hurt her.
[ ]
L1327 PN [ ] about her now what are you gonna do?
L1328 Bill Well I hadn't yet decided yet. Blow up or come out, one of the two.
L1329 PN Blow up or come out.
L1330 Bill Yeah.

Beth, a friend of Bonnie, gets on the line with Bonnie in episodes 35–37. The predominant frame for Beth is attunement, as she skillfully attempts to place her concern for Bonnie's well-being at the forefront in order to get Bonnie to surrender. Bonnie remains in the emotional distress frame, however, and interacting with Beth becomes, at times, too painful for her. At those moments, Bonnie abruptly changes the topic of conversation to more socially superficial topics. Because of their previous relationship, Bonnie expresses her true feelings and fears to Beth. While Beth provides a relationally empathic response, she does not sufficiently engage Bonnie in her emotional distress frame. Thus, the interaction with Beth becomes more painful for Bonnie, without the counterbalance of supportive communication that focuses on Bonnie's heightened level of fear or how she sees her situation (emotional distress). Further, Beth is unable to communicate information or support to Bonnie that would address the underlying action tendency (what plan can be made) of Bonnie's fear, as shown in the following dialogue:

Bravo Incident: Episode 35 (suicide): Lines 1354–1374

L1354 Beth = I just wanta see you guys come out of there.
L1355 Bill I'm just kiddin too baby. Ah well one of those things, babe.
L1356 Beth Yeah but nobody has to die over 'em you know.
L1357 Bill [Sighs] Hey Bonnie? [Talking in background]
L1358 Bonnie Aw you're kidding. Beth?
L1359 Beth Bonnie?
L1360 Bonnie Hi honey how ya do'n?
[ ]
L1361 Beth You gonna come out of there?
L1362 Bonnie Uh uh.
L1363 Beth How come?
L1364 Bonnie How come?
L1365 Beth Yeah.
L1366 Bonnie I, I don't want to go to jail baby.
L1367 Beth You'd rather get yourself killed.
L1368 Bonnie Yeah.
L1369 Beth You're kidding me.
L1370 Bonnie No.

L1371	Beth	Bonnie, all you got and you wanna die instead =
		[ ]
L1372	Bonnie	We ain't got nothin.
L1373	Beth	You got a lot of [muffled] =
		[ ]
L1374	Bonnie	[Heavy breathing]

This episode begins with Beth directly confronting Bonnie around Bonnie's reluctance to come out of the bank. Bonnie lets Beth know that she intends to commit suicide with Bill. After this initial, difficult conversation, Bonnie asks Beth about her pregnancy. Beth, however, soon changes the topic back again, when she asks Bonnie, "Why don't you come out?" [L1391], to which Bonnie quickly replies, "No, I ain't gonna do it. We'll let Betty out here pretty quick" [L1392]. Bonnie then informs Beth that she just called (from another bank phone) a friend and said goodbye, indirectly indicating Bonnie's desire for suicide. Beth responds by telling Bonnie that if she kills herself, "Well, you know, you don't really hurt yourself, you hurt all the people that love you" [L1405], to which Bonnie responds by saying, "Aw, yeah, well, they get over it. You know, it's better, it's better than spending a couple years in jail and getting out and having nothing to be, nothing again, you know" [L1406]. As Beth continues to confront Bonnie with her strong attunement-focused messages, Bonnie becomes more distraught, evidenced by heavy breathing, inappropriate laughter, and disjointed speech.

Episodes 35 (lines 1433–1462) and 37 present an emotionally laden discourse in which attunement closeness is focused on by Beth, but Bonnie's emotional distress is less effectively addressed. This S.A.F.E. frame disjuncture between Beth's attunement pleas and Bonnie's emotional distress (fear) heightens Bonnie's distress and results in Bonnie emotionally "pulling back" from Beth and, consequently, from Beth's primary request: for Bonnie to surrender. At this point, Bonnie switches the topic to how Beth heard about the robbery.

Bravo Incident: Episode 35 (suicide): Lines 1433–1462

L1433	Beth	Bonnie you know if you just come out nobody's gonna get shot nobody's gonna get killed.
L1434	Bonnie	Yeah honey I you know. I know that, I know that we could throw the gun out the front door and that dep come over and handcuff both of us and we'd both go off to jail.
L1435	Beth	Why?
L1436	Bonnie	I—[Laughs] Well I don't want to do that. I don't want to do it that way you know.
L1437	Beth	It's not worth dying over though you know Bonnie.
L1438	Bonnie	Mm hm.
L1439	Beth	It's not.

L1440 Bonnie It don't make no difference to me.
L1441 Beth It ought to, makes a difference to me.
L1442 Bonnie [Laughs] you got something to live for.
L1443 Beth So do you.
L1444 Bonnie No I don't.
L1445 Beth Ya you do Bonnie.
L1446 Bonnie Like what?
L1447 Beth You got yourself.
L1448 Bonnie Ah ha. [Laughs] Shit, I have that up a long time ago.
L1449 Beth Why?
L1450 Bonnie Cause a lost cause.
[ ]
L1451 Beth [muffled]
L1452 Bonnie Aw shit I saw him before I left and you know there ain't nothin. There ain't nothin there at all and there you know and ain't never gonna be.
L1453 Beth Well what do people have to do to show you that they care? You know.
L1454 Bonnie Oh honey I know you care and I really appreciate it and you know, but same time I expect you to understand how I feel about the whole deal.
[ ]
L1455 Beth I can't understand anybody giving up their life. I can't understand that Bonnie you know. I just can't. It's been eight years since my dad died and ya—you know, he hurt us more by it than he did himself.
L1456 Bonnie Yeah.
L1457 Beth Sure he got the easy way out but you know you hurt people by doing it.
L1458 Bonnie [Laughs] Really. Did you drive all the way up here from [City D]?
L1459 Beth Yeah.
L1460 Bonnie Aw honey who called up?
L1461 Beth Bonnie I heard about it and I came up. Nobody called me, nobody told me to...
[ ]
L1462 Bonnie Did ya hear about it on the radio?

Bravo Incident: Episode 37 (suicide): Lines 1479–1542

L1479 Beth Bonnie why don't you just come out of there ok?
L1480 Bonnie Honey not till three o'clock.
L1481 Beth Why?
L1482 Bonnie Cause that's the deal, you know. I mean, they didn't give us what we wanted, we didn't hurt nobody, you know. All I want to do is get out of here and we'd tried that and they wouldn't cooperate. [Mumbling]
[ ]
L1483 Beth You can get out of there.
L1484 Bonnie Yeah and go to jail.
[ ]
L1485 Beth What's the [muffled] =
[ ]
L1486 Bonnie An [ ] it. Why should I let them put me in jail?
L1487 Beth You're mature you know what's right and what's wrong.
L1488 Bonnie Shit ya I know. Well, that don't count now.
L1489 Beth It does count.
L1490 Bonnie Uh uh, it's too, it's done you know. If it was seven o'clock in the morning again you know and I had the chance to call it off, but it ain't. You know.
L1491 Beth You can call it off right now.
L1492 Bonnie Ha ha, no, not without paying for what I done.
L1493 Beth Everybody's gotta pay.
L1494 Bonnie Yeah, but I ain't going to jail [ ] honey, no way. Just no way.
L1495 Beth Well I don't understand.
L1496 Bonnie I'm sorry.
L1497 Beth But if I didn't love ya I wouldn't have called you know.
L1498 Bonnie I know.
L1499 Beth If I didn't care I wouldn't be here.
L1500 Bonnie I know.
L1501 Beth [ ] always makes me feel good you know, they come up here and care about ya and then ya say no I'd rather die.
L1502 Bonnie [Laughs]
L1503 Beth You know it doesn't make any sense Bonnie [ ], you're smarter than that.
L1504 Bonnie Well, did you ask about the cigarettes?
L1505 Beth No.
L1506 Bonnie Would ya?
L1507 Beth What'd ya need 'em for?
L1508 Bonnie To smoke. [Laughs] I'd like to have one 'fore I go. Shit, give me [muffled] Bill. [Sighs] Doesn't everybody deserve to have their last smoke?
L1509 Beth Bonnie don't be like this.
[ ]
L1510 Bonnie I mean even I deserve to have a last smoke.

L1511 Beth Don't I deserve to see you and have you come walkin out of the doors?
L1512 Bonnie [Laughs]
L1513 Beth Don't I deserve that?
L1514 Bonnie I don't know. Probably do, you know.
L1515 Beth I do. I really believe I do.
L1516 Bonnie [Laughs]
L1517 Beth You know I want to see you, I wanna, I want you to come out. Th—I want it bad. I wouldn't be here.
L1518 Bonnie I know, I'll think about it.
L1519 Beth And all the things you keep telling me about being positive toward life and you'll get through. Doesn't do me a bit of good to hear you talk like this you know.
L1520 Bonnie [Laughs]
L1521 Beth It doesn't and it's not funny. And I want you to know Bonnie I want you to come out.
L1522 Bonnie I ain't gonna do it right now. I ain't ready to go yet. I ain't ready for them to put those handcuffs on me yet. I got till three o'clock so I'm gonna enjoy it while I can.
L1523 Beth Well, you got a chance to live and a chance to die. And if you were smart you'd take the chance to live you know.
L1524 Bonnie Yeah.
L1525 Beth I mean so what you go to jail.
L1526 Bonnie [Laughs] Yeah.
L1527 Beth You may appreciate life a hell of a lot better when you come out.
L1528 Bonnie I doubt it. They just make you a worse con than you already are.
L1529 Beth No.
L1530 Bonnie Sure they do.
L1531 Beth No they don't Bonnie.
L1532 Bonnie [ ] for me.
L1533 Beth Will ya come out?
L1534 Bonnie Not till three o'clock.
L1535 Beth Will you come out at three?
L1536 Bonnie Maybe.
L1537 Beth Bonnie I wanna see you.
L1538 Bonnie I know huh.
L1539 Beth Bad. I really do. I'm not =
[ ]
L1540 Bill [Coughing in the background]
L1541 Beth =I'm not doing this for anybody but me.
L1542 Bonnie Ng'K. We'll see. Bill wants to talk to [PN].

In this heart-wrenching interchange, Beth seems to convince Bonnie to reconsider killing herself. However, Beth is functioning in a largely attunement frame, while Bonnie is predominantly operating within the emotional distress frame, evidenced by heightened levels of fear of prison and an inability to effectively problem solve her current situation. While Beth is therefore relationally present with Bonnie, Bonnie's heightened pain and anguish are not addressed. Further, because of the disjuncture between the attunement frame of Beth and the emotional distress frame of Bonnie, the relational empathy expressed by Beth toward Bonnie only further heightens Bonnie's distress, to the point that Bonnie can, literally, no longer talk with Beth because it is too disconnected from her emotional reality. Unfortunately, the emotional pain being experienced by Bonnie needed to be reduced by entering the emotional distress frame and engaging in supportive communication so that Bonnie can gain some degree of control over her fear. In effect, Bonnie was not able to "tell her story" and share more deeply how she feels. She maintains a perspective, then, that the situation is hopeless and in her emotionally distressed state of mind, *she would rather get rid of the emotional pain then live another day*. Unfortunately, while relationally engaging messages are sent by Beth, they are not helping Bonnie deal with her emotional pain and fear.

In episodes 38–42, the PN talks with Bill. Bill begins (episode 38) by asking the PN, "Hey, do me a fav—one, one last favor" [L1547], "would you send somebody with a pack of cigarettes by the front door and let Bonnie get 'em" [L1549]. The PN responds by attempting to make a deal, offering to exchange the cigarettes if Bill gives up his gun. To this request, Bill says, "Hell, what good's a hostage without a gun? (laughs) Hey, just, just do this for me, man; I'll turn her loose at three o'clock like I said I would. I just want somethin' to smoke" [L1571].

During this interchange, both the PN and Bill are operating in a substantive demand frame, focused on the peripheral substantive issue of how to get the cigarettes to Bill. Bill asks that the cigarettes by thrown up by the bank's door while the PN says they can put the cigarettes in the parking lot and Bonnie can go pick them up. While this discussion is framed substantively, a secondary frame emerges, namely, the lack of attunement (relational trust) between the PN and Bill.

In episode 39, Bill's concern is that Bonnie will be shot if she tries to pick up the cigarettes in the parking lot. In spite of reassurances from the PN, Bill does not accept this solution. Ultimately, the PN agrees to toss the cigarettes by the bank door so Bonnie can simply reach out and get them. During this time, the PN tries to convince Bill that he should not listen to Bonnie, "she's putting dumb ideas in your head" [L1632]. Predictably, Bill ignores this effort and continues to focus on how the police will deliver the pack of cigarettes. During the final interchange around getting the cigarettes, the lack of attunement between Bill and PN becomes apparent:

Bravo Incident: Episode 39 (getting the cigarettes): Lines 1659–1664

L1659	Bill	Oh, don't tell just be sure nobody tries to grab her when she...
L1660	PN	Have I lied to ya?

L1661	Bill	No.
L1662	PN	Do you trust me?
L1663	Bill	Ya, well I'm gonna have to.
L1664	PN	Alright well then tell her to open the door and get the cigarettes. I don't know what the hell she's scared of.

In episodes 40, 41, and 42, both the PN and Bill are operating in the substantive demand frame, focusing largely on the peripheral, substantive issue of Bill's efforts to reach, by telephone, his mother. While Bill expresses a desire to talk with his mother, he says, "Ya, she might not have much to say" [L1621] and that she will not be too upset with Bill. At this point, Bill again introduces a face frame into the conversation with the PN. That is, Bill is making an effort to call his mother in a situation that is extremely dangerous, and he essentially is saying, "*I don't have much of relationship with my mother, in fact, she probably won't be surprised—or upset with me because she knows I am a screw-up.*"

The PN, however, does not enter this face frame and further explore either Bill's reasons for wanting to talk to his mother or why Bill believes his mother will not be upset with him—in these circumstances. In fact, given Bill's assessment of his conversation with his mother, it is likely that Bill wishes to essentially "say goodbye," making it easier to end his own life. This is indirectly reinforced later when Bill comments, "I haven't talked to her [his mother] in about a year and I *need* to talk to her now" [L1696]. Somewhat later, Bill does suggest to the PN that talking to his mother is important to him. For example, when asked by the PN if he (Bill) is going to let the hostage go now, Bill responds by saying, "after I talk to my mother, then I'll let you know somethin'" [L1740]. Further, Bill lets the PN know that he and Bonnie have made a decision regarding whether they are coming out or committing suicide together:

Bravo Incident: Episode 42 (when releasing hostage): Lines 1807–1814

L1807	PN	Ah you still listening to the crazy girlfriend of yours?
L1808	Bill	Oh we got that settled.
L1809	PN	What ya gonna do?
L1810	Bill	Uh we gonna come out as soon as I talk to my mom.
L1811	PN	Ya gonna give up for sure.
L1812	Bill	Yeah.
L1813	PN	But ya gotta talk to your mom first.
L1814	Bill	Yeah.

At this point, Bill and Bonnie have already made a decision: namely, to kill themselves. However, rather than directly tell the PN that they decided to commit suicide, Bill verbally agrees with statements the PN makes about their coming out. Essentially, Bill consistently provides from this point forward very limited affirmative responses to the PN concerning their decision to give themselves up.

These very short responses are inconsistent with someone who has made an affirmative choice to live rather than die. One would expect increased positive affect (lessening of emotional distress), coupled with more self-face-honoring statements that would further justify coming out vs. suicide. In fact, this does not occur. Rather, Bill consistently simply expresses minimal agreement (e.g., "yeah") when the PN asks him if he is going to come out after the hostage is released.

In episode 43, the PN again provides instructions to the hostage upon her immediate release. Both the hostage and the PN operate within the substantive demand frame, which at this point in time is helpful to Betty, as she believes that she, in fact, is going to be released shortly.

In episode 44, Bill finally talks to his mother. He does not, however, tell his mother anything about his current situation. Further, in his conversation with the PN, Bill shares very little information about his phone call to his mother. Essentially, the brunt of the conversation in episode 44 between the PN and Bill revolves around the police negotiator's efforts to confirm the agreement with Bill: namely, that Bill will release the hostage and that Bill and Bonnie will give themselves up. Bill's responses are consistently phrased in terms of very short, affirmative answers (e.g., "yeah, we'll come out").

In episode 45, an extended conversation between Bill and the PN takes place, largely within the substantive demand frame, around protocols for releasing Betty (a central, substantive issue) and Bill's request for another packet of cigarettes (a peripheral substantive demand). As the PN and Bill get closer to releasing the hostage, Bill requests that he and Bonnie be given 20 minutes after the hostage is released (to talk and finish some cigarettes) before they come out. Again, the PN asks Bill if they are coming out, to which the following interaction takes place:

Bravo Incident: Episode 45 (arrangements for hostage release): Lines 1986–1997

L1986	PN	Yeah [Background—Everybody else just stand clear of there.]. Ok. Alright send Betty out.
L1987	Bill	Ok.
L1988	PN	And we're gonna give you—we'll give you 20 minutes.
L1989	Bill	Ok.
L1990	PN	And then you're gonna surrender.
L1991	Bill	Right.
L1992	PN	Ok.
L1993	Bill	You got the key with ya. Hey, we don't we'll do that and then ah give me 20 minutes um we'll come out.
L1994	PN	Alright.
L1995	Bill	You know.
L1996	PN	You're not thinking about this suicide thing anymore.
L1997	Bill	No uh uh.

While Bill confirms he and Bonnie are going to surrender, there is no progress made within either the face frame for Bill or the emotional distress frame for Bonnie to substantiate surrender as a committed option taken by Bill and Bonnie. At the end of this episode, when the hostage is finally released and Bill and Bonnie are given 20 minutes, Bill informs the PN that he is going to make one more phone call and then will call the PN back.

In episode 46, the PN receives a phone call from a newspaper reporter (Bob). The following interchange takes place:

Bravo Incident: Episode 46 (20 minutes alone): Lines 2057–2065

L2057	PN	Sir I'm sorry I can't talk to you I'm expecting a phone call you're going to have to...
L2058	Bob	we've got him on the line ok he says, tell him not to rush this bank because I don't want anybody else to get hurt, but me and Bonnie. Tell 'em to leave us alone they can come in here and get us after a while. Either way if they come through the door we're dead but I don't want anybody else to get hurt. That's right off. He's saying it. [Sighs].
L2059	PN	Tell me again.
L2060	Bob	Ok he—this is word for word. Tell him not to rush this bank because I don't want anybody else to get hurt but me and Bonnie.
L2061	PN	He's [ ] thinking about this suicide thing.
L2062	Bob	Sounds like it.
L2063	PN	And then.
L2064	Bob	Ok, and he says leave them alone and they'll come in ah you know they come in here and get us after awhile. Either way if they come through the door we're dead. And he stills says nobody to get hurt.
L2065	PN	Ok.

The reporter also comments that "He's also told, ah, my man on the phone here that he's gonna call, ah, him back so he can hear the gun go off" [L2082], to which the PN again says, "So he's talkin' about suicide, huh?" [L2083].

The final episode (47) takes place between Bill and the PN. At this point, the PN now knows that Bill and Bonnie are going to kill themselves, and he attempts one more time to convince Bill not to commit suicide:

Bravo Incident: Episode 47 (to be buried together): Lines 2093–2117

L2093	PN	= well, you're gonna get 'em all wrapped up. So tell you what, it'd be a dumb thing to do and you're probably gonna regret that for the rest of your life. And = [ ]
L2094	Bill	How am I gonna regret it?
L2095	PN	= you're gonna regret it. Killin that girl and thinkin about yourself. See what I want ya to do. You walk out there and you throw that

		gun out. And we'll do just like we talked about earlier. And I'll come over there and get ya and we'll walk on out. Alright?
L2096	Bill	No I gotta call that dude back.
L2097	PN	Aw to hell with him.
L2098	Bill	No, talk to him while he's gonna do something.
L2099	PN	What's he gonna do?
L2100	Bill	Well he's gonna contact some people [ ].
L2101	PN	Um so you're gonna talk to with, what's he gonna do?
L2102	Bill	He's gonna contact some people for me.
L2103	PN	What your relatives? Tell 'em that you're gonna kill yourself up here.
L2104	Bill	No he ain't gonna tell 'em that.
L2105	PN	What's he gonna tell 'em?
		[ ]
L2106	Bill	He's gonna contact them and tell 'em what I want done.
L2107	PN	What do you want done?
L2108	Bill	Huh?
L2109	PN	What do you want done?
L2110	Bill	Well =
		[ ]
L2111	PN	What do you want done?
L2112	Bill	I just wanna make sure me and Bonnie get buried together.
L2113	PN	Get buried together. Well, [muffled].
L2114	Bill	Well you don't know nothin about tah =
		[ ]
L2115	PN	What?
L2116	Bill	I said you know it's not right [ ].
L2117	PN	Mh hm. What's the purpose of all that. You know ah this thing isn't gonna last forever, you know you're gonna get, you gonna do a little bit of time and we both know that but tah what the hell. It's gonna end and life goes on. You can solve these problems. If you let your problems, ah do you in you know you've had it. You can't do that you've gotta come off the side a little bit. A best way to do this is stand up like a man.

In this final interchange, the PN desperately attempts to persuade Bill to surrender. Unfortunately, Bill and Bonnie have already made up their minds and have made arrangements for their own burials. The PN continues to try to convince Bill, from a substantive demand framework, that prison will not be that bad and he can overcome this situation. For Bill, the issue is not the length of a prison sentence (a substantive concern), but rather a face issue coupled with emotional distress, particularly for Bonnie. As this episode ends, gunshots are heard, resulting in the double suicide of Bill and Bonnie.

OVERALL S.A.F.E. FRAME ANALYSIS

This is an incident in which a long-time criminal and his girlfriend break the law one more time. They attempt to rob a bank and, in the process, shoot a police officer and end up taking hostages inside the bank where they subsequently release all except Betty, the bank manager. Near the end of the incident, Bill lets Betty go, after which he kills Bonnie and then commits suicide.

During the initial conversation between Bill and the police negotiator, Bill clearly expresses his desire to not get "locked up." Bill has been in prison previously and does not want to go back again. Bill's resistance to accepting the inevitability of his returning to jail remains throughout the event. This resistance is well founded as he is savvy about what the sentencing outcome would likely be as an accomplice to attempted murder of a police officer and attempted bank robbery. For Bill, he is looking at many, many years behind bars. During negotiation, Bill often functions within a substantive demand frame as he attempts to find an acceptable solution to justify surrender rather than suicide. Due to lack of progress in the substantive demand frame, Bill attempts to shift the conversation to a face frame, repeatedly making comments that he "messed it up" and he "blowed it." Thus, for Bill, his focus is predominantly within a substantive demand frame followed by directed efforts at self-face attack behavior and the need to talk about his sense of failure (a face frame). Suicide seems to be a viable option for Bill, given his assessment of the bleakness of the rest of his life behind bars.

The situation is not as certain for his girlfriend, Bonnie. Apparently, this is her first criminal act. Nevertheless, she would likely be charged with attempted murder and as an accomplice to attempted bank robbery. Bonnie would also probably receive a prison sentence as well, the length not as predictable. Bonnie, however, apparently has no such prior involvement with the U.S. prison system. Bonnie is experiencing debilitating fear and remains in an emotionally distressed state throughout the ordeal. Bonnie's fear compromises her ability to effectively problem solve during the event. She is literally consumed by her fear of the consequences of going to prison. From this emotionally distressed perspective, suicide with her boyfriend represents a solution to her all encompassing and overriding fear that is associated with surrender.

Bill is realistic in his appraisal of the consequences of their criminal actions and likely views suicide as a better solution than a very long prison sentence. In contrast, Bonnie is incapable of making such an appraisal as she experienced interaction with the police negotiator and TPIs through the lens of overwhelming fear of prison. The action tendency of Bonnie's fearful emotional state is to avoid or escape, in this case, through suicide. Yet Bill or Bonnie has not completely decided to end their lives. One core theme throughout this incident is whether Bill and Bonnie truly have reached the "end of the line" in their lives or whether there is some possibility—ever—of a better life if they surrender. If they were fully committed to killing themselves, they would have done so within a few minutes of the arrival of the police. The fact that they had not yet committed suicide coupled with their voluntary participation in negotiating with the police and friends provides evidence that suicide was not a completely forgone conclusion.

The police negotiator and the TPIs who talked at various times with Bill and Bonnie predominantly functioned within a substantive demand frame. Some of the TPIs, however, did communicate to Bill and/or Bonnie more within an attunement frame, attempting to establish a bond of trust sufficient to encourage surrender.

When Substantive Demand Frames Converged

There were times during this situation in which the police negotiator and the TPIs were grounding their communication within a substantive demand frame and Bill was also centered within the same S.A.F.E. frame. In other words, Bill was focused on negotiating substantive demand issues and the police negotiator and the TPIs were also focused on the same concerns. Why then, did the situation not de-escalate and lead to a peaceful surrender?

The primary reason is that communicating with another individual in the same S.A.F.E. frame is a necessary but not sufficient requirement for de-escalating a critical incident. What is needed is to be able to employ frame specific negotiation strategies in order to "work on" the frame issues to the point that some progress (resolution) of the frame issues results. Thus, while Bill and the police negotiator (and the TPIs) at times functioned within the same substantive demand frame, there was a lack of actual "negotiation" on specific substantive demands made by Bill in which Bill might experience a sense of progress. The result is that Bill became more resigned to the fact that there is no minimally acceptable "solution" to his going to prison that would allow him to surrender. For Bill, the police negotiator did not "work through" either in a bargaining manner or a problem-solving process the substantive demands made by Bill.

In this regard, the substantive issue that was most important to Bill was his demand to talk to a federal prosecutor who will guarantee that he (and Bonnie, presumably) will be charged federally and, therefore, will be sentenced to a federal prison rather than a state penitentiary. Bill did not trust the police or the court system in general. While Bill stated that he did not want to get "locked up," he was adamant about wanting to be locked up in a federal prison. Therefore, Bill demanded that he personally speak with a federal attorney about where (jurisdiction) his criminal case would be handled.

At this point, in order to make substantive demand frame progress, the police negotiator needed to directly engage Bill in discussing this demand. One option might have been to contact a federal prosecutor and allow Bill to talk to this person, presumably in order to "bargain" federal jurisdiction.[9] A second strategy might have been to identify the underlying "interests" of Bill in being sentenced to a federal prison. Finding out, for example, that Bill's underlying interest may have been personal safety would have allowed the federal prosecutor or possibly the police negotiator to then problem solve how to ensure Bill's safety rather than simply meeting a demand for incarceration in a federal facility.

Unfortunately, the police negotiator and the TPIs did not work with Bill on this substantive demand. Rather, the police negotiator simply asserted that this demand (for federal incarceration) is accepted. Because attunement was not present between Bill and the police negotiator, this confirmation by the PN was not acceptable. Bill likely felt that he stood a better chance of having this demand fulfilled if he could talk directly to a federal prosecutor who will provide some guarantee that meets his demand. The TPIs for the most part simply tried to minimize the situation rather than provide any viable approach or solution to Bill's substantive concerns about going to state vs. federal prison. The result is that the police negotiator and the TPIs consistently repeated that it would be better if Bill and Bonnie gave themselves up, but did not engage the substantive demands Bill asserted. The result is that a sense of real progress in the substantive demand frame did not come to fruition. The situation therefore continued to slowly escalate.

When S.A.F.E. Frames Diverged

There were other times during the negotiation when Bill attempted to shift the conversation to a face frame. It is possible that the face frame may have been most central to Bill. However, whenever he introduced this frame, with statements such as "I've messed it up," or the many comments about needing to commit suicide, the police negotiator (and the TPIs) did not shift to this frame and ask Bill to elaborate. Rather, the PN and the TPIs avoided responding to these self-face attack statements by again asserting the substantive demand frame response of "it will be better if you come out now." At other times, the police negotiator primarily responded to Bill with face-attack statements, such as, "well, that's just dumb." When the more substantive demand frame of the police negotiator and the TPIs diverged from the face frame being tentatively asserted by Bill, the result was an escalation of the situation, to the point that the police negotiator comments at the end that he does not have anything more to say to Bill.

There were other times when, for example, friends of Bonnie attempt to convince Bonnie to surrender. For some of the friends, they remained within a substantive demand frame and simply kept pleading with Bonnie that she should come out. For other friends, they attempted to frame their pleas for surrender in terms of their relationship with Bonnie (attunement). During these heart-wrenching interactions, Bonnie becomes more emotionally distraught as the added "burden" of her friendship compounds her deep emotional distress. When this "relational card" is played by her friends,

Bonnie attempts to move the conversation to "lighter" topics in order to avoid further attunement interaction. Bonnie makes this effort because her core S.A.F.E. frame of emotional distress is not being acknowledged by the police negotiator or her friends. Bonnie needed supportive, emphatic communication focused on her underlying fear. She needed to talk about her situation, including her sense of the hopelessness of it. Once this "emotion work" was undertaken, a sense of progress may have been experienced by Bonnie, at which time she might have been able to look at her options outside of the fear frame. That is, suicide was a solution to her fear (emotional distress). As her fear is lessened, she may have been able to look at suicide in a different light—a light that allowed surrender rather than death.

CHAPTER 9

The Charlie Incident: A Russian Agent

BACKGROUND

"Chuck" was 33 years of age when he shot and killed his father near his parents' home, after which he fled into their garage. Chuck had a long history of mental illness, having been diagnosed since the third grade as a paranoid schizophrenic. On this day, his delusional claim was that his father is a spy for the Russian intelligence service (KGB) and he killed his father on CIA orders. Chuck had been off his medication when this incident occurred. After shooting his father, he went into the home. His mother ran out the side door to a neighbor's house and called the police.

During the first two hours, a police negotiator attempted to communicate with the subject using a bullhorn. When the subject refused to continue talking, the tactical unit inserted three canisters of tear gas into the garage and a throw phone. Negotiation was then initiated with the subject and two hours later, the subject surrendered. No further loss of life occurred.

Table 1.1 (Chapter 1) identifies this incident in terms of a single male, suffering from paranoid schizophrenia (mental instability incident), who had earlier in the day shot and killed his father. There were no hostages or third-party intermediaries involved in this situation. The event lasted four hours and resulted in the subject surrendering.

An initial topical analysis is presented followed by an episodic assessment of the communicative dynamics between Chuck and the police negotiator. The chapter concludes with an overall S.A.F.E. frame analysis.

TOPICAL EPISODE ANALYSIS

The conversation between Chuck and the police negotiator (PN) in this incident is comprised of nine episodes defined by conversation topic. Table 9.1 summarizes these episodes. When the event begins, the efforts of

Table 9.1 Topical Episodes in the Charlie Incident

Episode # & Line #	Topic Shift by	Topic Description
1: 1–118		*Delusional explanation: KGB & CIA*
	PN	The PN initiates telephone contact with Chuck.
	Chuck	Chuck shifts conversation to a disjointed, lengthy explanation for why he killed his father that included a brain tumor, the KGB "replacing" his real father, the CIA pressuring Chuck to kill his "fake" father, and Chuck's need for a "hot shot" (lethal dose of heroin and morphine) so he can end the pain from the brain tumor.
	PN	The PN shifts conversation to how Chuck can get a "hot shot" in order to end his life.
	Chuck	Chuck shifts conversation back to why he needs the "hot shot." Chuck expresses desire to not harm local police officers.
2: 119–136		*Surrender in a motor home*
	PN	The PN changes the topic to how Chuck can surrender without anyone getting hurt. Chuck offers the solution that he will walk out and the police can bring him downtown in a motor home.
3: 137–152		*Delusional explanation: Brain tumor at military hospital*
	Chuck	Chuck returns to his delusional story, describing how he has been diagnosed with a brain tumor at an Army hospital.
4: 153–160		*Removal of media from scene*
	Chuck	Chuck makes a demand that the police remove the television media from the area.
5: 161–328		*Delusional explanation: Drug bust & gasoline*
	Chuck	Chuck returns to telling his delusional story, focusing on how he made a deal to live quietly and then receive a hot shot.
	PN	The PN focuses on how to get Chuck to a psychiatric hospital.
	Chuck	Chuck changes the topic and describes how he made a drug bust. Chuck then describes how he is sitting in gasoline. Chuck also tells the PN he soiled himself when the tear gas was inserted.
	PN	The police negotiator asks Chuck if he would be willing to talk to the initial negotiator who was on the bullhorn when the event began. Chuck agrees.

Table 9.1 (continued)

Episode # & Line #	Topic Shift by	Topic Description
	Chuck	Chuck shifts back to his story, telling the PN of a conspiracy in the city where five secret agents were sent to clean up the city.
	PN	The PN asks Chuck how he got gasoline over himself. Chuck says he was in the Army. The PN comments he was also in the military. The PN offers food to Chuck. Chuck declines.
	Chuck	Chuck reiterates the story of killing his father. The
	PN	PN responds as one veteran to another, requesting that Chuck surrender. Chuck explains how he knows he has a false birth certificate.
	Chuck	Chuck asks the PN to get a pair of pants from his truck, parked outside. Chuck then continues with his delusional story by stating he does not really hold the land title to his home.
6: 329–355		*Winchester truce & cuffs*
	PN	The PN asks Chuck how we can get Chuck transferred to the psychiatric hospital so he can get cleaned up.
	Chuck	Chuck offers the Winchester truce method of surrendering.
	Chuck	Chuck then offers another surrender plan: the police can throw him the handcuffs and he will put them on and come out.
7: 356–374		*Guidelines for surrender*
	PN	The PN asserts they both have to follow police guidelines for surrender.
8: 375–397		*Buck knife*
	Chuck	Chuck offers to throw his buck knife out the window.
9: 398–494		*Surrender ritual*
	Chuck	The PN and Chuck communicate about getting the handcuffs inside to Chuck and how Chuck should walk out. Chuck walks out and is taken into custody.

the initial police negotiator to talk with the subject using a bullhorn are largely unsuccessful as Chuck generally refuses to respond. After two hours, three canisters of tear gas are inserted into the garage, where the subject is barricaded. The subject was able to withstand the tear gas, in part, by opening up the door of a refrigerator that was in the garage. The cold air from the refrigerator helped, evidently, to keep the tear gas from debilitating the subject. Subsequently, the negotiation team was able to make telephone contact with Chuck. It was at this point that negotiations were consistently initiated and audiotaped. There was no more use of tear gas or other tactical actions directed toward the subject.

The negotiations began with the PN introducing himself to Chuck (episode 1). Immediately, Chuck begins telling his story. His explanation of his previous situation (i.e., what happened to him) is quite complex and is unfolded throughout the remaining two hours of the incident.[10] This story is delusional, offering a number of reasons why he shot his father earlier in the morning.

During the disjointed telling of his story (episode 1), Chuck makes a substantive request from the PN for a "hot shot," which is a lethal dose of heroin and morphine. The hot shot was requested in order to end the pain Chuck claimed he was experiencing as a result of a brain tumor. The PN listens throughout the story and then attempts to get Chuck to focus on finding a solution for peacefully surrendering and getting him what he wants (a hot shot).[11] Chuck shifts the topic back to telling his "story," emphasizing that he does not want to harm police officers, as the CIA did not request him to kill any police.

The PN then shifts the topic, this time asking Chuck how we can get him "out of there" so no one gets hurt. At this point, the subject offers to surrender via a rather complicated process of bringing a motor home and a police cruiser to the garage (episode 2, *surrender in a motor home*).

In episode 3, Chuck returns to tell his (delusional) story, this time focusing more directly on how he was diagnosed with a brain tumor at a military hospital. In contrast to Chuck's previous delusional focus, in episode 4, he becomes more rational and asks the PN to move the media (who were covering the incident) "out of sight."

Once this demand is made, an extended dialogue between the subject and the PN takes place, in which a back-and-forth process of topic shifts occurs between the subject and the PN (episode 5). Chuck returns to continuing his elaborate story, this time talking about how he wants to simply and quietly live out his remaining years, after which he will take the hot shot. The PN attempts to change the topic by talking about how to get Chuck to a psychiatric hospital. Chuck then changes the topic back to his story, now describing how he made a drug bust to help the local police, and later revealing that he is soaked in gasoline and had soiled himself when the tear gas was inserted. The PN shifts the topic by asking the subject whether he would be willing to talk with the initial negotiator. Chuck agrees, although the initial police negotiator is never put on the telephone during the incident. In fact, the initial police negotiator interacts with Chuck again only at the very end of the incident, talking to the subject through the bullhorn as the subject exits the garage.

Following this brief exchange, the subject again shifts the conversation back to his delusional story, this time talking about five secret agents who are in town to take care of a conspiracy. The PN asks Chuck how he got gasoline all over himself. Chuck explains to the PN that he is ex-Army and he followed the Army manual when the tear gas was inserted in the garage. The PN shares that he is also ex-military. The PN then asks Chuck if he is hungry. Chuck states that he does not eat and therefore does not want food.

Chuck changes the topic back to telling his story, again talking about how and why he killed his father. The PN shifts the topic by asking Chuck to surrender. Chuck continues his story, explaining how he found out he has a false birth certificate, where the PN can find a pair of pants for Chuck to change into (in his truck parked outside), and how the land title to his home is false and owned by other people.

Episodes 6–9 are concerned with various ways Chuck can surrender. In episode 6 (*Winchester truce & cuffs*), the PN asks Chuck about helping him get transferred to a psychiatric hospital where he would be able to get cleaned up. Chuck responds by proposing that he surrender by "Winchester truce." When the PN does not immediately accept this solution, Chuck then suggests that the police throw him a pair of handcuffs and he will put them on.

The PN follows this up by presenting a few guidelines for Chuck to follow when he surrenders while wearing the handcuffs (episode 7, *guidelines for surrender*). At this point, unexpectedly, Chuck offers to throw his big, buck knife out the window (episode 8, *buck knife*). The PN asks Chuck to wait to do this so the tactical people are not surprised. Finally, in episode 9 (*surrender ritual*), the handcuffs are thrown into the garage by the tactical officers, Chuck places his weapons on the car hood, puts on the handcuffs, and walks out of the garage, at which time he is apprehended.

EPISODIC S.A.F.E. ANALYSIS

This incident begins with the fatal shooting by the subject of his father. After the police arrive, attempts to communicate with Chuck by bullhorn take place over a two-hour period of time. Chuck is generally unresponsive to these communication efforts; consequently, the tactical unit inserts three canisters of tear gas into the garage where the subject is barricaded. Also inserted was a throw phone. The police negotiator then calls the subject. The PN asks Chuck if he can call him Chuck, after which the subject responds "yeah."

Given the level of previous violence as well as the insertion of the tear gas, it would not be uncommon for a person in this situation to be experiencing heightened levels of stress and perhaps fear that the tactical unit was going to assault the garage. Yet the subject sounded remarkably calm when finally contacted by the PN on the throw phone. Chuck says to the PN in a straightforward manner, "Yeah, I got ya, I got ya on the phone" [L11].

Desire to Tell His Story

Without transition, Chuck then says, "Let me tell what happened." This simple statement unequivocally communicates two key ideas. First, given the dangerousness of the situation, the comment reflects an unusually high disregard for outside circumstances (that is, activities that may be occurring outside of the subject's mental thoughts or internal monologue). Second, this comment clearly communicates the message that Chuck wants to talk to the PN. The PN responds, "Ok, explain what happened" to which Chuck replies, "Ok," and sighs. The PN reassures the subject by saying, "I just got here, Chuck. Let's go through this, let's work it out" [L23]. Talking very fast, Chuck then explains that he is a military veteran and went to Los Alamos (New Mexico) and got sick. He says he went to a military hospital and they found he had a brain tumor. While there, the CIA offered Chuck a deal. Chuck was to kill this Russian agent whose name had the same initials as his father's (and who was, in fact, his father). In describing this situation, Chuck comments:

Charlie Incident: Episode 1 (delusional explanation: KGB & CIA): Lines 38–50

L38	Chuck	Exact look-alike of [name deleted], who was my father by the way.
L39	PN	Ok, Ok.
L40	Chuck	Now, they give me a name,
L41	PN	Un-huh
L42	Chuck	I have brain tumor cancer,
L43	PN	Ok, when did you find this out, Chuck.
L44	Chuck	This month; they had an inkling of it, they took all the tests down there at Los Alamos
L45	PN	At Los Alamos?
L46	Chuck	And then they promised me a hot shot, i.e. enough poison to down a bull elephant if I put down—I'm talking to you man!
L47	PN	Ok, good.
L48	Chuck	and they promised me a hot sh- they promised me a hot shot if I put down [name deleted]...(PAUSE)...
L49	PN	Ok, I understand that. Now when—who promised you this? Can you tell me that?
L50	Chuck	CIA and s... so and they gave me a number, ok? 5551239 That was a- (inaudible)

As the subject tells his story, the PN provides positive responses (e.g., minimal encourages, paraphrasing, and open-ended questions), indicating he is listening to Chuck and is interested in hearing how Chuck sees his situation. As Chuck concludes this part of his story, he says, "Now I'm not, no brave man or nuthin' like that, but I'm dyin' and I don't want to die like an animal and haven't ate for a year. Can't eat" [L58].

A Face Frame

While early in the negotiation process, Chuck has framed his story largely in terms of face concerns. That is, Chuck consistently makes references to the predicament he is in and how a series of prior events have conspired to makes things difficult for him. He presents this thematic story in terms of core characteristics of his self-identity that he feels needs validation by the PN. While this thematic focus on "self as victim" is clearly characteristic of a common, persecutory delusional theme associated with paranoid schizophrenia (American Psychiatric Association, 1994), it is communicatively expressed by Chuck in the form of face behavior, notably self-face attack and self-face-defend acts. That is, there is a discourse "logic" to Chuck's delusional state. This logic is a core focus on self-presentation or face in the context of a delusional explanation of events. Importantly, it is the validation of Chuck's self-image that is the interactional response from the PN that Chuck desperately desires.

The PN continues to listen to Chuck as he rambles on with his explanation of his situation. The subject remains in this face frame and the PN consistently engages the subject in this frame from the beginning of negotiation. Chuck then adds more information to this delusional explanation:

Charlie Incident: Episode 1 (delusional explanation: KGB & CIA): Lines 74–86

L74	Chuck	. Look, I'm, look the thing about it is =
L75	PN	Ok,
L76	Chuck	= [name of mother deleted], the bitch that I was gonna shoot that raised me.
L77	PN	Yeah!
L78	Chuck	She admitted, openly today, that they didn't mean to kill [name of father deleted] in 1958 at [City A]
L79	PN	Uh-huh
L80	Chuck	And she's been walking the streets for 28 years with that son-of-a-bitch and he's been calling himself my father.
L81	PN	I see.
L82	Chuck	Now you tell me what he k- helped kill him and you tell me that when the CIA tells me that and presents proof- fingerprints uh, lets see, fingerprints, signature and footprints =
L83	PN	Ok!
L84	Chuck	= because [name deleted] worked at Los Alamos in World War Two.
L85	PN	Ok, can you tell me who your doctor was down at Los Alamos?
L86	Chuck	It was just that- no, I can't.

Chuck indicates that he intended to kill his mother because she knew that Chuck's "real" father was killed in 1958. Again, the story is disjointed as it is told, moving without transitions from statements about his mother walking the streets for 28 years to the CIA having proof (fingerprints, signatures, and footprints), presumably of the fact that the man Chuck killed was a Russian agent, not his real father. However, the face frame implication of the statement that the CIA had this "proof" is, "*after seeing all this overwhelming evidence against my father and mother, can you understand how I must feel and why I did what did?*"

The PN patiently listens and provides supportive responses that validate the self-image Chuck so desperately needs to have acknowledged by the PN. This self-image is clearly delusional, yet it is anchored in core personal characteristics important to Chuck. Some of these personal qualities of his self-image are that he wants to die with dignity; he suffers great pain and hardship; he has been harmed; he is in a difficult situation and he made the best decisions he could, under the relentless pressure of the CIA and others.

Chuck states, reflecting his developing awareness that the PN is listening to him, "I don't have any more information for you, Ok?" [L88]. The PN responds with a simple "Ok." This is a transitional moment in the dialogue between the subject and the PN, reflecting convergence between the parties regarding a sense of progress in meeting the face needs of the subject.

A Shift to Attunement

Because Chuck felt his face needs were validated, he then offers a cooperative message (attunement) to the PN when he says, "Now look, I'm talking, I got the rifle laid down, let's everybody stay calm and I'll talk to you" [L90]. The PN quickly responds, "Ok, well no, be assured, Chuck, we are going to stay calm, we want you to stay calm" [L91]. Chuck initiated this reciprocated cooperative act with the PN. This attunement move further de-escalates the situation, as evidenced by Chuck's commitment to keep his rifle down and to stay calm.

Shift to a Substantive Demand Frame

Chuck then explains that the CIA paid him (one hot shot) to kill this Russian agent (his father) "cause he was a undercover KBG agent" [L96]. The PN, by making progress in validating the subject's face needs and attunement concerns, now shifts the conversation to a more substantive demand frame, which the subject accepts. The PN comments, "but unless we get you out, we cannot get you to the CIA, we can't have them come to you" [L60]. The subject then responds, "The thing about it is, if I go out, where do I go?" [L98], to which the PN says, "we will take you downtown and we'll arrange for the CIA to come and meet you" [L99]. Shortly thereafter, the PN says, "What I need to know is, if I can arrange for them to meet you downtown with the hot shot for what went down today, can we get you out, peaceful surrender" [L103]? The subject responds, "I'll surrender if they come up on the phone and guarantee it" [L105].

A little later on, Chuck says, "Now, I'm not gonna become a drug addict for anybody" [L114]. He then says he was not paid to kill a cop. The PN responds with a substantive demand message, "Chuck, I don't want you to kill anybody, what I want you to do is help me work this out so we can get you what you need; if you need the hot shot, we'll get you that, give us time to contact the people" [L117]. The subject then says, "I'll give you time" [L118], sending a message of cooperation around the substantive concern of time to the PN.

The PN continues within the substantive demand frame (episode 2, *surrender in a motor home*), by commenting, "Ok, but also let's talk about how we're going to get you out of there where none of us, none of the police officers get hurt and you don't get hurt" [L119]. At this point, Chuck now joins the PN in actively problem solving a peaceful solution to this volatile situation. Because of the alignment of the PN and the subject within the same S.A.F.E. frame (i.e., substantive demand), the incident is further de-escalating. To the question asked by the PN, the subject says, "it's very simple" [L120], and he proceeds to describe a surrender approach that involves the police driving a motor home to the police cruiser, presumably parked near the garage, then Chuck leaving the garage, after which he is taken downtown in the police car. While this "surrender plan" may sound feasible to the subject, the PN responds by explaining that the police cannot let an officer walk into an area of open cover. The PN then pointedly reassures Chuck that the tactical people "are not going to take any hostile action toward you" [L134].

In this shared, substantive demand frame, Chuck is lucid and followed the suggestions of the police negotiator. While Chuck's "solution" to the problem was not feasible, it reflects an emerging, de-escalating pattern. This interchange between Chuck and the PN indicates that the sense of progress made within the face frame (through validation of the subject's self-image) has permitted the PN to briefly shift to negotiating relational trust (attunement) and then shift with the subject to a substantive demand frame, resulting in a commitment from the subject to surrender.

A Return to Face Concerns

However, Chuck is not yet ready to come out; primarily because, in his mind, he has not been able to tell his whole story. Thus, while the PN gets commitment from Chuck for a conditional surrender, the subject nevertheless returns to a face frame and continues telling the PN more about his situation (episode 3). The following list reflects this continuing unfolding of Chuck's face-based explanation:

Charlie Incident: Episode 3 (delusional explanation: brain tumor at military hospital): Lines 137–150

L137 Chuck Well the thing is that they informed me so I don't know, see, what I'm trying to say this is was a military hospital I was at.
L138 PN Right!
L139 Chuck So I'm not- it could be army security, it could be FBI, it could be Secret Service, I don't know. They said they were CIA aut-authorized. They showed me their b- authorization cards and, and when you're diagnosed as brain tumor cancer you're gonna b- you're gonna- gonna grasp at a couple of straws to do two things =
L140 PN Yeah,
L141 Chuck in '58, where John Wayne caught cancer?
L142 PN Right,
L143 Chuck That's what they diagnosed it as; the same cancer, I was there, ok? So listen, I...I...I've been having this for 28 years, this pain.
L144 PN Ok, Chuck, today are you in pain right now? Do (inaudible)
[ ]
L145 Chuck I am in pain right now.
L146 PN Ok, where do you hurt at, cause I am gonna get a doctor on the (inaudible)
[ ]
L147 Chuck My gut, my head, I have a h- I have a 24 hour headache, I finally had to start taking Tylenol...and I've been throwing up every d- I have an ulcer too.
L148 PN It sounds like you're really hurting and I...I sympathize with that but (inaudible)
[ ]
L149 Chuck Actually- Actually my s- actually the tear gas really cleared up my sinuses.
L150 PN It cleared up my sinuses too and I was...I was on the other end down here.

The subject is again offering a convoluted explanation that functions to honor or restore his self-image in the eyes of the PN, presenting his self-image in terms of a noble man who is dealing with a great deal of pain. The PN continues to engage the subject in the face frame by validating that he understands and sympathizes with the fact that Chuck is hurting.

Again, following this validation, Chuck moves into a (nondelusional) substantive demand frame (episode 4), and says, "Do me a favor, get those fucking news vultures outta here, I learned to hate th- hate them t- hate them" [L155]. The PN responds that he will talk to somebody to get the media to move back out of sight. This peripheral substantive demand made by the subject is agreed to by the PN, demonstrating cooperative action between the parties and functioning to build relational trust (attunement) between the subject and the PN. In part, this is reflected in Chuck beginning his demand with the phrase, "do me a favor," signaling this peripheral demand functions as a relational request for help.

A Divergence in S.A.F.E. Frames

Chuck then returns to his delusional story (episode 5) within a face frame and talks at length about how he does not want to die like an animal and why he wants a hot shot. At this time, however, the PN attempts to redirect the subject to a substantive demand frame focused on surrender. During this extended episode, the PN makes more directed efforts within a substantive demand frame to influence the subject and move Chuck to completing the surrender they talked about earlier.

However, the subject does not move into the substantive demand frame with the PN, but simply talks past the PN and continues to embellish his story. This additional information that Chuck feels a need to tell the PN involves details about how the subject made a drug bust; how money that was due him was never delivered, and how, as a result, the Mafia sent him a .22-caliber bullet. Again, while this explanation of his circumstances is irrational, Chuck adds, "So I'm not, look, I'm not, I been cooperating with the law by turnin' in drug dealers, so you tell me who the hell's somebody's out there, out to kill me, so you, uh, understand what I'm saying" [L279]. Again, the moral of his wandering story is to present his self-image in a positive light to the PN (e.g., I am a moral, law-abiding citizen).

Chuck then says, "and you can find out I'm not out ta kill no damn law, I just was sent to kill one man and even though I may have hated the son-of-a-bitch father for 28 years, you know?" [L183]. Rather than respond with a validation of the self-image Chuck is projecting as the PN successfully did before (e.g., I see that you want to help the police, but you are not recognized for your efforts), the PN directly attempts to shift the subject to a substantive demand frame by responding, "Ok, Ok, Chuck. What about—you know the CIA—what about us taking you straight to the [psychiatric hospital] and then contacting them [CIA] there" [L184]; to which Chuck says, "prison ward" [L185], reflecting a disconnection between what the subject was talking about and the police negotiator's response.

During this interchange, the PN is operating within a substantive demand frame while the subject is engaging in face-frame behavior. As a result of this divergence in frame alignment, the subject becomes more agitated, and the situation begins to escalate to the point that the PN comments, "I mean, we need to just slow it down to where you give us time" [L192].

Chuck then discloses to the PN that he is sitting in a pool of gasoline and he soiled his pants:

Charlie Incident: Episode 5 (delusional explanation: drug bust & gasoline): Lines 199–203

L199	Chuck	= and this is the, this is—I'm sitting here now in gasoline, soaked in gasoline, I shit my pants, pissed—I pissed my pants, and I'm sitting here running out of cigarettes, now.
L200	PN	Ok, what a- if you're soaked in gasoline, Chuck, you don't want to be smoking cigarettes.
L201	Chuck	Why not?
L202	PN	Well, because it's not—You know, you're talking about not wanting to be in pain and I don't want you in pain, that's what I'm trying- I got people working on other phones, working on getting hold of the people you need gotten hold of and working with arranging [psychiatric hospital].
L203	Chuck	Ok!

Convergence within a Face Frame

With the disclosure that Chuck is sitting in gasoline, the PN responds to the subject's comments by reassuring him that he (the PN) does not want harm to come to Chuck, that Chuck should be careful smoking around the gasoline, and that the PN is working to help Chuck by trying to find CIA people to meet him at the psychiatric hospital. The PN, in short, shifts into the face frame of the subject, who is communicating the underlying message "*I'm in a lot of trouble, I am scared, I am embarrassed at soiling my pants, and I don't want you or others to see me this way.*" The police negotiator's comments of recognition of the subject's situation de-escalates the event. With progress now being made in the face frame, the situation begins to de-escalate. The PN asks Chuck if he would be willing to talk to the initial negotiator. The subject agrees to this request, indicating relationally co-operative behavior.

Chuck then returns once more to elaborating his story, this time by adding that there are five secret agents in the city, explaining that these agents have proof that some of the "brass" were on the take (see the following list). This time, the PN remains in this face frame with the subject, reinforcing that he understands his situation and reassures Chuck that the police do not want to hurt him.

Charlie Incident: Episode 5 (delusional explanation: drug bust & gasoline): Lines 219–222

L219	Chuck	That's right, the cops sha- and, and they got proof that. . . uh- some of the brass was on the take, quote, now I'm not saying it's local, you understand what I'm saying, they, ok, this is what's wrote on the record with the federal government, now I'm not knowing what's going on, I'm just told one thing. Now have you ever seen a government operative that ever was told the truth half the time?
L220	PN	Probably no,

L221	Chuck	So now you understand why I'm sitting right here with a 12 gauge shotgun, one .22 and I'm sitting here and I haven't fired at you have I?
L222	PN	No, and we haven't fired at you, Chuck, we don't want to fire at you. [ ]

The situation returns to a de-escalating pattern. The subject now explains how he poured gasoline on the tear gas canisters, based on advice given in an Army manual (while this may well be a delusional explanation, it was quite fortunate that the gasoline did not ignite). Finding out that the subject is ex-Army, the negotiator responds that he is ex-Air Force. Chuck then explained how his work in the Army was cryptology; the negotiator commented that the subject "held a pretty important position" [L240], again validating the self-image of the subject.

A Shift to Attunement

As the subject and the PN discuss further how much gasoline is on the floor, the PN shifted the conversation to an attunement frame and made a number of statements to the subject expressing his concern and consideration for the subject. For example, the PN asked the subject to be sure not to throw a match on the floor. Building on this tentative progress in attunement, the PN asks Chuck if he is hungry. The remaining dialogue reflects negotiation around issues of trust between the subject and the PN:

Charlie Incident: Episode 5 (delusional explanation: drug bust & gasoline): Lines 246–251

L246	PN	I wouldn't either, I don't want to see you hurt. How hung- you said you were hungry you had (inaudible) [ ]
L247	Chuck	No.
L248	PN	You're not hungry?
L249	Chuck	I'm not hungry, I haven't ate all day, but I'm not hungry, I got a dollar in my pocket but I'm not hungry...
L250	PN	Ok, I was just—if you were hungry I was gonna see about working in get- getting you some food. [ ]
L251	Chuck	I ain't gonna trade for it. Let's be honest, I'm not exactly a trusting person right now after getting shit—look, for 28 years this man has been sitting here pretending to be my father and he's- and they, and they have signature, fingerprints, and footprints because my old man cooked at Los Alamos during World War Two and uh, and their cooks went through a security check out there do you understand what I'm saying?

As evidenced by this interchange, the subject reminds the PN that he does not trust the police right now.

Return to a Face Frame

Following this, Chuck returns, again without transition, to a face frame where he continues his explanation of his situation, reiterating information about how his father was a KGB agent. At one point, Chuck says, "I've come up here to find out what the- they said and I'm sitting here broke and I came here to find what the hell happened to my Social Security my one- my, my, agent Orange check; I wan in- look, I'll be honest" [L259]. The PN interrupts and asks, "were you in Nam, Chuck?" [L260]. Chuck sighs and says, "I was in Korea" [L262]. As Chuck continues with his story, the PN says, "I hear ya, being ex-military, I understand that" [L266].

The interchange in the following list indicates the attunement work the PN is engaging in with the subject. At this point in the event, the PN is listening to the face-framed story that the subject is telling, but he is responding from an attunement frame:

Charlie Incident: Episode 5 (delusional explanation: drug bust & gasoline): Lines 273–274

L273	Chuck	Oh- and th- I- can agree to that, I can see your point I just said at the poi- pres- the earlier conference it was put under the door, Army insulation style and that's fine but I, but see I, I don't trust doctors because they keep wanting to give you all these damn, uh, heroin, strychnine heroin...a heroin and morphine based drugs that make you higher than a kite and loonier than hell if ya do that just put me in [City B] and let me die like an animal an I don't want to die like that.
L274	PN	Chuck, as one veteran to another, this is [name deleted] talking to you, I don't want to see that happen to you and what I do want to accomplish is that you come out and I'll go with you wherever—you know, I'm not gonna let them take advantage of another veteran, you tell me what you need and I'll make sure you get it. [ ]

Chuck, however, does not reciprocate the relational invitation made by the PN when the PN reassures Chuck that he will not let anyone take advantage of a fellow veteran. In fact, Chuck is so consumed in explaining his story through the face frame, he likely does not notice the relational message being communicated by the PN.

Chuck then continues with explaining his situation, this time talking at length about how there were three different names on his birth certificate, and the land title to his parents' home was supposedly in Chuck's name, but he found out it was not. Further, Chuck claimed that the title showed he owed $150,000 on the home. During this extended explanation, the negotiator returned to the face frame and provided minimal encouragers and validating statements about Chuck's situation.

A Move to a Substantive Demand Frame: The Surrender

After going through an extensive explanation (again) of his dire circumstances, Chuck shifts his communication to a substantive request, asking the PN to get a pair of pants from his truck, which was parked nearby. The PN, after listening for quite a while to this complicated, delusional story, responds that they will get Chuck his pants. The PN then continues in a substantive demand frame and says, "You know, I can understand that you want to get cleaned up, uh, we can clean, we can let you get cleaned up on the ambulance before we go to the psychiatric hospital" [L328]. The subject agrees, saying "I can get cleaned up in the shower at the psychiatric hospital" [L329].

The PN and the subject now remain in the substantive demand frame (episode 6). In fact, from this point forward (episodes 6–9), the PN assumes a directive role concerning the surrender of the subject. The subject actively cooperates with the PN in identifying and agreeing to the instructions being given by the PN for safely surrendering.

However, while both parties converge within the substantive demand frame, the problem-solving efforts of the PN and the subject are not without difficulties. The following list reflects the substantive frame discussion around the "Winchester truce" and the "cuffs" solutions offered by the subject:

Charlie Incident: Episode 6 (Winchester truce & cuffs): Lines 334–355

L334	PN	Well, Chuck, what we need to do is see about workin' it out to where we can transfer you from there to [psychiatric hospital] in a nice safe way to where we can get in contact with the people you need to contact-
		[ ]
L335	Chuck	well, why don't co- I think you can get contact the CIA, they sort of stay open on weekends.
L336	PN	No, I know we can, but I'm sayin' that they're that we're gonna have to arrange to get you from here to [psychiatric hospital]=
		[ ]
L337	Chuck	thats-
L338	PN	= so we can get you in contact with them
L339	Chuck	I'll put it this way,
L340	PN	yeah,
L341	Chuck	You come in with a holster gun, I'll hold the rifle-
		[ ]
L342	PN	I-
L343	Chuck	Wait a sec.
L344	PN	Uh-huh,

L345 Chuck You hold the gun, butt out, straight ahead, you don't trust me, I don't trust you let's say.
L346 PN Well
L347 Chuck It's called a Winchester truce, I look at you, you hold that gun out you point it straight at the ground, and I say fine, lets take a walk.
L348 PN Ok, Chuck, if,
[ ]
L349 Chuck Or you can throw a pair of cuffs in, and I'll put them on the front.
L350 PN Ok,-
[ ]
L351 Chuck Not the back-
L352 PN Uh, would you do that, but ok, listen to me as far as, we do have, have some rules that, you know, are set down by our department; I'm not going to be able to go face to face with you, but if,
L353 Chuck Wait a second, what I'm saying is you get a 12 gauge for a pair of cuffs when you come in without a weap- when you come, when, when, when ya toss one pistol out then I'll toss the next one and you keep the sni-snipers down,
L354 PN Yeah, no problem.
L355 Chuck Mm-k you put that down on the deal then I'll, then well, then we'll talk.

The PN, feeling the handcuff option is acceptable, responds that there are some guidelines that have to be followed (episode 7), to which the subject says, "Ok, what's yours?" [L357]. The PN then explains that a police officer cannot go "face-to-face" with the subject, but the handcuffs could be tossed into the garage. The subject could then put them on and walk out, where he will be met by the tactical officers and transported to the psychiatric hospital where he can get cleaned up. Chuck responds with the question, "Guarantee"? And the PN says, "Guaranteed." The subject then asks, "with at least a 72 hour stay?" [L365], to which the PN says (I am fairly sure with complete confidence) "yeah, no problem" [L366].

Once this agreement is reached, the following interchange takes place:

Charlie Incident: Episode 8 (buck knife): Lines 375–385

L375 Chuck Here, this is a buck...
L376 PN Yeah,-
[ ]
L377 Chuck Ok!
L378 PN Who...
[ ]
L379 Chuck Tell him to watch out.
L380 PN This is a what?
L381 Chuck A Buck Knife.

L382 PN Ok, what are you doing, throwing =
[ ]
L383 Chuck I-
L384 PN = don't throw something out until I can tell you're doing it- Ok, let me tell them it's coming out, ok? I don't want you to excite them.
L385 Chuck Ok,
[ ]

The PN then makes arrangements with the tactical officers for Chuck to throw his knife out the window. Chuck complies. Following this, the PN now arranges for the handcuffs to be thrown into the garage (episode 9). The subject is completely agreeable to the suggestions made by the PN and remains lucid and rational:

Charlie Incident: Episode 9 (surrender ritual): Lines 398–407

L398 PN Ok, now you want them to throw in a set of cuffs?
L399 Chuck You can throw in a set of cuffs, I'll put them on the front.
L400 PN Hang on, hang on, (Negotiator to one of the perimeter units... Negotiator to one of the perimeter units, tell them to throw a set of cuffs in to him...ok...ok, he wants the cuffs, I want to give it to him-)
L401 Chuck It's your rules, not mine.
L402 PN I know, I'm workin' on it.
[ ]
L403 Chuck Now wait a minute, I'm trying to stay within your perimeter.
L404 PN I hear ya, (PN: go down n' toss them to him if you have to but I told the man and I—we're being straight down the line with him I —have them in there). There's another negotiator coming down there in a blue jacket, he's going to throw the cuffs to ya, ok?
L405 Chuck Ok!
L406 PN Just give him a minute, he's 3 houses down, have ta- he's gonna have ta he's gonna have to run all the way down there.
L407 Chuck No, I can give him more than a minute.

At this point, both the PN and the subject are cooperatively problem solving within the substantive demand frame. Within a few minutes more, the subject exits the garage and is taken into custody (and transported to the psychiatric hospital).

OVERALL S.A.F.E. FRAME ANALYSIS

Chuck was a 33-year-old man who shot and killed his father near his parents' home. He then walked into his parents' home, looking for his mother. She saw what he did and fled to the next door neighbor's home where she immediately called the police. After six hours, the police negotiator was able to convince Chuck to peacefully surrender.

Negotiation with a Mentally Ill Individual

This is a clear incident in which the subject suffered from a mental disorder, having been diagnosed since the third grade with paranoid schizophrenia. Further, this mental disorder was manifest during the six hours of negotiation. Chuck maintained a number of delusions, including (1) his father was a Russian KGB agent, (2) his mother knew all along that this Russian agent was not his real father, (3) the CIA contracted with him to kill this KBG agent (who was his father), (4) he claimed he had a brain tumor, (5) he had been taken to a hospital in Los Alamos, New Mexico, (6) he was given a promise to receive a lethal "hot shot," (7) he helped the police in a drug bust, (8) the Mafia sent him a .22-caliber bullet, (9) he had three birth certificates, and (10) the land title to his parents' home was not, as he was told, in Chuck's name. In addition, Chuck grounded these delusions within a "self as victim" viewpoint.

There are two observations concerning negotiation dynamics with a mentally ill subject. First, while Chuck often inhabited his delusional world, he did not always make sense of external stimuli in terms of his internal, delusional mind-set. In other words, there were multiple moments during the negotiation that Chuck evidenced nondelusional perceptions and appraisals of his situation. During these moments, the negotiator was able to influence Chuck toward a peaceful surrender.

Second, even when Chuck was experiencing the world around him through his delusional state, he nevertheless processed stimuli and made cognitive appraisals through more stable S.A.F.E. frames. Chuck told his story in ways consistent with face frame patterns. He accomplished this by engaging in significant self-face-honoring behavior (e.g., self-face defend/restore messages). His communication evidenced a fundamental need to project an enduring set of personal/group qualities he identified as descriptive of his self-image. While these qualities were generated from a delusional platform, they nevertheless comprised a stable "self-image" that communicatively was projected to the police negotiator. Each of the many "stories" Chuck told was made coherent in terms of this projected self-image.

Third, Chuck engaged in patterned social interaction with the police negotiator through the face frame in a manner that indicated a core need to have this projected self-image *validated (acknowledged) by the police negotiator*. In short, Chuck was delusional in much (but not all) of the content of his communication messages with the police negotiator, but he was lucid in the "meta-messages" he conveyed to the PN and the manner in which he verbally constructed meaning with the PN. Chuck "negotiated" with the PN through the face frame, and this negotiation was patterned according to S.A.F.E. model principles. While Chuck inhabited a delusional world, his interactive dynamics with the police negotiator was patterned and predictable in terms of S.A.F.E. interpretive frames.

Finally, when the police negotiator did not shift into the dominant frame of the subject, the subject became increasingly agitated and the situation escalated. When the police negotiator shifted into the main S.A.F.E. frame of the subject and negotiated using S.A.F.E. strategies grounded in that specific frame, a sense of progress arose and the situation de-escalated.

A Core Interactional Pattern

A fundamental interaction pattern emerged between the subject and the police negotiator. This de-escalatory pattern can be described as follows:

1. The subject begins to "tell his story" in his own words. This story is comprised of an oftentimes lengthy explanation of his situation, framed around face needs.
2. The police negotiator responds to the subject within a face frame and as the subject is telling his story, the police negotiator responds with face-validating statements that express an understanding of the challenges and concerns of the subject.
3. Progress in face frame negotiation results. The subject then briefly shifts to the attunement frame, in which the subject and the police negotiator communicatively and behaviorally express cooperation toward one another.
4. The subject, on a number of occasions, shifts back to a face frame and continues to explain his situation. The police negotiator responds with face-validating messages. A mutual sense of progress results, and the subject again moves to an attunement frame, reinforcing his growing trust toward the police negotiator.
5. Building upon a sense of attunement progress, the police negotiator is able to shift the conversation to a substantive demand frame, engaging Chuck in figuring out how he can safely surrender. Chuck engages in this problem-solving effort with the police negotiator.

This incident was potentially tornadic, with a mentally ill subject who had just killed his own father. The police tactical team initially inserted three canisters of tear gas into the garage in which Chuck had barricaded himself. Yet the subject refused to surrender. The subject, however, had a need to tell his story. His story was delusional and often told in a fragmentary and disjointed fashion. To an outside observer, this behavior may appear simply "crazy" and *therefore unpredictable.* Yet an analysis of the discourse patterns between Chuck and the police negotiator reveals a *predictable pattern of meaning-making* engaged in by Chuck and the police negotiator. What provided coherence and, therefore, some sense of predictability to the interaction was the observation that Chuck operated in S.A.F.E. interpretive frames. The dominant frame for Chuck was face. When the police negotiator entered this face frame with Chuck, stable patterns of communication resulted. Chuck needed to tell his story and even more fundamentally, needed to have his face needs validated. Fortunately, the police negotiator engaged in communication that acknowledged Chuck's situation and his "sense making" of that situation. The police negotiator's ability to fluidly shift with the subject from the face frame and then to an attunement frame finally enabled the police negotiator to influence Chuck to shift into a substantive demand frame, at which time the subject actively problem solved a peaceful surrender (throwing in the handcuffs).

CHAPTER 10

The Delta Incident: A Deadline to Detonate

BACKGROUND

"David" was a young man in his early 20s who hijacked a small airplane while en route to another city in the United States, threatening to blow up the aircraft. The subject had a history of drug and alcohol abuse and had attended a substance abuse rehabilitation program earlier. Once the airplane landed, he released the passengers but held hostage the pilot and the copilot. Negotiations continued for four hours after which David surrendered. No one was injured or killed.

In this chapter, a topical analysis is presented, followed by an episodic analysis of the communicative dynamics between David and the hostage negotiator. The chapter concludes with an overall S.A.F.E. frame analysis of the event.

TOPICAL EPISODE ANALYSIS

Once the airplane landed, the police tactical team secured the area, establishing a perimeter around the aircraft. Initially, there were efforts to establish communication with David by the police negotiation team using the airplane's radio system. However, this system was unreliable (due to low battery power), with voices fading in and out, making extended communication difficult. During this time, the subject demanded food and to talk to Diane, a female friend. Due to difficulties in safely bringing food to the airplane, locating Diane, and problems with the radio, these demands had not yet been met when the police were able to begin audiotaping the negotiations. There appears to be about a one-hour period of time between the time the airplane landed and more reliable communications between the subject and the police negotiator (PN) were established. The audiotape of the situation begins as the police are completing hooking up ground electricity in order to use the on-board radio in the cockpit. Table 10.1 presents a summary of the discussion topics between the PN and David.

Episode 1 (*establishing communication*) reflects David's frustration in not receiving food or being able to talk with his friend, Diane. As the radio fades in and out, there are long pauses during which efforts are made to finalize the ground power system so the radio can be reliably used.

In episode 2 (*locating Diane*), the subject expresses his frustration with not being able to talk to Diane. The PN attempts to reassure the subject that he should be patient. The PN tells David that he is working on getting food to the subject and finding Diane.

In episode 3 (*talking with Diane*), the PN shifts the conversation away from David's demand to talk with Diane to asking questions about the bomb the subject claims he has on board. After providing minimal information about the bomb, David shifts back to talking about his frustration with the PN for not bringing Diane to him. David then asks to talk with his mother. The PN questions David where his mother works and her contact information. The subject again demands to have Diane brought to the airplane so he can talk to her. The PN responds by telling David that she may not want to come on the plane. The PN then says that he could talk to her by radio.

The PN shifts the conversation to David's previous military service (episode 4, *military service & lying*). David then asks the PN why he keeps telling lies and is delaying having Diane brought to the aircraft. The PN explains that she is in the airport and it takes time to get her to the radio.

In episode 5 (*demand to see Diane*), the PN continues to reassure David that Diane is coming; David, however, becomes increasingly agitated because he is not able to see or talk with his friend. David then terminates communication with the PN and puts the pilot on the radio to talk to the PN. The PN quickly assures the pilot that their families have been contacted. David again gets back on the radio and demands that the food be brought immediately.

Diane arrives and the PN permits her to briefly talk with David (episode 6, *Diane briefly talks to subject*). In episode 7 (*the bomb*), the PN interrupts the short conversation between David and Diane to tell the subject that food is on the way and to ask David about the bomb he says he brought on the airplane. The PN finds out the copilot's husband has a heart condition, and he is worried about his wife. The PN then asks if she (copilot) can be released. David emphatically rejects this request. During this time, food is finally brought to the airplane. The PN then turns over the negotiation to another police negotiator (PN2), who talks to David for a minute or two, after which the PN returns and continues discussion with David, again asking about the bomb.

The PN once more asks David to release the copilot, and this time, David agrees (episode 8, *release of copilot*). The PN offers to help David with his

Table 10.1 Delta Incident: Topical Episodes

Episode #	Line #	Topic Shift by	Topic Description
1	1–73		*Establishing communication*
		N/A	Communication through the airplane radio system has deteriorated to the point that it is almost impossible for the PN and David to hear one another. The PN is informing David that they are hooking up ground power in order to continue communicating with the airplane's radio system.
		David	At different times, David expresses his frustration with the delay in not receiving food and not being able to talk to his friend, Diane.
2	74–101		*Locating Diane*
		David	David demands to see and talk to Diane.
3	102–169		*Talking with Diane*
		PN	The PN asks David about the bomb.
		David	David shifts conversation to finding Diane.
		David	David asks to talk to his mother. The PN requests contact information. The PN promises to find David's mother.
		David	David returns to his demand to see Diane. The PN tells David that Diane may not want to go onto the airplane. The PN says Diane can talk to him by radio.
4	170–193		*Military service & lying*
		PN	The PN asks David about his military service. David asks the PN why he keeps telling lies. The PN explains that Diane is in another part of the airport, and it takes time to bring her to the phone.
5	194–276		*Demand to see Diane*
		PN	The PN continues to reassure David that Diane is coming. David becomes increasingly agitated because he has not yet talked with Diane. During a brief conversation with the pilot, the PN reassures the pilot and the copilot that their families have been contacted. David demands that police bring food immediately. The PN reassures the subject that the food is coming.

Episode #	Line #	Topic Shift by	Topic Description
6	277–293		*Diane briefly talks to subject*
		PN	The PN tells David he has Diane and she can talk to him briefly. Diane talks to David.
7	294–367		*The bomb*
		PN	The PN interrupts the conversation between Diane and the subject and tells David the food is on the way.
		PN	The PN asks the subject for more information on the bomb.
		PN	The PN finds out the copilot's husband has a heart problem and asks if she can be released. Subject declines. Food is delivered.
		Pilot	The pilot tells the PN that if Diane could talk to the subject, the situation would end peacefully. The PN does not respond.
		PN	The PN tells David he is going to step out to talk to Diane. PN2 becomes the primary negotiator.
		PN	The PN returns and continues to talk to David, asking him questions about the bomb.
8	368–536		*Release of copilot*
		PN	The PN asks David to release the copilot. The subject agrees.
		PN	The PN offers help for David.
		David	Communication takes place with the pilot as the go-between. David demands Diane be brought in visual sight. The PN agrees. The PN asks the subject to leave the black bag that contains the dynamite inside the airplane and release the pilot.
		David	The discussion over where Diane will be visible escalates the situation. David demands to see his mother. The PN says she is not at the airport yet. David becomes significantly agitated. He expresses distrust toward the PN. The PN attempts to calm David down.
		PN2	PN2 takes over negotiation. David sets a deadline of 30 minutes to bring Diane and his mother to him or he will blow up the airplane. PN2 continues to tell David that they are working on meeting his demands. David counts down the time.
		PN	The PN comes back on the radio and continues negotiation with David.

Table 10.1 (continued)

Episode #	Line #	Topic Shift by	Topic Description
		PN2	PN2 takes over communication and continues to try to reassure David that Diane and his mother will arrive. David becomes emotionally distressed.
		PN	The PN comes back on the radio and tells David, with 10 minutes left of the deadline, that Diane can talk to him.
9	537–561		*David talks with Diane & surrenders*
		Diane	Diane talks to David. Diane offers to help David and reassures him that she can be trusted. David walks off the airplane and is taken into custody. No one is injured or killed.

problems, but the subject rejects this invitation. David becomes more agitated as he wants to see and talk with Diane one more time. Communication then takes place between the PN and the pilot, who shuttles information between the subject and the PN. David demands Diane be brought out on the tarmac so he can see her. The PN agrees to this demand. The PN asks David to leave his "black bag" that supposedly contains dynamite inside the airplane and release the pilot. David declines.

David becomes emotionally distressed at this point and angrily demands to see his mother and Diane. The PN attempts to calm David down. For a brief time, PN2 takes over negotiating with David; however, the subject remains highly agitated and angry, now threatening to blow up the airplane in 45 minutes unless Diane is brought onto the airplane. The PN returns and continues to try to calm the subject. PN2 then replaces the PN once more and also attempts to reassure David that his mother will arrive shortly and arrangements are being made for David to see Diane. David becomes highly distressed. With only ten minutes left to the deadline, the PN comes back on the radio and tells David he can talk to Diane.

Episode 9 (*David talks to Diane, surrenders*) begins with Diane talking and reassuring David that he can trust her. David expresses his core need for help with his substance abuse problem. David then walks off the airplane and is taken into custody by the police. The pilot exits immediately thereafter. No one was injured or killed during this volatile event.

EPISODIC S.A.F.E. ANALYSIS

This is a volatile situation, where an individual claims he has a bomb and expresses his willingness to detonate it. The event begins with difficulties in establishing communication between the hijacker on the airplane and the police negotiation team, due to low battery power to the airplane radio. Prior to the establishment of reliable ground power to maintain the radio connection, David requested food and also demanded that his friend, Diane, be brought to the airplane so he can talk to her. Neither of these demands were met by the police, in part, because of poor communication via the radio and also due to difficulties in locating Diane.

As the ground power is turned on (episode 1), the two-way radio system becomes more reliable. Nevertheless, because it is a two-way radio system, both the subject and the PN often signal when they are initiating contact (e.g., "PN to David") and when done talking (e.g., "10-4"). The following list captures David's frustration with what he considers the delay in having his demands met.

Delta Incident: Episode 1 (establishing communication): Lines 1–5

L1	David	Establishing communication, requesting S.O.S., get the God damn power here, bring the fuckin' steak and the eggs. 10-4.
L2	PN	David I just found out that your steak and eggs, uh, have just arrived and I want to find out from you how you want them delivered.
L3	David	I've already established that you're really pissing me off. I want em brought out on the same cars that they're goin', on, establish electricity with, should take no more than two men to do it! I want one once the car gets here to bring me electricity, one to bring the steak and eggs to the fuckin' window. If someone comes through the pilot's window and sticks a gun up, pulls, uh, sticks the gun up, it all goes up. I'm being calm. You all are being a little bit irrational in a type situation like this, you're not dealing with your average (pause) hijacker. 10-4.
L4	PN	Well I understand the fact that you're very intelligent, and I appreciate that. We're just about ready to bring the food out to you now, here's the way it's gonna be done David, now listen up ok.
L5	David	10-4, I told you how it was gonna be done, you tell me how you want to do it and then I'm gonna tell you how it's gonna be done, and I want to know where in the hell Diane is.

Substantive Demand vs. Attunement Frames

As the radio system becomes operational (with reliable electrical power), a divergence in predominant S.A.F.E. frames emerge between the subject and the PN. The subject is highly frustrated with the delay in getting food, electricity for the radio (that also cools down the temperature in the aircraft), and in locating his friend, Diane. In response to David's demands, the PN adapts a substantive demand frame as a way to exchange (bargain) food and talking with Diane for the release of the pilot and the copilot, and ultimately, the peaceful surrender of the subject. The PN asserts this instrumental bargaining framework as the method through which the subject can get his demands met.

However, the subject is functioning within an attunement frame and therefore is interpreting the PN's messages in terms of relational power, trust, and consideration. For David, food is a peripheral demand, while talking with Diane is his central, substantive request. This central demand (to talk with Diane) is relationally framed and therefore is "negotiated" (from David's attunement framework) in terms of demonstration of trust and consideration between the PN and the subject. This relational demand, however, is not "bargainable" in the sense of making a trade, because it is not instrumentally grounded. In essence, the "demand" to talk to Diane is functioning for David as a relational "need" to talk to Diane.

The PN, however, is "negotiating" with David within the substantive demand frame and therefore communicates to the subject that a deal can be made. For example, the PN uses such phrases as, "here's the way it's gonna be done, David, now listen up" [L4]. The subject does not respond to the instrumental meaning of what the PN says (i.e., here is how the police can safely deliver the food you asked for). Rather, because the subject is operating within the attunement frame, he asserts that *he* will decide how the food will be delivered, saying, "10-4, I told you how it was gonna be done, you tell me how you want to do it, and then I'm gonna tell you how it's gonna be done, and I want to know where in the hell Diane is!" [L5]. In short, for David, the negotiation is about trust, power, and consideration (i.e., attunement); therefore, David's sensitivities are aligned toward responding to the PN's messages with these criteria in mind.

As a result of divergent frames, the situation escalates. The PN does not, however, shift from his substantive demand frame (working out a deal) to an attunement frame (responding to David's *need* to talk to Diane). Rather, he remains in his instrumental frame and asserts how the police will bring the food to the captain's window. David counters by again stating that *he* will tell the police how the food will be brought to the airplane.

During this initial interaction, the pilot periodically comes on the radio and informs the PN that the battery power is getting low and the radio will shortly be unworkable. The PN assures the pilot they are doing everything they can to restore power to the radio and the airplane.

Somewhat later, the PN again tries to bargain with the subject, saying, "I have everything all set to go, what I'd like you to do is to let, uh, the co-pilot walk out of the plane and I'll bring the shipment (food) right over to you, right now, OK?" [L24]. This focus on "trading" the copilot for food simply does not relate to the dominant attunement frame of the subject. As a result, the subject responds to this offer by saying, "Negatory! Negatory!...I'm not letting anyone go, besides, uh, we're gonna stay here, you're not talking me out of two people who are on the plane with me.... I'm getting a little pissed off, I'm a little hungry, 10-4" [L25].

A Need to Talk to Diane

David then goes on to emphasize that talking with Diane is very important to him. However, the *reason* he needs to talk to Diane is not addressed by the PN. For David, he does not view "talking with Diane" through a substantive demand lens; that is, he does not want to talk to Diane in order to "make a better deal" with the PN. Rather, talking to Diane is about attunement (trust, feeling understood, and "being heard"). The subject makes this point repeatedly, becoming more and more frustrated, saying at one point with heightened frustration, "11:00, 11:35 was when we landed, it is now 1:35, the clock is running. Find Diane, find someone *who's willing to talk* to me, okay! 10-4! 10-4! Out!" [L67]. Unfortunately, the subject does not feel the PN is "willing to talk to him" (i.e., engage in attunement negotiation through listening, cooperation, and trust-building actions).

As a result of these divergent frames, the situation continues to escalate. This divergence in S.A.F.E. frames between the PN (who wants to strike a bargain) and the subject (who needs to talk to Diane to establish trust and "tell his story" in this volatile situation) continues throughout the event. Further, the reason David feels he needs to talk to Diane is not explored by the PN. It is this lack of understanding concerning why David needs to talk to Diane that lies at the core of the escalation as this event develops.

A Continuing Escalation

David continues to insist that he talk to Diane, accusing the PN of deliberately delaying getting him food, and, more importantly, keeping him from talking with Diane (episode 2). After each plea from David to talk to Diane, the PN responds that he is doing everything he can to locate Diane and get food to the airplane. Unfortunately, this "we're working on it" strategy employed by the PN communicates distrust and lack of consideration to David—two critical aspects of the attunement lens through which David is interpreting the situation. The PN remains within the substantive demand frame rather than focusing on establishing trust and consideration through reciprocal cooperative acts. The subject frames his communication in terms of trust/distrust and consideration/no consideration concerns (attunement), resulting in an escalating situation as evidenced in the following list:

Delta Incident: Episode 2 (locating Diane): Lines 86–92

L86	PN	David now listen to me, I've done everything I can to help you right now and I'm trying to get you some food, all I want you to

		do is to hang tight, trust me, that's all you have to do, we're gonna get Diane here, right now she's in, she's en route to the airport, okay.
L87	David	10-4. She's en route [ ], but tell me where she's en route from, she works for the Governor and she knows I'm here, she's gonna get here and she's gonna get here as quick as possible, now, tell me where she's en route from, she works here in [City A], she lives in [City B], tell me where she's en route from, damn it, I'm tired of sittin' here for a fuckin' two in a half fuckin' hours, hour in a half, I'm tired of sitting, repeat tired of sitting, and asking you to help me, tell me where Diane is.
L88	PN	David, I've told you that she's on her way right now, we have located her, she was gone to lunch and we found her, we're trying to get her here as soon as we can, just stay calm, stay cool and uh, let's help each other out on this thing, okay.
L89	David	You could establish communication between she and I, don't bullshit me, you keep fuckin' bullshittin', you're pissing me off, the longer you bullshit me, you're pissing me fucking off! [pause]
L90	PN	PN to David
L91	David	David to PN, come in PN, I'm tired of fuckin' with ya.
L92	PN	Okay, the food is ready to be brought out to ya David and Diane is coming just, just hang tough that's all I ask you to do. It's a two-way street um, okay.

This interaction pattern again reflects the disjuncture between the more substantive demand frame of the PN (who views this bargain as a "two-way street") and the attunement frame of David.

The PN then tells David that he is bringing the food, at which point the subject corrects the PN, saying, "the food will not be brought out without Diane. 10-4! 10-4! Will release all hostages when talk to Diane, Diane is my ticket off this plane. I'll talk to Diane; anybody else, refuse 10-4!" [L95]. The situation continues to escalate as the PN responds, "I understand. When Diane comes out, are you coming off the plane and talk to her or what?" [L98], to which the subject says, "Negatory! Diane will come on the plane and talk to me" [L99]. The PN continues, "Suppose she doesn't wanna talk to you" [L100], to which David, clearly more agitated, threatens, "Suppose she doesn't! Suppose I have to do what I have to do. 10-4!" [L101].

An Abrupt Shift

In response to this clear escalation in threat, the PN abruptly shifts the topic and says, "David, let me ask you about that instrument that you got on board, you say it's a bomb?" [L102]. This is a jarring switch of topics, without even minimal transition (episode 3). Rather than focus on "why" the subject feels such a strong need to talk to Diane, the PN shifts the topic to gathering more information on the bomb.

Why might the PN shift the topic so dramatically? One likely answer is that this shift in topic is reflective of the disjuncture between the substantive demand lens used by the PN to negotiate and the attunement frame dominant with the subject. More specifically, the shift of topic represents a response to the escalating dialogue with the subject by the PN from a "bargaining" (substantive demand) frame. From this perspective, the PN is trying to move the subject off a topic that is getting too "hot." This explanation is consistent with the previously identified divergence of S.A.F.E. frames between the PN and the subject.

A second possible explanation also reflects this same divergence in S.A.F.E. frames, but arises from a different consideration. One requirement all crisis/hostage negotiation teams have is to gather "tactical intel" (e.g., intelligence concerning the lethal force available to the subject). This would be especially important when an individual has hijacked an airplane and claims he has a bomb. What kind of bomb, how is it detonated, how powerful is the bomb? Could it blow up the airplane and damage property or kill people within a 200-yard radius? A 1,000-yard radius? A two-mile radius? These and other questions are critical intel for making decisions as a critical incident develops.

There are times when Incident Command may instruct the PN to "ask the subject about his weapons." This "instruction" may come at a time, for instance, when the tactical unit is considering moving some of its officers to a more advantageous position—a movement that may make the officers vulnerable to the weapons (i.e., bomb) possessed by the subject. In the current situation, it is possible that this abrupt shift in topic may reflect such an instruction.

Nevertheless, from an interactional perspective, the PN's effort to shift to talking about the makeup of the bomb communicates a lack of consideration (low attunement) toward the needs and concerns of the subject. As a result, the situation escalates in tension. However, this escalatory outcome needs to be weighed against the possible value of the intelligence that is gathered. The underlying reason for the PN introducing the topic of the bomb at this particular juncture is not known. What is known, however, is that this abrupt shift in conversation further alienates the subject and reduces trust toward the PN. The following list presents this abrupt shift in topic and its interactional impact:

Delta Incident: Episode 3 (description of bomb): Lines 102–104

L102	PN	David let me ask you about that instrument that you got on board, you say it's a bomb?
L103	David	All communications will be disestablished at this point, this flight will, flight nineteen sixty two from uh, [City C] to [City A] all

communications are disestablished. I'll tell you exactly how my bomb works, a 120° is what it takes to set off the electronical control on it, 140° Fahrenheit is what it takes to set off the dynamite, now, if you want that on your hands then live with it, if you don't, get me some fuckin' help, I'm tired of negotiating with you [ ].

L104 PN We're really not negotiating, you haven't given me anything, I'm the one who's giving up everything David. I'm trying to get the girl here, she's on her way, so just hold on, okay?

This segment (episode 3) is revealing insofar as both David and the PN are now more overtly expressing their frustrations with one another, frustrations that arise from the discord between the substantive demand frame of the PN and the attunement frame of the subject. For David, he is fundamentally trying to say to the PN, "*I am very frustrated with you. I don't trust you, and you do not have any consideration for me. I need to talk to Diane; she is a way for me to leave this airplane safely, and you don't care about this at all!*" The PN responds with equal frustration when he says to David, "We're not really negotiating, you haven't given me anything, I'm the one who's giving up everything, David" [L104]. What the PN is trying to say is, "*Look, David, you told me what you want and I am trying to get it for you, but you have to give me something in return. If you don't do this, how will we ever be able to peacefully end this incident?*"

Diane Can Help Me

At this point, the subject turns over the radio to the pilot for a brief discussion with the PN. However, David comes right back on the radio and again reasserts that he needs to see Diane, that he trusts her. The PN then asks David whether Diane knows him. David responds, "uh, and get the help I need, it's a shame that someone who has the drug rehab problem has to go to such extremes. I apologize for, I apologize to the American public, but maybe, even if I die here..." [L110]. For the first time, David makes explicit that his desire to talk to Diane is about his drug abuse problem, and he is hinting that holding up the airplane is an extreme way of getting the help he wants.

As his frustrations increase, David also now overtly talks about suicide. The PN directly responds to this suicide threat, saying "nobody's gonna die anyplace, Okay. We're gonna be able to work this thing out to everybody's satisfaction, all I want you to do is trust me, okay?" [L113]. Following this statement, David and the PN argue with one another around the issue of trust, with the PN asserting that the subject should trust him and the subject indicating he does not trust the PN. From David's point of view, his main need—to talk with Diane—has not been met, and the PN has not demonstrated cooperation toward David's attunement needs. That is, for David, the PN has not communicated or demonstrated a sense of understanding for David's overwhelming drug addiction and his desperate need for help. Because of this lack of alignment in S.A.F.E. frames, as this incident goes on, David becomes increasingly angrier when the PN attempts to bargain with him.

The subject then asks to talk with his mother. The PN responds by asking David for information on how to contact the subject's mother. After giving the PN this information, the subject again returns to his frustration in dealing with the PN. He says, "I'm tired of dealing with you p-people, who are trying to talk me into releasing people. I'm gettin' a little pissed off, the more and more I get pissed off, the less and less either of our circumstances, we'll all die..." [L136]. Following this outburst, the subject becomes too angry and gives the radio to the pilot.

Great News

After a long pause, the PN demands to talk to David because he has some "great news." When he gets the subject back on the radio, the PN says he now has Diane with him. However, rather than present the good news of locating Diane in terms of building relational trust and helping the subject deal with his problems, the PN "frames" Diane in terms of a bargaining chip, which increases the subject's frustration:

Delta Incident: Episode 3 (talking with Diane): Lines 152–155

L152	PN	Okay, now you listen to me, she's here, she does not want to come on the plane, she's not going to go in the plane, I can't force her to go in the plane. What I can do, is I can place her in a position where you can see her, do you follow me?
L153	David	10-4!
L154	PN	Alright now you listen to me, I promised you that I would get her here. What are you gonna do for me once I let her, uh, expose herself to you like that, are you gonna let the uh, co-pilot off the plane or what?
L155	David	We're, what are you gonna do for me if my demands are met, I told you my original demands to the guy who superseded you, now if you want my demands met then fine you'll meet um, if you don't, then fuck it, you're given up three lives, God Damn You!

When the PN realizes the subject will not bargain, he changes tactics and offers to allow Diane to be visible (but safe) so David can see her. David counters with "quit lying to me, if you're talking to Diane, put her on the radio, with me, she's in no danger, if she gets on the radio with me, she's in no danger, repeat no danger if she gets in radio contact with me" [L163]. Again, the opportunity presents itself for the PN to inquire into why David feels he needs to talk to Diane. However, the PN does not directly respond to David's demand to talk with Diane.

Rather than put Diane on the radio, the PN shifts the topic of conversation and asks David, "were you in the military?" [L170]. The subject then describes his work in the military as classified (episode 4). The PN comments, "I understand, now tell me a little bit about this drug rehabilitation deal that you're in on" [L176]. The subject then says, "put Diane on the damn radio and I'll talk to her" [L177], to which the PN responds, "first you're gonna talk to me a little bit, because she's on her way, okay? Tell me about the program" [L178]. However, David does not feel he can trust the PN, saying "big fucking deal. Why do you keep lyin' to me, I'm tired of you lyin' to me. Come on be real" [L179]. The PN then asks David to stand by and he will have Diane ready to talk.

Telling Lies

For the next few minutes, David implores the PN to explain why he is lying to him. David says at one point, "why don't you be honest and objective with me and tell me you can't meet my demands, okay. Be honest and objective and we'll go from there" [L184]. Later on, he says, "I don't want anybody to get hurt either, but I'm tired of you all lyin' to me" [L188]. To each of these statements, the PN again explains that these things take time, that Diane is at another location and she is being brought to the PN. These explanations are consistently rejected by the subject as untruthful. As they continue talking, the same pattern emerges: The subject asks for an explanation for why the PN is "lying," and the PN essentially responds with variations of the "we are working on it" explanation (episode 5), reflecting a continuing disjuncture between the attunement needs of David (to trust the PN) and the substantive demand focus of the PN.

Finally, the PN confirms Diane is at the airport to which the subject replies, "She's at the airport. That means within fifteen minutes you should be able to have her out at least on the runway in front of me where I can look at her and talk to her eye to eye" [L197]. The negotiator expresses some support for David, saying, "I'm concerned about you and I'm concerned about everybody else on board, uh, as far as Diane is concerned, I'm trying very hard to get her here" [L198]. Unfortunately, the subject at this point does not believe the PN and responds, "I'm tired of being bullshitted" [L199].

As David continues to demand to talk to Diane, the PN summarizes his understanding, from a substantive demand frame, "I understand and uh, what you're saying to me is that you're agreeing to uh, to defuse the bomb and to throw the caps out if we'll let you, uh, talk to Diane and, and see her, is that correct, David" [L204]. David then confirms this by commenting that he will feel more at ease talking to Diane and if she boards the plane, then everyone will walk out alive. The PN agrees, but cautions David, "I can't promise you that she will board the plane, I can't make her go on board with you, you'll have to talk to her yourself, okay?" [206].

The PN and David have reached an understanding of sorts. For the PN, this is an agreement based on a bargain he made with David. For David, while he claims he does not want anyone to get hurt, he has a desperate, relational *need* to talk with Diane.

Briefly, David turns over the radio to the pilot who talks to the PN. The subject returns to the radio and again asks where Diane is. The PN responds that she is on her way. The PN also informs David that they are still trying to reach his mother. The PN then talks to the pilot until David again takes over the radio and says, "I mean it when I told you to, God damnit, I'm getting pissed off, GOD DAMNIT!" [L236]. David is by now quite upset and is yelling at the PN to bring the food and bring Diane. The PN continues to reassure the subject that both are on their way. The following dialogue reflects the same divergence in S.A.F.E. frames that continues to escalate the situation:

Delta Incident: Episode 5 (demand to see Diane): Lines 267–271

L267	PN	Okay, the foods coming out to you right now, my friend. [pause] David do you see the truck?
L268	David	Diane was here at the airport just a little bit ago you, you uh, obviously, you uh, you all have screwed her up, ah, she's not comin', tell me what the deal is, I want to know, Now!
L269	PN	Okay, the deal is this. I have her right here in my office right now, that is the deal, will you listen to me for instance, okay buddy.
L270	David	Negatory!
L271	PN	Alright David, what do you want? What do you want, you tell me what you want.

This interaction reflects more overt irritation of the PN with the "unreasonableness" of the subject and, similarly, the subject's frustration with the PN. Relationally, they are quite distant from one another.

A Conditional Conversation

Following this interchange, Diane is permitted to talk to David (episode 6). However, the PN places conditions on the radio contact, saying "all I'm going to do is, is to put her on the radio to identify herself for a second and then I'm gonna talk to you just to show you that I'm for real, do you understand that?" [L277]. From the bargaining (substantive demand frame) perspective of the PN, this is a "qualified" compromise by the PN to let David talk to Diane and is designed to give David a "taste," so that a better deal can be worked out. For David, talking to Diane is a way to establish trust in this situation and ask for help. The following dialogue presents the interchange between David and Diane.

Delta Incident: Episode 6 (Diane briefly talks to subject): Lines 288–294

L288	Diane	David, this is Diane
L289	David	Baby.
L290	Diane	David.
L291	David	I'm listening to ya Diane baby.
L292	Diane	What's goin' on?
L293	David	I'm just tryin' to get help Diane, that's all I want is help and I'm willin' to let the pilot and the co-pilot go, I'm gonna come off of here if they'll put me into a drug rehab where I can get help, I've tried my best, I tried my best to write a letter, I, I send, tried to send a congressional letter yesterday before I left the drug rehab. They refused to accept it, I've done, I've exhausted all means of getting help, Diane, I'm sorry that I have to get to this point that I need help. It's, the, this is what I have to do.
L294	PN	PN to David.

As this brief interaction clearly shows, David needs to talk to Diane, he trusts her, and he sees her as someone who can help him with his drug problem. As he begins to tell Diane "his story," however, the PN ends the conversation and again tries to "cut a deal" with David. The subject rejects any sort of deal for surrendering in large part because from his attunement perspective, talking to Diane is a relational need, and not something that is really bargainable.

Following this, the PN shifts the topic back to the type of bomb the subject has built (episode 7). As the subject talks more about his military service and the bomb he built, he becomes more and more agitated, to the point where the PN asks David to "talk a bit slower. It's hard for me to understand you, okay" [L310].

After talking about the bomb some more, the PN shifts the topic and tells David that the copilot's husband has heart trouble and asks David if he would release her (copilot). At this time, he refuses. By now the food has finally arrived. The PN is talking to the pilot when the pilot comments that if "Diane would come out here and talk to him [David], this whole thing would be over in five minutes" [L335]. The PN does not respond to this suggestion. For a very short time, the PN says he is going to talk to Diane and a second police negotiator (PN2) takes over talking to David. The PN then returns and resumes talking to David about how the bomb works. The PN again asks David to release the copilot. This time, he says he will. Shortly thereafter, the copilot is freed. David makes a point of saying that he is releasing the copilot because her husband has a heart condition. Again, David is making explicit with this statement that he has not bargained the release of the copilot because he now has received food. Rather, he is indicating that he freed the copilot because he has concern for the well-being of the copilot and her husband. The PN, however, does not recognize that David is reaffirming his rejection of bargaining as a means of incident resolution.

After the copilot leaves the airplane, the PN thanks David and says, "what I wanna do, try and get some help for you. I wanna do something for you, that's what I'm saying, because you've done something for me and uh, I really appreciate that, okay" [L370]. While this statement is certainly more supportive than previous expressions of consideration toward the subject, the statement is, nevertheless, a conditional expression of support within a substantive demand frame. What the PN is essentially saying is, "*thank you, David, for releasing the copilot; I gave you food and you gave me a hostage.*" This results in continued disconnection between David's framing of the situation and the instrumental focus of the PN.

Introduction of the Surrender Ritual

The PN now moves to complete the bargain (episode 8), saying, "this is what I'm gonna do for you. I know that you wanted to uh, see Diane and I know that you want to get out of there and everything is gonna be alright, so here's what I wanna do, here's the way I wanna conclude this thing" [L372]. The PN then says David can see a doctor and get psychiatric help and in return asks David to leave the bag of dynamite in the airplane and walk out.

The PN then asks the pilot if he could ask David "why he wants to see Diane please, he's talked to her in the cockpit, I mean, ah, she's here, she's waiting on him to walk off the plane, would you ask him that please, that's very important to us" [L395]. David then responds, angrily, "I'm waiting to recognize someone that I fuckin' know. If you can't understand that, you can't understand my fuckin' demands, I'm tired of fuckin' deal with you, okay, God damnit!" [L398]. The pilot then says to the PN, "I think he [David] just wants to be assured that uh, she is uh, definitely here and he can recognize her and uh, and uh, the way he feels with her, uh, being out there, she'll may look after him and order to uh, get him the uh, help that he needs" [L400]. Rather than support this "paraphrase" of David's attunement needs, the PN says he needs to consult with his superiors. This lack of acknowledgment from the PN sharply communicates to David that the PN fundamentally does not "understand" what David wants or needs.

Hearing this, the subject now becomes emotionally distressed, becoming so angry that his ability to productively cope with the situation is compromised. He responds, "Why did you ask me to do somethin' uh, ask me to do somethin' that you know you can't do, I'm tired of you fuckin' bargain me, I've bargained to the point of no return. There's no fuckin' bargain, all bargain has been stopped, you've got my God damn demands; all communications are stopped!" [L405]. The situation continues to dangerously escalate:

Delta Incident: Episode 8 (release of copilot): Lines 410–415

L410 PN Okay, would you mind replaying this to uh, David please, uh, ask him uh, as soon as, uh, as we uh, show him to Diane, I would like very much to have him let you walk down the ramp and walk off the plane and there after uh, I'd like him to walk down. Over.

L411 David That's negatory, I'll walk down with the pilot, we'll go arm and arm.

L412 PN David I have promised you. I have promised you that nothing will happen to you, I've promised you that. I'm very concerned about you, and I'm very concerned about the Captain, and I want you to listen to me if you will. All I want you to do is to walk off the plane, walk off the plane with the Captain, that's fine. Okay, will you do that for me right now?

L413 David Do What!

L414 PN I will show you Diane, all I want you to do is to walk off the plane and then we can talk eyeball to eyeball, okay?

L415 David As I said if my demands are not met, I'm gonna blow this son-of-a-bitch up, I'm gonna head it towards you. Take your fuckin' choice [PN]!

As this incident has developed, the divergent frames of the PN and the subject have led to substantial misperceptions. The PN believes the situation has de-escalated, some bargaining has worked, and the subject is now ready to come out. However, for David, until he is able to establish relational closeness (attunement) with Diane and at least begin to tell his story and enlist her support in getting him help for substance abuse, he is unwilling to surrender. Given David's core need to relationally connect with Diane, having the PN simply "show Diane" to David would likely not be a sufficient attunement move (cooperative act), because the subject needs to establish relational trust with Diane before he will peacefully come out of the airplane. Thus, for David, the situation has drastically escalated, and he is not at all ready to surrender.

Further, David is becoming so upset as to begin to experience emotional distress, as reflected in his final comment, "take your fuckin' choice!" [L415]. The pilot, perhaps sensing that the situation may be close to getting out of control, comments on the radio to the PN, "uh, listen, uh, I'm uh, right here with him, uh, I can guarantee you that, uh, if you just put her [Diane] out in front of the truck and, uh, we both walk off and leave the bag on, nothing's gonna happen" [L418]. The PN responds that there are a number of things to take into consideration and they are working on it. A little later, David yells, "I'll take my God damn Uzi and I'll fuck you up!" [L424]. These comments reflect a situation where David has reached a state of emotional distress: a level of anger and frustration that needs de-escalation through listening, allowing him to tell his story, and appeals to the action tendency of his core emotional distressed state of anger.

Seeing Diane: A Final Goodbye?

In terms of the police simply following the advice of the pilot and allowing David to see Diane before he surrenders, there are, in fact, important considerations as alluded to by the PN that may explain why the PN balks at letting David actually see Diane *before he surrenders*. One consideration is whether David intends to commit suicide. It may be that David only wants to say "one final goodbye" to Diane and/or his mother and then will complete the suicide act by detonating the bomb. For individuals who are suicidal, it is not uncommon for them to want to have a close relative or friend "witness" their end. A second consideration is that David may wish to kill Diane, in which case, if he can see her, he can shoot her (while David to this point is only threatening to detonate a bomb, it is not known with certainty whether he also possesses a firearm). The reluctance to have Diane come out where David can see her is likely grounded in either of these possibilities.

Nevertheless, the situation is now rapidly escalating. While David did indicate he would blow up the airplane and he is not afraid of committing suicide, in fact, his threats to detonate the bomb have been said to reinforce his strong need to talk with Diane more than a desire to kill himself or kill others. Further, after making such threats, David has consistently stated his desire to not harm anyone. In addition, his initial radio conversation with Diane indicated they did, in fact, have a close and trusting relationship: one in which David would not likely try to kill her if he had a "good shot." Therefore, while it is unlikely that letting David "see" Diane prior to surrender would result in negative outcomes, it would be prudent for the police to attempt to have David surrender and then let him see or talk to Diane once he is safe and in custody.

This explanation concerns making Diane "visible" to David only; it does not address the strategy for allowing Diane to talk by radio once more with David. In fact, from a tactical point of view, it is far safer for everyone to have David talk to Diane by radio than to move her closer to the airplane in order for David to see her clearly.

With this in mind, the PN attempts to calm David by saying, "let me put Diane back on to talk to you. Just hold on for a second, I'll get her back over here, okay" [L421]. David responds, "How long does it take you, four fuckin' hours to do somethin' like this, that's the reason our government's in control with a bunch of fuck heads like you, runnin' the son-of-a-bitch" [L426].

A Deadline to Detonate

The subject is now filled with so much anger and frustration that the situation is perilous:

Delta Incident: Episode 8 (release of copilot): Lines 449–454

L449	David	I fuckin' met my moral obligation to you and to the fuckin' democratic society we live in, and God damnit I've asked you for two fuckin' simple demands and you haven't met um yet [ ] wait to be kind to you, keep fuckin'.
L450	PN	We've done this, you've asked for four demands, and I've met two of them, I'm working on the other two right now, all you have to do is to continue to trust me and I'll have those worked out.
L451	PN	This is PN to David.
L452	David	Go PN, Go!
L452	PN	Okay, listen David just, just settle down for a minute, I want you to know that I have to go over and talk to my boss for just a second, just a few minutes and, and I'll be right back to you, and then we can have this thing resolved, please, please wait on me okay?
L454	David	Let me tell you somethin' [PN], I've been waitin, I've been sittin' here. I hijacked this plane at approximately uh, hijacked it 9, 11.2 noticeable miles before we got here. I place the time at approximately 11:30, now, it is now 3:15, I'm tired of fuckin' doin', I'm givin' you to fuckin' 4:00, your fuckin' times runnin' out buddy, you got 43 fuckin' minutes as the clock struck twelve jus then, 43 fuckin' minutes to meet, meet my demands, have my mother standin' out there by that fuckin' thing and have Diane standin' out there, I'll get off this fuckin' plane, and I'll walk off here with this Captain, otherwise I'll blow the son-of-a-bitch up. You got it? That's your, that's my fuckin', you go toward either phones now buddy.

The substantive demand, bargaining frame being asserted by the PN, coupled with the delay in allowing Diane to talk with David, has created a very combustible situation, with the anger of the subject driving his interaction with the PN. In addition, he has now set a deadline—43 minutes or he will blow up the airplane.

Various cars and trucks have been slowly moving closer to the airplane. The subject is aware of this and yells to the PN, "I'm tired of meeting your demands, I went as far as I can go, you've got mine, I want to see my mama and I want to see Diane out there by the damn fuel truck, when I see them, I'll walk over, off with this son-of-a-bitch, with the pilot, keep pushin' your God damn safety men, keep pushin' them a little closer, keep tryin' to get em within position and your gonna fuck up, your gonna blow the whole God damn thing up, promise me" [L460].

The PN continues to ask the subject to calm down, and he attempts to reassure David that he is working on getting Diane to talk to him. During this time, the PN tells David that he has to talk to his boss again, presumably to gain permission to have Diane talk to David once more.

The second police negotiator (PN2) briefly takes his place and talks primarily to the pilot. The subject interrupts and says, "I've done all my talkin', my fuckin' pilot is not talkin', you meet my demands or else. You've got 40, 39 minutes left." A little later, David asks for cigarettes and reminds PN2 that they now have 23 minutes. PN2 and the subject continue talking, with PN2 indicating that they are working on getting Diane to talk to David and the subject vehemently declaring his demands and asserting the deadline is getting closer.

The PN returns to briefly talk with David followed again for a short time by PN2. Whether talking with the PN or PN2, however, the same substantive frame dominates the two police negotiators, with both playing for time and delaying putting Diane on the radio to talk with the subject.

David's anger subsides and is replaced by a resigned acceptance that unless he gets his demands met by 4:00 P.M., he is going to detonate the bomb. For example, he says, "I'm not really worried about getting me and uh, the pilot off the plane, that's beyond my control, that's up to you all, you all decided our fate, you all want him to walk off the plane first, you all wanna put a bullet in my head, I know exactly what you all want to do" [L510].

After this statement, the PN returns to talk with the subject. However, the discussion continues in the same vein, with the subject counting off the minutes. At one point, David says, "I'm cutting off all communications, you've got 16 minutes and 33 seconds. It's up to you" [L522]. PN2 then comes on the radio again and is able to reestablish communication with the subject. PN2 continues to reassure David that they are doing everything they can. Predictably, David rejects this explanation, no longer offers explanations, and simply asserts his demand to talk to Diane, all the while continuing to count down the time.

Diane Arrives

The PN returns to negotiate with the subject. He tells David that Diane is available to talk to him. The following dialogue presents the full conversation between David and Diane:

Delta Incident: Episode 9 (David talks with Diane & surrenders): Lines 537–561

L537	David	Ha Diane.
L538	Diane	How ya doin' buddy?
L539	David	[laugh] I'm doin pretty good, 10 minutes and countin down.
L540	Diane	Oh, don't talk to me like that.
L541	David	What else am I suppose to say Diane?
L542	Diane	David, please I wanna help you. Everythings gonna be okay, I promise you that.
L543	David	You promise me Diane and I'll get off this plane, I tried my best, I, I uh, went in as far as to write a congressional letter to my United

		States Senator yesterday while I was in the drug rehab, but they refused to accept it.
L544	Diane	David you know I have contacts in politics, I will get you any help you want, anybody you wanna talk to, no one, everything's gonna be okay, I wanna help you, I wanna see you.
L545	David	Help, don't you think so.
L546	Diane	Don't you trust me? Don't you trust me?
L547	David	Yes I trust you Diane; if I didn't trust you, I wouldn't have called you to begin with.
L548	Diane	Come on David, you trust me, you know that I'm not gonna tell you a lie, You know I'm right here with you, I'll be with you the entire time.
L549	David	Alright Diane, I'm willin' to get off this plane, and I'll get off and I'll leave my bag on it. There's a white truck sittin, sittin over there and I'll walk straight toward it, the Captain and I will walk toward it together.
L550	Diane	Come off, off David, come on off.
L551	David	An, I'm okay, but I just, I just uh, I need help and I've, I've begged for it an I'm sorry that I have to go to such extreme's to get it, but that's just the way it is.
L552	Diane	Come on, off David, I'll help you, I'll go with you every step of the way, every step of the way, anything you want me to do, trust me. Now, please now, please you can come right direct to me.
L553	David	Come out to the truck
L554	Diane	I'm, I can't David. You've got to let that thing out, come off the plane and I'll be right there for you within a few seconds.
L555	David	You promise.
L556	Diane	You got my word on it. You trust me, now, please do it now and you got me every step of the way, all night long, however long it takes.
L557	David	Go wrong.
L558	Diane	Nothin' goes wrong, you will be safe with me right in my hands.
L559	David	[ ], they just shoot me.
L560	Diane	Trust me David. trust me! I'm here to help you and then you call me to help ya, I'm here to help you. [pause] Please David now, help me, come on out here and help me, get off the plane now, come on baby please, do it for me. [pause] David please. [pause]
L561	PN	Okay, he's off the airplane now.

Diane begins talking with David by focusing on David's needs, saying, "how ya doin', buddy?" David replies, "you promise me Diane and I'll get off this plane." David then begins to explain his situation and Diane listens, offering help with contacts in politics. She reinforces to David that he can trust her and she will not lie to him. More importantly, she speaks directly to his fears and concerns when she says, "I'm right here with you, I'll be with you the entire time." He explains that he needs help and he apologizes to Diane for hijacking a plane in order to get help. She continues to assert her concern for David and that he can trust her. In short, she deepens attunement with the subject to the degree that he peacefully comes off the airplane.

She concludes by saying to David, "Trust me David, trust me! I'm here to help you and then you call me to help ya, I'm here to help you. . . . get off the plane now, come on baby, please, do it for me. David, please" [L560]. Diane and David are squarely within the attunement frame, he poignantly wanting the relational trust that only Diane can provide, and she offering unconditional support to help him. David's core attunement need is now, finally, being directly addressed. After a brief pause, David exits the airplane to live another day.

OVERALL S.A.F.E. FRAME ANALYSIS

This event is a very dangerous and volatile situation, with David, a young, emotionally distraught man, threatening to detonate a bomb on a hijacked airplane that landed at an airport in the United States. Upon landing, David releases all the passengers, but keeps the pilot and the copilot as hostages. Communicating through the cockpit radio to the police negotiators, David demands to have food brought to the aircraft and he also asks to talk to Diane, his friend. For over one hour, communication is sporadic due to a low battery for the airplane cockpit radio. Once the police establish reliable ground electricity to the airplane, negotiations are more consistently undertaken. By then, however, David's frustration has grown as the police had yet to deliver food to the plane nor have they indicated they will allow David to talk to Diane.

It is understandable why the tactical team has not delivered food to the airplane. Detonating a bomb would instantly kill any of the police officers who were near the aircraft. Similarly, talking to Diane, at this early stage in the event, is ill-advised. David could be wanting to commit suicide. In this case, it is not uncommon for suicidal individuals to request to see or talk with a loved one as a way of saying a "final goodbye." Once they talk to that person, they are more likely to kill themselves. Alternatively, David could previously have had a fight with Diane. In this case, David may wish to "see" Diane, perhaps so he can shoot her, and then, perhaps take his own life and others by detonating the bomb. Therefore, it is understandable that David's demands were not met immediately.

Why did David hijack an airplane? What does this situation "mean" to David? What is the problem David believes he is solving through this violent act? As the event unfolds, David becomes increasingly upset at the "delay" in letting him see or talk with Diane. David is interpreting and responding to communication from the PN and actions from the tactical unit in terms of attunement. For David, his actions have placed him in a desperate and dangerous situation. This desperation is grounded in his inability to get help for a substance abuse problem that he feels is taking over his life. He believes the police have little, if any, consideration for his welfare, stating at one point that he thought the police would like to put a bullet in his head. David is viewing and responding to this situation in terms of mistrust toward the PN and a lack of consideration for what David sees as important (i.e., talking to Diane).

Talking to Diane represents a way for David to get the help he needs by enlisting the support from someone he trusts and someone who genuinely empathizes with his substance abuse problem. As David repeatedly says throughout this escalating incident, "it's a shame that someone who has the drug rehab problem has to go to such extremes" [L110]. For David, he has a "relational" need to talk with someone he trusts (Diane) so he can get the help he needs for his substantive abuse difficulties.

In contrast, the PN communicates throughout this incident in a substantive demand frame. He is looking to "make a deal" so that David will peacefully surrender. For the PN, negotiation is viewed in terms of bargaining. He operates with the maxim, "don't give up something without getting something in return." As this incident develops, the PN is continually asking David to state what he wants. The PN grounds his interaction with David in terms of trading David's demands for food and talking with Diane for the release of the hostages and ultimately, a peaceful surrender. What is important to the PN throughout this crisis is "where we are at on meeting demands." The PN views David's demand to talk to Diane as a bargaining chip, the most important bargaining chip the PN controls. Therefore, the police negotiator's goal is to allow David to talk to Diane only after he surrenders. In this way, the PN is able to instrumentally use (manipulate) David's request to talk to Diane to gain concessions, namely, the release of the pilot and the copilot and the surrender of the subject.

Because David and the PN are operating within very different S.A.F.E. frames, they become increasingly frustrated with one another. For David, his frustration is framed in terms of "not being listened to." For the PN, his frustration is framed in terms of David's unwillingness to agree to peacefully surrender in return for talking to Diane.

As the incident escalates, David approaches an emotional distressed state, with anger for a period of time dominating his interaction with the PN. During this time, David attaches a deadline to his demand to talk with Diane. He also more overtly threatens to blow up the airplane. Somewhat later, his anger is replaced by a sense of resignation that the PN may not let him talk to Diane, in which case, he will end his and the hostage's lives. This explosive and escalating disjuncture continues, with the PN becoming more frustrated because he cannot get David to make a deal and the subject becoming more agitated because he cannot talk to his friend, Diane (to establish sufficient trust to allow him to surrender).

Core Interactional Pattern

The interactional pattern that emerged and solidified between David and the PN that escalated the situation can be summarized as follows:

1. David makes a relational request (e.g., to talk with Diane in order to trust someone in this volatile situation and gain her help with his drug addiction problem, an attunement frame).
2. The PN stalls for time and looks for ways to bargain what David wants (e.g., talk to Diane) with obtaining the release of the hostages and the surrender of David (substantive demand frame).
3. David interprets this bargaining-oriented communication (substantive demand frame) as relationally insulting (low attunement) and lacking in consideration of what is important to David.
4. David becomes increasingly agitated.
5. As David's agitation increases, the PN changes the topic of conversation rather than enter the attunement frame of David.
6. David's perception of the PN as untrustworthy in enhanced and his agitation increases.

With ten minutes to go on David's deadline, the PN allows Diane to talk to David. The interactional pattern between Diane and the subject that de-escalates the situation can be described as follows:

1. Diane expresses genuine interest in David and how he is doing (an attunement message).
2. David responds by sharing his need for help to deal with his substance abuse problem (a relational or shared concern Diane and David have with one another).
3. Diane reinforces her concern for David's well-being. She then asks David to confirm whether he trusts her.
4. David unequivocally states that he trusts Diane.
5. Diane frames her request that David surrender in terms of assuring David that she will be there for him when he comes out of the aircraft. Diane does not frame her request that David surrenders in any bargaining fashion. Rather, she empathizes with David and restates her relational commitment toward David.
6. David then surrenders.

This interaction between David and Diane clearly illustrates the relational moves that take place between both people that result in David's surrender. Diane enters the attunement frame with David, focusing on the relational bond between her and David. She asserts that David can trust her and she offers to help David with his drug problem. With someone now in the same attunement frame, David tells a little bit of his story and explains that he hijacked an airplane because he did not know of any other way to get the help he needs. As he tells this story, Diane offers unconditional support for David. She does not argue with him nor does she question the sanity of his actions. Rather, she relationally assures David that he has her "every step of the way, all night long, however long it takes" [L556]. With this relationally based assurance, David agrees to put down the bomb and peacefully walk off the airplane.

CHAPTER 11

Extending the S.A.F.E. Model: Where Do We Go from Here?

INTRODUCTION

The use of more formal negotiation (diplomatic) approaches for resolving violent, interstate confrontations has a long history in our global community. However, it is astounding to realize that the systematic application of negotiation to resolve critical incidents was only first initiated in 1972 by the New York Police Department (Boltz & Hershey, 1979; Hammer & Weaver, 1998). It is not surprising, therefore, that hostage and crisis negotiators—practitioners and researchers alike—have been at the forefront of defining this valuable approach to violence mitigation and crisis resolution. Critical incident management (CIM), with its new, equal partner of negotiation, has emerged in the twenty-first century as essential for effectively responding to the unexpected and unwelcome violence that often characterizes a crisis situation.

Within law enforcement, there has been a significant maturation of both theoretical sophistication and applied practices in how hostage/crisis events are defined and their preferred methods of resolution. Hostage/crisis negotiation is now an established facet of law enforcement's overall approach for responding to potentially violent situations.

Traditional typology, instrumental, and expressive approaches to crisis negotiation reflect an evolving philosophy of how negotiators should ply their trade. Yet, as discussed earlier in this book, while these approaches provide insight into some important facets of the conflict dynamic in crisis situations, they also suffer from limitations in theoretical comprehensiveness as well as application. The proposed S.A.F.E. model extends these existing approaches by focusing on how "communicative frames" function in escalating and de-escalating violent confrontations among police negotiators, third-party intermediaries (TPIs), subjects, and hostages/victims.

Further, the S.A.F.E. model identifies specific S.A.F.E. frame "tracking" protocols for determining escalation and de-escalation and further delineates various negotiation strategies within each S.A.F.E. frame for de-escalating the crisis situation. In this final chapter, implications for further development and implementation of the S.A.F.E. model are examined.

PREPARING FOR A MAJOR CRITICAL INCIDENT: STATUS OF THE S.A.F.E. MODEL

It can be argued that traditional, diplomatic approaches for resolving interstate conflict are inadequate in effectively responding to violent, critical incidents. In part, this is due to the fact that the nature of global conflicts has changed in three astonishing ways. First, there has been a shift from interstate violence (i.e., nation-to-nation warfare) to nonstate actors (i.e., global terrorist networks). Traditional forms of interstate coercion and influence, such as sanctions, are simply less effective against nonstate actors, whose infrastructure is continually changing and geographic location is often unknown. Second, there has been a shift from state-controlled weapons of mass destruction (WMD) to nonstate actors with global reach gaining access to WMD. Thus, the specter of cataclysmic devastation is now in the hands of individuals and groups who have little to no constraints placed on them from the international community. Third, violent conflict has shifted from traditional military targets and control of land (geography) to civilian targets for the purpose of creating fear and disruption. What was once unthinkable is now an everyday reality, whether it involves the systematic murder of volunteer Red Cross/Crescent workers, the beheadings of civilians, or the suicide bomber who casually enters a café and kills dozens of patrons.

Each of these seismic shifts in the way violence is conducted indicates that critical incidents are becoming key escalation events that the world system must address in new and innovative ways. Traditional, slow-moving, formal, diplomatic processes are simply not up to the challenge of rapidly managing and responding to these types of large-scale, crisis events.

The United States has taken note of these dramatic shifts; on February 28, 2003, President George W. Bush released Homeland Security Presidential Directive/HSPD-5, *Management of Domestic Incidents*. This directive instructed the Secretary of Homeland Security to develop a National Incident Management System (NIMS) to use in domestic incident management and emergency prevention, preparedness, response, recovery, and mitigation efforts and to support actions taken to help state and local government.

In 2004, the Department of Homeland Security began implementing the NIMS system throughout the United States. This massive effort is divided into four phases. Phase 1 involves staff training in basic incident command concepts and in understanding the national incident management system.

The S.A.F.E. model is becoming an important tool for many police hostage/crisis negotiators. Today, I conduct, through my organization (Hammer Consulting S.A.F.E. Hostage Operations, LLC), advanced hostage/crisis negotiation training for law enforcement in the S.A.F.E. model. To date, over 30 police agencies have already completed this training and at least another 30 or more are scheduled for training in 2007.

Under the oversight of Mr. William Hogewood, the ATF was the first federal law enforcement agency to embrace the S.A.F.E. model for its negotiators. Today, all of the ATF hostage/crisis negotiators are equipped to use S.A.F.E. strategy in critical incidents. It was not too long after I completed training these agents that a demanding incident arose in which the ATF used the S.A.F.E. model to help resolve a difficult incident.

Standoff in Bowling Green, Kentucky

On October 29, 2004, ATF agents attempted to serve a warrant to 41-year-old Russell Sublett outside Bowling Green, Kentucky, when Sublett fled in his car. State police and ATF agents followed. Sublett then drove through "stop sticks" set up in the road to disable his car, later stopping his vehicle in the middle of the road. The authorities arrived and Sublett, using a semiautomatic pistol, exchanged gunfire with the police. He then carjacked another vehicle and crashed into the home of his former employer, where he barricaded himself inside. Fortunately, no one was home at the time. ATF agents, working alongside other law enforcement officers, then began negotiation.

Sublett was having trouble coping with his current situation, having been recently fired from his job, experiencing difficulties with his 12-year-old son, and having previously been indicted for a number of crimes, including robbery, assault, and resisting arrest. During the three-day standoff, he fired 200 rounds at police. Fortunately, no officers were injured or killed. During the gunfire exchanges, Sublett was wounded.

Negotiator's discovered through talking with Sublett that he was emotionally distraught and wanted very much for the police to kill him (suicide by cop). During the ordeal, his wife commented that "he's not coming out of that house alive. He's not going out peacefully" (Fellwock, 2004). The ATF incident commander stated, "We're not doing anything to force an outcome" (Fellwock, 2004). As a result, the negotiation team was able to talk to the subject and "hear his story." The subject, after three days, changed his mind from suicide by cop to surrender. The predominant S.A.F.E. frame for the subject was face and, secondarily, emotional distress. The negotiator described the situation as follows:

> When we first got him talking...he began with FACE and emotion. The negotiators, who I directed to work S.A.F.E. throughout, went with him in that

> frame. After that we seemed to move to building "attunement," trust relations....I think working "face" and some "emotional" frames and then easing through the weak demands, building trust and relationship was the key. The roadmap was traveling with him in each frame.... (Negotiator, 2004)

USING S.A.F.E. IN OUR FAMILIES, ORGANIZATIONS, AND COMMUNITIES

This book focuses on how the S.A.F.E. model can be used to develop negotiation strategy, de-escalate, and peacefully resolve violent confrontations in situations that call for a response from law enforcement. Hopefully, very few of us will face the life-and-death conflicts that are described in this book. We do face, often on a daily basis, situations that demand deeper, conflict resolution skills that many of us lack. The S.A.F.E. model and the S.A.F.E. frame negotiation strategies described in this book can be very helpful in dealing with some of the difficult events that often arise in our lives.

More commonly, we may have disagreements with others that can lead to misunderstandings and poor communication. We may have problems in working with others that can result in lower performance. We may face situations where our friends or family members are experiencing substantial emotional distress and we are not sure how to help. We may have a close friend disclose that he or she was a victim of domestic abuse, sexual assault, or even attempted murder, and we are unable to be supportive at this critical moment. We may have children who have substance abuse problems and find it is easier to refer them to a professional than to engage in a difficult, yet authentic, conversation about their use of drugs or alcohol.

In these and many other "difficult" situations, understanding what "frame" a person is in can allow us to connect to that person. The S.A.F.E. model can help us move into his or her frame or perspective and use strategies within that frame that allow us to "move with" rather than "move against" the other person. This permits a sense of progress to emerge from our interaction—and this progress enables more effective resolution of the difficult issues being discussed.

In today's harried and stressful world, the ability to engage in difficult conversations is a skill everyone must develop. The S.A.F.E. approach offers one framework for having a more satisfying, genuine, and productive conversation.

CONCLUSION

It is certainly not an understatement to claim that crisis/hostage negotiation is dramatically distinct from other more normative forms of conflict management and negotiation. Heightened levels of emotional excitation, intense public scrutiny, the possibility of physical harm, even death, mutual distrust, the likelihood of one party suffering from extreme mental and emotional stress, and the seeming intractability of the situation all converge to create a situation that demands the most knowledgeable and highly trained professional. Experience has clearly shown that tactical resolutions to these incidents often fail to produce the desired results, frequently resulting in the loss of life to hostages, police, and suspects. Negotiation is, therefore, the desired alternative.

Although the S.A.F.E. model is originally conceived for analyzing the conflict discourse of domestic U.S. crisis negotiations, it holds significant promise for understanding the dynamics of intercultural incidents (Hammer, 1997; Hammer & Weaver, 1994; Weaver, 1997). An informed understanding of how different cultural groups communicate in conflict contexts around the issues of face, instrumentality, relational concerns, and emotion will better equip negotiators to manage crisis incidents involving cultural backgrounds different from their own. Useful in this regard is the cross-culturally valid, innovative Intercultural Conflict Style (ICS) model and assessment inventory. This model describes an individual's core approach for solving problems and resolving conflicts in terms of direct or indirect strategies for addressing disagreements, and emotional expressive or restrained approaches for dealing with emotional upset that often arises in problem-solving or conflict situations. The ICS inventory provides individuals with a profile of their core approach for addressing conflict when they, themselves, are under stress (Hammer, 2002b, 2002c, 2003).

Saving lives is the name of the game. The S.A.F.E. model represents a valuable framework for understanding the conflict dynamics of crisis negotiations. The 1972 Munich Olympic games; Attica; Ruby Ridge, Idaho; and Waco, Texas: we need not add any more names to this list. It is my hope that the S.A.F.E. model will aid law enforcement in its efforts to realize nonviolent resolutions to all future crisis incidents. I also hope it can provide a useful framework for effectively resolving other situations where difficult conversations need to be undertaken.

APPENDIX A

The S.A.F.E. Model: Underlying Assumptions and Theoretical Foundations

ASSUMPTION #1: A FOCUS ON GOALS

There are ten key assumptions associated with the formulation of the S.A.F.E. model. The first theoretic assumption is that the S.A.F.E. model, as a communication-based approach, adapts a perspective where messages are "taken seriously as the practical tools they are for ordinary actors" (Tracy, 1989, p. 411). This perspective is based on the idea that communicators pursue a variety of *interaction goals* and these goals are reflected in the conversational messages employed by the participants (Tracy, 1989). The S.A.F.E. model, therefore, is grounded in the view that during times of conflict and crisis, individuals are oriented toward one another and the difficult situation they face largely in terms of achieving particular interactional goals with one another.

Three interaction goals that have been proposed as central to human communication and particularly relevant to conflict interaction and crisis negotiation are instrumental concerns, identity (face) concerns, and relational concerns (Clark & Delia, 1979; Roloff & Jordan, 1992; S. Wilson & Putnam, 1990). Identity goals denote a concern for one's own and/or the person's projected image or face (Goffman, 1967). Relational goals represent individual concerns for the quality of the relationship with the other (Donohue & Roberto, 1993; Roloff & Jordan, 1992). Instrumental goals concern the objective or tangible wants and demands of the individual.

Finally, given the earlier conceptualization presented on the core characteristics of a "conflict dynamic" (see Chapter 1), emotion (emotional distress) is identified as the fourth interaction goal of participants (Adler, Rosen, & Silverstein, 1998; Barry & Oliver, 1994; Jones, 2000, 2001).

ASSUMPTION #2: A SOCIAL CONSTRUCTIVIST PARADIGM

Second, the S.A.F.E. model is situated within the general social constructivist paradigm (e.g., Kelly, 1963; Maturana & Varela, 1987; Von Foerster, 1984). The underlying perspective of this paradigm is that people actively construe their social reality and this construal process is interactively situated. This suggests that a focus on how police negotiators and subjects in a crisis event "make meaningful" their interaction (interpretation and behavior in situ) with one another is a central concern of the S.A.F.E. framework.

Within this more general social constructivist paradigm, the S.A.F.E. model is consistent with the pragmatics theory of human communication. A pragmatics focus emphasizes the influence of communication on human behavior (Watzlawick, Bavelas, & Jackson, 1967). However, communication is not viewed from this platform as simply the exchange of information between parties. Rather, communication from this perspective is defined broadly to include

> not only the words, their configurations, and meanings, which are the data of syntactics and semantics, but their nonverbal concomitants and body language as well. Even more, we would add to personal behavioral actions the communicational clues inherent in the *context* in which communication occurs. (Watzlawick et al., 1967, p. 22)

ASSUMPTION #3: GROUNDING IN SOCIAL INTERACTION

Third, the S.A.F.E. model has its origins in interactional communication and the work of such scholars as G. Bateson (1954/1972), K.N.L. Cissna and E. Sieburg (1981), H.E. Ruesch and G. Bateson (1951), and P. Watzlawick et al. (1967). Briefly, the interactional view suggests that human communication is a transactional process between two or more individuals engaged in interaction with one another in which messages and meaning are jointly created and shared. The emphasis is on the reciprocal dynamic relationship of the interactants rather than on the condition or psychological state of either party. In this sense, meaning emerges from the experience emanating from mutual interaction (Walter & Peller, 1992; Watzlawick et al., 1967). This view highlights the emergent meaning-making process of social interaction. Further, this underscores the view that understanding human behavior can be profitably examined in terms of the interactants' message behavior, rather than in terms of a set of predetermined states or psychological characteristics of an individual. In short, the process of making meaningful a particular experience involves mutual participation in the conversation.

In examining crisis negotiation dynamics, this suggests an interactive assessment of the communicative behavior of both the perpetrator and the negotiator, rather than solely on the incident typologies, psychological disposition, or substantive demands of the suspect (Hammer, 2001; Hammer & Rogan, 1997; Hammer & Weaver, 1994; Rogan & Hammer, 2002). The key question from this perspective is how messages (discourse) serve to create shared meaning in such a way as to escalate or de-escalate the contentious interaction dynamics between the police negotiator and the subject.

ASSUMPTION #4: MESSAGES CONTAIN BOTH REPORT AND COMMAND LEVEL MEANING FOR FRAMING INTERACTION

Fourth, the S.A.F.E. model, consistent with this interactional view of communication, distinguishes two fundamental levels of meaning in communication (Bateson, 1954/1972; Cissna & Sieburg, 1981; Ruesch & Bateson, 1951; Watzlawick et al., 1967). On one level are what Bateson (1954/1972) views as the implicit and explicit cues about language and its meaning, what he terms as "metalinguistic" communication, given that it serves as commentary about actual language forms. Bateson defines the second level meaning in terms of verbal and nonverbal messages that say something about the quality of the relationship between communicators, which he labels as "metacommunication." The metacommunicative level functions as a map of human interaction, which also guides human behavior.

Bateson (1954/1972) and Watzlawick (1967) identify a similar set of core dimensions of meaning, with human communication seen as consisting of "report" (or content) and "command" (or relational, emotional) levels of information. The report dimension refers to the specific information or data that are being exchanged (the instrumental substance of the message), while the command dimension provides meaning about how the report dimension should be understood in terms of the relationship between the parties. More specifically, the command dimension speaks to how the interactants see themselves in relation to the other person, how they feel toward one another, and how they view the other person relative to themselves. Further, the command level provides information about how a person's messages should be interpreted, given the nature of the relationship.

In this way, command level communication gives instructions about how to understand report level data. Thus, the command dimension is "communication about communication" and is therefore consistent with Bateson's (1954/1972) notion of metacommunication. For example, a hostage taker who says to the police negotiator, "Just when are you going to bring my wife here? This is taking too long!" is not simply commenting on the delay in bringing his wife to the scene (a report message), he is also stating that he feels angry and believes he is being manipulated (a command message).

Consistent with the thinking of Bateson (1954/1972), the metacommunication or command level of communication serves as an overarching interpretive "lens" or "frame" for making meaningful the message content (report) of communication engaged in by the conflicting parties. It is this idea of a frame that provides coherence and coordination to human interaction.

Broadly speaking, Bateson (1954/1972) defines a frame as "a class or set of messages (or meaningful actions)" (p. 186), which functions as a map providing cues about how the interaction is to be defined and how to interpret the communicative acts within the specific context. At a general level, framing is the process by which people attach idiosyncratic definitions, interpretations, and meaning to a class of objects, persons, and events (Watzlawick et al., 1967). According to Lewicki, Saunders, and Minton (1999) frames "are abstractions, collections of perceptions and thoughts that people use to define a situation, organize information, determine what is important, what is not, and so on" (p. 31). Yet frames do not exist as abstract forms disconnected to how people behave. As B. Gray (2006) cogently points out, "How we frame a situation also affects how we respond to it" (p. 194). Frames, then, *are the lenses or interpretive sets through which people perceive and respond to a particular situation, issue, or problem.*

D. Tannen (1986, 1993) offers a sociolinguistic perspective on frames, which builds upon the work of Bateson (1954/1972) and E. Goffman (1974). According to Tannen (1993), frames are "cognitive structuring devices" by which "one organizes knowledge about the world and uses this knowledge to predict interpretations and relationships regarding new information, events, and experiences" (p. 16). D. Tannen & C. Wallat (1993) suggest that frames, as expectations for interaction, function on multiple levels, from the broadest level of interaction context and activity, "to ideas about episodes and actions, to objects and people" (p. 41). In other words, frames function to define both the context of interaction as well as the content of verbal communication.

On the broadest level, frames are viewed as interpretations of interaction that serve to define the activity in which individuals are engaged. At a more precise level of meaning, frames reflect a person's expectations about the issues at hand. At this more specific level, the linguistic cues that a person uses essentially denote their definition of and expectation for specific issues (content) of communication. While frames can be explicitly stated in language (e.g., "this is play" vs. "this is fight" behavior), most frames are more subtle and dependent upon interpretation of linguistic and paralinguistic cues (Tannen, 1986).

According to L.L. Putnam and M. Holmer (1992) the act of framing is a communicative process whereby individuals create verbal descriptions and/

or representations of an issue or relationship. L.E. Drake and W.A. Donohue (1996) suggest that framing entails assigning a particular quality to an issue as reflected within a communicator's linguistic choices (p. 301). Although framing involves attributing a relatively stable interpretive orientation toward self and other's communicative behavior within particular interactive contexts, frames are co-created, maintained, and changed through the linguistic choices the parties make in interaction with one another (Drake & Donohue, 1996).

While individuals frame events and issues in a fairly stable manner, these frames are subject to potential influence and modification based on the level of convergence with another person (Hammer, 2001; Putnam & Holmer, 1992). Research has demonstrated that disputing parties operating from divergent frames are more likely to engage in distributive (competitive) interaction and not achieve resolution, while those operating from convergent (cooperative) frames are more successful in reaching a resolution to their conflict (Drake & Donohue, 1996). Furthermore, individuals in conflict tend to operate from a single dominant frame as a means to express their concerns, but may change frames as a consequence of frame satisfaction during negotiation. This suggests that, when applied to crisis negotiation, individuals can shift frames more easily after some degree of issue resolution has been achieved within the existing discourse frame. In contrast, attempts to shift frames too early can result in conflict escalation (Hammer, 2001).

ASSUMPTION #5: FOUR CORE FRAMES ARE CONTESTED IN CRISIS DISCOURSE

Fifth, building upon the conceptualization of the four communicative goals discussed previously (assumption #1), the S.A.F.E. model identifies four core frames that provide interpretive meaning and structure for understanding conflict interaction. These frames are (1) substantive demands: a frame within which one or more of the parties understands and acts largely in terms of the specific demands and wants expressed; (2) attunement concerns: a frame within which one or more of the parties understands and acts largely in terms of relational distance and closeness experienced. This typically involves framing interaction in terms of power imbalances, issues of trust and mistrust, and affiliation (liking, respect, and caring) toward one another during a conflict interaction; (3) face needs: a frame within which one or more of the parties understands and acts largely in terms of their sensitivities toward their own self-image and how that self-image is perceived by the other party during a conflict interaction; and (4) emotional distress: a frame within which one or more of the parties understands and acts largely in terms of the degree of emotional arousal (typically negatively valenced) being experienced during a conflict interaction.

ASSUMPTION #6: ALL BEHAVIOR HAS MESSAGE VALUE

Sixth, the S.A.F.E. framework is consistent with the axiom "one cannot not communicate," identified within the pragmatics of human communication perspective (Watzlawick et al., 1967). This suggests that any perceived behavior is potentially meaningful and, therefore, has potential message "framing" value. Even noncommunicative behavior (e.g., refusing to continue talking) is itself a coherent "message" interpretable by the other party and can contribute to the emergence in discourse of an overarching interpretive frame.

ASSUMPTION #7: INDIVIDUALS MAKE INTERACTION "MEANINGFUL" THROUGH FRAMES

Seventh, the S.A.F.E. model is consistent with the interactionist axiom that parties punctuate (make meaningful) events (Watzlawick et al., 1967). This axiom suggests that message exchanges between parties are sequenced such that each utterance in the sequence is both a stimulus and a response. In effect, the punctuation of message exchanges enables a string of interactive behavior to be grouped or punctuated into larger units of meaning, which is characterized in the S.A.F.E. model as an interpretive frame. This interpretive frame in turn functions to make meaningful more discrete units of behavior enacted between the parties.

ASSUMPTION #8: MEANING MAKING IS GROUNDED IN MICROBEHAVIOR

Eighth, the S.A.F.E. model is grounded in the microanalysis of the molecular elements of linguistic and paralinguistic cues (Hammer, 2001). It is via these molecular level cues that coherence and meaning are manifest in discourse (Tannen, 1986). These microlevel behaviors include both verbal and nonverbal elements.

ASSUMPTION #9: THE S.A.F.E. MODEL IS NOT "STAGE" ORIENTED

At a broad level, there are some general "stages" of a critical incident that have relevance and applicability to the development of negotiation strategy in a critical incident. M.J. McMains and W.C. Mullins (2006), for example, identify four possible stages of a critical incident. In the precrisis stage, the police negotiator and the subject are engaged in relatively normal social interaction, stress levels are low, and everyday planning processes are operating. In the crisis stage, a serious threat is encountered, stress levels are high, emotions are volatile, and planning is interrupted. It is typically at the crisis stage that the critical incident arises and the police response unit is called to the scene. In the accommodation/negotiation stage, more effective problem solving emerges, stress levels are reduced, and emotional distress is stabilized. During this phase, the subject is willing to consider a number of more productive alternatives (e.g., surrender) to resolve the crisis situation. The resolution stage is the "period during which a person works out the solution to his or her problem, a new equilibrium is reached and a variety of needs can be addressed" (McMains & Mullins, 2006, p. 82). Clearly, such a broad framework shows value in describing a "meta-trend" that takes place within a critical incident. For example, there is certainly a resolution phase in all crisis incidents, insofar as a peaceful resolution takes place through a surrender ritual, while a tactical resolution is initiated through a surprise assault.

The S.A.F.E. model does not, however, emphasize a set of stages or phases in characterizing crisis discourse. In this sense, the S.A.F.E. framework is not consistent with other, far more detailed "stage" approaches articulated for understanding conflict interaction (e.g., Gulliver, 1979; Roberts, 1991). More to the point, the S.A.F.E. model challenges such prescriptive approaches for understanding conflict in general and crisis negotiation in particular by positing that conflict escalation/de-escalation processes are enacted by parties as they communicatively negotiate the core elements of substantive demands, attunement, face, and emotional distress. The S.A.F.E. model views this process in fluid terms, defined by the interactional moves of the parties rather than a preset structure of what is often conceived of as "problem-solving" phases.

There is some indirect support for this view in research findings regarding the stability of specific crisis negotiation stages during crisis incidents. M.E. Holmes and R.E. Sykes (1993) examined the "fit" of P.H. Gulliver's (1979) phase model of negotiation in "simulated" hostage negotiation scenarios compared to actual hostage negotiation incidents. In this more detailed, problem-solving model, Gulliver (1979) identifies eight stages posited to generalize across various conflict situations. These stages include search for an arena, agenda identification, explore range, narrow range, preliminaries to bargaining, final bargaining, ritualization, and execution. Sixteen incidents were coded in terms of this stage model. The main finding from the Holmes and Sykes (1993) study, summarized by R.G. Rogan and M.R. Hammer (2006) is that

> [s]imulations most closely match the phase structure detailed in Gulliver's model, while authentic negotiations are characterized by a more disorderly and disorganized progression. Holmes and Sykes posited that the training demands present in simulations seem to create an order and conformity to negotiation dynamics not present in authentic incidents. (p. 464)

While the S.A.F.E. model does not describe a preset order of stages in a crisis event, it also does not preclude the possibility that a more orderly (and predictable) phase structure may emerge in crisis negotiations. Should this occur, the S.A.F.E. framework would point to explanations for this observed pattern within the discourse and meaning-making interaction that takes place between the negotiator and the subject. The S.A.F.E. framework rejects, however, a priori stages of problem solving that somehow exert a structuring influence that is not reflected in a socially constructed manner and observable through the discourse of the parties involved.

ASSUMPTION #10: DISCOURSE IS A DEVELOPMENTAL MECHANISM FOR MEANING MAKING

Lastly, the S.A.F.E. model views negotiation as a process rather than a static transfer of information between parties. This suggests that "communication" as a process is active and developmental and functions as a mechanism through which meanings and behaviors change as a result of conflict interaction between the parties. L.L. Putnam & M.E. Roloff (1992) summarize this perspective when they state that a communication perspective toward conflict negotiation (what they term bargaining)

> [o]perates from different assumptive ground than does a political, economic or psychological view of bargaining. The assumptive ground derives from attention to elements that are typically ignored in extant literature, specifically, the micro-processes and patterns of bargaining interaction; the dynamic or evolving nature of negotiation; and the systems of meaning enacted through individual, situational, and cultural factors that shape the process. (p. 8)

Overall, the S.A.F.E. model of crisis negotiation is grounded in the constructivist/pragmatics perspective of human communication, is based on four conflict foci that constitute communicative frames that operate as discursive and interpretive structuring devices (Hammer, 2001; Hammer & Rogan, 1997; Rogan & Hammer, 2002), and these frames function to focus (make meaningful) the negotiation discourse between negotiator and the perpetrator. As R.G. Rogan, M.R. Hammer, and C.R. Van Zandt (1997) conclude,

> This communication-oriented approach to studying crisis negotiation is founded on an interactive assessment of the situation as it unfolds and is created through the discourse of the negotiator and the hostage taker. As such, the model represents a powerful and responsive alternative for evaluating the dynamic interplay of perpetrator and negotiator message behavior, potentially resulting in more successfully negotiated incidents. (p. 3)

Overall, these ten assumptions provide the theoretical foundation for the more applied articulation of the S.A.F.E. model in Part 2 of this book. These assumptions are pragmatic considerations that equally lend support to the S.A.F.E. model.

APPENDIX B

Testing the S.A.F.E. Model: A Discourse Analytic Approach

THE DISCOURSE DATA: FOUR CRISIS NEGOTIATION INCIDENTS

Systematic analysis and measurement of communicative behavior was undertaken on four crisis negotiation incidents. I first provide a description of the selection criteria for the actual incidents (sample) examined and then review the methodology used to analyze the discourse present in these four hostage-taking situations.

Audiotapes and transcripts of four crisis incidents were obtained based on the valuable assistance provided by members of the FBI hostage negotiation unit. Altogether, 50 crisis incidents were reviewed for possible analysis. Of these, four incidents were selected for in-depth analysis, based on both conceptual as well as pragmatic criteria.

Criteria for Selecting Incidents

The first criterion focused on the breadth of incident "type." Given the information presented earlier concerning the kinds of instrumental- and expressive-oriented crisis situations law enforcement negotiators typically encounter, incidents that included political goals (e.g., terrorist incidents), prison inmate uprisings, incidents involving hostage takers who have clearly defined mental disorders, emotionally distraught hostage takers (e.g., domestic disputes), and suicides were reviewed. Based on this review, a final set of incidents was selected representing a range of different challenges negotiators face. The final sample included, therefore, a domestic dispute, a mental instability situation, a personal crisis event, and a criminal act. These situations are considered the more frequent types of crisis incidents faced by police negotiators (Hammer, Van Zandt, & Rogan, 1994; Rogan, Hammer, & Van Zandt, 1994).

The second criterion focused on the range of outcomes in a crisis incident. The sample of incidents includes outcomes of a negotiated peaceful surrender and a suicide by the subjects. Within this range, it is possible to examine escalation and de-escalation patterns across "successful" incident outcomes (i.e., peaceful surrender) to "unsuccessful" negotiated outcomes (suicide).

A third criterion involved the range of violence associated with the incident. Therefore, incidents were selected in which a hostage taker had previously killed someone before the negotiation began to incidents in which nobody was killed or injured either before, during, or after the incident.

A fourth criterion focused on whether hostages were held (a hostage situation) or not (a barricade incident). Incidents were selected that included both hostages being held (adults and children) to situations in which no hostages were being held captive.

A fifth criterion included incidents in which negotiation was solely between one police negotiator and one hostage taker to incidents in which there were multiple "third-party" negotiators along with the primary police negotiator as well as multiple hostage taker/negotiators.

A final criterion focused on the duration of the incident. The four hostage events ranged from four hours to seven hours in length.

Two additional pragmatic criteria were also included in selecting incidents for analysis. First, it was necessary to obtain a complete audiotape of a crisis incident. If there was substantial missing audio of an incident, the incident was excluded from further analysis.

Second, sufficient information from the negotiations and/or subsequent police reports (when available) of the outcome of the incident needed to be available. In some cases, this information is directly obtained from the audiotape (e.g., when a gunshot is heard on the hostage taker's phone). In other cases, the hostage taker and negotiator as recorded on the audiotape make an agreement to surrender, but additional confirmation was needed to determine whether the perpetrator actually did surrender at that time. The four incidents selected met these criteria.

Issue of Confidentiality

One important issue related to the analysis of audiotaped hostage incidents concerns the sensitivity of the researcher to police departments that have permitted the researcher access to the incidents. Based on my interactions with police negotiators and the Crisis Management Unit of the FBI, the following research procedures were employed:

1. All audiotaped/video-taped incidents were kept in strict confidence among the research team members. Access to these tapes was limited to designated project researchers.
2. All taped incidents and their transcripts were located in a safe, locked cabinet unless being used for coding or analysis.
3. Once coding was completed, the audiotaped/video-taped incidents were returned to a locked cabinet.
4. All appropriate Human Subjects Committee requirements as specified by the American University were followed regarding issues of confidentiality and protection of human subjects.

Demographic Information

To the extent possible, and without compromising the confidentiality of the actual incidents, demographic information is presented in Table 1.1 in Chapter 1 on each of the four incidents. In addition, further background information is reviewed in the book chapters that present the results from each incident. Table 1.1 presents information concerning (1) incident name (all incidents were simply labeled using U.S. military designations ("A" = Alpha; "B" = Bravo, etc), (2) incident type (criminal, domestic dispute, personal crisis, or mental instability), (3) gender of perpetrator, (4) gender of police negotiator, (5) third parties involved, (6) violent acts (if and when violence occurred; before, during the incident) and who (relationship) was killed or injured, (7) hostages (whether hostages were held and type of hostage held: family member, friend, or stranger), (8) time negotiated (length of time the incident is negotiated), and (9) outcome of crisis event (suicide or surrender). This contextual information provided background information for the analysis of the incidents.

Qualitative Discourse Analysis

Discourse Analysis is a term used to describe a qualitative methodological approach that analyzes texts and discursive practices (Van Dijk, 1997). This approach is relatively new and encompasses a wide variety of interdisciplinary interests (Tracy, 1991). Common across this diversity of interests, however, is a focus on how individuals actually use language to accomplish interactional goals and a commitment to examine connected discourse (texts) in context. As K. Tracy (1991) comments, "this commitment to connected text stands in contrast to research practices of equating language study with the study of sentences and of examining words, sentences, and single utterances out of their textual and social context." (Tracy, 1991, p. 179)

When the focus is on oral discourse, the initial step is the audio or video recording of the discourse followed by a written transcript. Then close analysis takes place culminating in a written report that includes discourse excerpts to support insights. What most centrally distinguishes discourse analysis from other methods is "its commitment to recording and transcribing the specifics of talk, as well as using it in the research report to evidence claims" (Tracy, 1991, p. 200).

Discourse analysis has been employed within such law enforcement contexts as jury deliberations (Manzo, 1993), courtroom interaction (Aronsson, 1991; Penman, 1987, 1991), investigation of crime (Rabon, 1994), police interrogations (Linnell & Jonsson, 1991) and cross-cultural threat assessment (Hammer, 2002a).

Action Implicative Discourse Analysis

The qualitative approach used in this study is centered in the metatheoretical work of R.T. Craig (1989) and R.T. Craig and K. Tracy (1995) who view communication as a practical discipline. As Craig (1989) suggests, "as a practical discipline, our essential purpose is to cultivate communication *praxis,* or practical art, through critical study" (p. 98). Viewing communication in this way suggests that theory development takes place in an interactive process of theory and practice that includes detailed accounts of practice, identification of issues and dilemmas individuals face in interaction, and reflection identifying more general principles of practice.

Craig and Tracy (1995) further elaborate on this view of communication as a practical discipline by articulating what they term "grounded practical theory." The goal of grounded practical theory is to "provide reasoned normative models—rational reconstructions—that inform praxis and critique" (p. 265). The notion of praxis is viewed by the authors as practical action, which "depends on an interpretive understanding of situations and requires deliberation about purposes and moral standards (normative reflection) as well as means (technical rationality)" (p. 249).

Grounded practical theory, then, focuses on a reflective reconstruction of a practice. This reconstruction of a practice takes place at three levels: (1) the strategic level, in which the specific communicative strategies are identified, (2) the problem level in which the interactive problems or dilemmas are identified that influence the use of specific communication strategies, and (3) the normative principle level, in which the normative ideals of the practice and more general principles are generated for the resolution of the identified problems and dilemmas.

This theoretical stance suggests that "communication problems typically arise because communicators pursue multiple, competing goals or purposes such that conflicts among goals often emerge to block ongoing discourse and require reflective thinking" (Craig & Tracy, 1995, p. 254). Grounded practical theory focuses theoretical attention at the problem level of practice and methodological attention toward close analysis of the discourse of the interactants.

Consistent with the view of communication as a practical discipline and borrowing heavily on the tenets of grounded practical theory, this research study employs a modification of a qualitative methodology, termed Action Implicative Discourse Analysis (AIDA) developed by K. Tracy (1995, 1997a).[12] This approach is grounded on the notion that because communicators have multiple goals, they oftentimes face problems or dilemmas in interaction with others. Thus, the primary level of analysis focuses on the interactional problems or dilemmas participants face. Once the interactional problems are reconstituted, analysis moves to both a more concrete level (identification of communicative strategies and techniques interactants use to deal with the identified dilemmas) and a more abstract level (articulation of a set of idealized principles that aid in problem resolution). AIDA, therefore, is an approach for understanding "problematic communicative practices—the character of interactional problems, the conversational strategies used to address them, and participants' situated ideals about appropriate responses to them" (Tracy, 1995, p. 198).[13]

In addition to close analysis of the situational discourse, AIDA also incorporates interview discourse as a way to ascertain the beliefs of the participants about the situated problems, as "a metadiscourse about the interactive discourse" (Tracy, 1995, p. 199). Tracy contends that "reconstruction of the problems and situated ideas of a practice primarily draws on the interview discourse. In contrast, formulation of existing conversational strategies is based on analysis of the interactive discourse in a problematic situation of interest" (Tracy, 1995, p. 199). On this aspect, the current study diverges. Given the nature of the crisis negotiation incidents, it was not possible to conduct interviews either with the hostage takers or the law enforcement negotiators. Therefore, the reconstruction of the problems and situated ideals of the practice (crisis negotiation) relies on analysis conducted of the discourse of the hostage taker and the negotiator in each incident examined.

Tracy (1995) summarizes the approach of AIDA according to the following five features: (1) communicators' action is taken based on the way they frame a situation's problems, (2) analysis reconstructs the interactants problems/dilemmas as experienced in the situation as well as the specific communicative strategies and situated ideals, (3) understanding of a particular situation is enhanced through analyzing the discourse of the situation and discourse about the situation (e.g., interviews), (4) analysis is fundamentally interpretive with the purpose of generating grounded practical theory, and (5) an intermediate level transcription detail is appropriate for the type of analysis employed.

In the present study, the following elements of analysis were undertaken: (1) transcription of communicative interactions between hostage takers and negotiators (including transcription of third-person interactions as well), (2) segmenting transcriptions into topic level units of analysis, (3) identification of "problematic" interactions, misunderstanding, and/or conflict escalation/de-escalation dynamics within topic and between topic units, (4) interpretive analysis of discourse patterns, including various conversation discourse elements as topic shift patterns as well as meaning and form of communicative goal behavior (substantive demands, attunement, face, and emotional distress), (5) integration into an analytical framework of relevant literature to generate initial hypotheses, (6) testing tentative formulations against the transcribed "data," with a particular focus on those "problematic" or disruptive discourse interactions, (7) reinterpretation of original patterns/hypotheses, and (8) further testing/validating of formulations with the data.

Comparisons among the Four Crisis Incidents

In addition to incident-specific analysis, grounded in the identification of S.A.F.E. discourse patterns of escalation and de-escalation, comparative analysis across incidents was also completed, specifically examining differences in outcomes.[14] That is, comparative analysis was undertaken regarding identification of S.A.F.E. patterns of escalation and de-escalation that emerge in those incidents that were "unsuccessfully" negotiated insofar as suicide was the outcome (Alpha and Bravo incidents) compared to "successfully" negotiated outcomes of surrender (Charlie and Delta incidents).[15] Differences that emerged in this analysis were incorporated in the formulation of S.A.F.E. tracking protocols and negotiation strategy recommendations summarized in Part II. This analysis of S.A.F.E. discourse patterns was undertaken to shed light on the general question, are there differences in interaction patterns between police negotiators and perpetrators that emerge in suicide vs. surrender outcomes?

NOTES

1. The terms "hostage" and "crisis" incidents are used interchangeably throughout this book. This, in part, reflects the transition to the broader practice of critical incident negotiation in which references were historically made to the practice of "hostage negotiation" and more recently to either "crisis" negotiation or "hostage/crisis" negotiation. When it is important to distinguish incidents in which hostages are held (to obtain some goal) vs. incidents where an individual is held against his/her wishes (a victim), then the appropriate term of hostage or victim is employed. The term "subject" is primarily used (although at times, the term "hostage taker" may also be used) throughout this book to broadly refer to all individuals who engage in barricade standoffs with police, regardless of whether hostages or victims are actually held.

2. All names of individuals used in the book are changed in those cases where actual discourse is presented (e.g., audiotapes of the incident). In addition, in order to protect the identities of the individuals in these events, changes have been made in demographic information presented (e.g., city, street address, telephone numbers). Actual names of individuals and accurate demographic information is used in the book when descriptions of incidents are presented based on public (e.g., newspaper) accounts and no audiotapes or transcripts of the actual events are available.

3. This finding is based on the FBI's definition of a hostage incident as involving a perpetrator who is holding an individual or individuals in order to obtain a substantive concession from the authorities, while a nonhostage incident involves a perpetrator who is holding an individual or individuals without the intent of obtaining concessions from the authorities. In this case, the individual being held is a victim, not a hostage (McMains & Mullins, 2006).

4. These "wildly contradictory diagnoses" of David Koresh, the leader of the Branch Davidians, cited by J.S. Docherty (1998) include (1) suffering from a seizure disorder, (2) antisocial personality disorder, narcissistic personality disorder, and paranoid, (4) not psychotic, (5) a functional, paranoid-type psychotic, (6) suffering

from delusional beliefs, (6) not suffering from delusional beliefs, (7) suicidal, and (8) not suicidal.

5. Given one aspect of this study focused on the mental health of the perpetrators, the degree to which the "sample" is generalizable is critically important. However, how these incidents were identified and included in the database is not stated. The results can be considered to possess greater generalizability if these incidents (1) represent all of the crisis incidents that occurred during a period of time in a particular locale or (2) represent a random sample of a larger population of incidents. However, if the sample was not constructed with this in mind, then the results may not be representative of crisis situations more generally (Wilson & Putnam, 1990).

6. Relational Order Theory (ROT) also examines a second dimension, which is termed interdependence. This dimension, however, is more focused on the instrumental aspects of negotiation dynamics. Interdependence is viewed within ROT in terms of the degree to which conflicting parties are able to demand rights and impose obligations on each other. As such, the interdependence element of ROT essentially is another way of describing the frame of substantive demands. For this reason, I limit the discussion and application of ROT to the interpersonal distance/closeness dimension (termed affiliation in Relational Order Theory).

7. A throw phone is a specially designed telephone system in which a hard-cased telephone receiver is typically "thrown" through a window or open door to the subject to use when talking to the police negotiator. This maintains a dedicated line of communication between the police and the hostage taker.

8. In all incidents presented in Chapters 6–9, the names of the individuals have been changed to maintain confidentiality. Further, "PN" is used to refer to the primary police negotiator in these incidents and PN2 is used to refer to a second police negotiator who may talk to the subject.

9. In fact, any such "promises" are considered given under duress and therefore are considered legally invalid. However, the federal prosecutor may well have thought it was more advantageous to prosecute Bill and Bonnie federally rather than through the state system.

10. The subject's overall topic of conversation was "explaining his previous situation." Within this topic, the subject referred to a wide variety of subtopics throughout the negotiation. When the subject changed the topic away from his previous situation, a separate episode was identified.

11. The police negotiator, attempting to listen and develop a relationship with the subject, discussed how "we can get a hot shot." The PN had no intention, obviously, of providing the subject with a lethal cocktail. Rather, the PN was attempting to build rapport within the delusional story presented to him by the subject.

12. Action Implicative Discourse Analysis, while largely developed through a detailed examination of academic colloquium discourse (Tracy, 1997a; Tracy & Baratz, 1993; Tracy & Naughton, 1994), has also been applied within the law enforcement context to an analysis of 911 calls (Tracy, 1997b).

13. K. Tracy (1995) suggests that (1) the end goal of qualitative, Action Implicative Discourse Analysis (AIDA) research is "understanding human action and cultivating practice rather than scientific explanation, (2) knowledge is socially constructed, (3) qualitative methods are better suited than quantitative approaches to address many of the most important questions about language and social

interaction, and (4) other criteria than reliability are important in assessing qualitatively derived scholarly claims (pp. 195–196). As general characteristics of qualitative research approaches, I would agree. My discomfort lies in the implied sense of incompatibility of qualitative and quantitative analysis of conversation. It is my contention that the basic tenets of AIDA are not inherently "at odds" with quantitative research approaches.

14. It should be noted that the perpetrators were male in three of the four situations, whereas the Bravo incident had both a male and a female perpetrator involved. In all four cases, the police negotiators were men. Other third-party negotiators in the incidents were both male and female.

15. For purposes of this study, negotiated surrender outcomes can be usefully viewed as "successful" compared specifically to suicide outcomes, which can be appropriately if tragically characterized as "unsuccessful" in terms of a negotiated result. However, while examined in this study, it is important to *not* equate the outcome of a "tactical rescue/assault" with a lack of success in negotiation. Suggesting that negotiation was not successful because a tactical assault was undertaken in a particular incident is oftentimes an unwarranted conclusion. In these situations, there is not typically clear, objectively verifiable evidence that negotiation was not effective, other than the fact that at a particular moment, the hostage taker had not yet surrendered. A decision to "go tactical" is made for a variety of reasons beyond the assessment of negotiation progress. Other factors that influence a tactical decision include the window of opportunity, the element of surprise, and an overall assessment as to the probability that a tactical rescue operation will save lives. Thus, caution is in order when using the labels of "successful" and "unsuccessful" concerning tactical resolutions.

REFERENCES

Adler, R.S., Rosen, B., & Silverstein, E.M. (1998). Emotions in negotiation: How to manage fear and anger. *Negotiation Journal, 14,* 161–179.

American Psychiatric Association. (1994). *Diagnostic and statistical manual of mental disorders: DMS-IV* (4th ed.). Washington, DC: American Psychiatric Association.

Andersen, P.A., & Guerrero, L.K. (1998). Principles of communication and emotion in social interaction. In P.A. Andersen & L.K. Guerrero (Eds.), *Handbook of communication and emotion* (pp. 49–96). San Diego, CA: Academic Press.

Anonymous. (2006). *The D.C. sniper case.* Paper presented at the Annual Baltimore hostage/crisis negotiation conference, Baltimore, MD.

Aronsson, K. (1991). Social interaction and the recycling of legal evidence. In N. Coupland, H. Giles, & J.M. Wiemann (Eds.), *"Miscommunication" and problematic talk* (pp. 215–243). Thousand Oaks, CA: Sage.

Associated Press. (2006, November 23, 2006). Police: Gunman, hostage die in Chicago standoff. *CNN.Com: Quoting Associated Press.*

Auerbach, A.H. (1998). *Ransom.* New York: Holt & Company.

Bargh, J.A., Chen, M., & Burrows, L. (1996). Automaticity of social behavior: Direct effects of trait construct and stereotype activation on action. *Journal of Personality and Social Psychology, 71*(2), 230–244.

Barry, B., & Oliver, R.L. (1994, June). *Affect in negotiation: A model and propositions.* Paper presented at the International Association for Conflict Management Conference, Eugene, OR.

Bateson, G. (1954/1972). *Steps to an ecology of mind.* New York: Ballantine Books.

Bilsky, W., Muller, J., Voss, A., & Von Groote, E. (2004). Affect assessment in crisis negotiations: An exploratory case study using two distinct indicators. *Psychology, Crime & Law,* 1–13.

Boardman, S.K., & Horowitz, S.V. (1994). Constructive conflict management: An answer to critical social problems. *Journal of Social Issues, 50,* 1–244.

Boltz, F., Dudonis, K.J., & Schulz, D.P. (1990). *The counter-terrorism handbook: Tactics, procedures, and techniques.* New York: Elsevier Science Publishing.

Boltz, F., & Hershey, E. (1979). *Hostage cop.* New York: Rawson Wade.

Borum, R., & Strentz, T. (1992). The borderline personality. *FBI Law Enforcement Bulletin, 61,* 6–10.

Britt, T.W., & Shepperd, J.A. (1999). Trait relevance and trait assessment. *Personality and Social Psychological Review, 3,* 108–122.

Brown, B. (1977). Face-saving and face-restoration in negotiation. In D. Druckman (Ed.), *Negotiations: Social-Psychological perspectives* (pp. 275–299). Beverly Hills, CA: Sage.

Brulliard, K. (2006). Standoff in Loudoun began over gas tab. *Washington Post,* p. B01.

Bureau of Justice Statistics. (2006). National crime victimization survey violent crime trends: 1973–2005.

Burleson, B.R., & Goldsmith, D.J. (1998). How the comforting process works: Alleviating emotional distress through conversationally induced reappraisals. In P.A. Andersen & L.K. Guerrero (Eds.), *Handbook of communication and emotion* (pp. 245–280). San Diego, CA: Academic Press.

Bush, R.A.B., & Folger, J.P. (1994). *The promise of mediation.* San Francisco, CA: Jossey-Bass.

Butler, W.M. (1991). *Hostage taking and barricade incidents in the United States: A nationwide survey and analysis.* University of Vermont.

Buvinic, M., & Morrison, A.R. (2000). Living in a more violent world. *Foreign Policy* (118), 58–71.

Call, J.A. (1999). The hostage triad: Takers, victims, and negotiators. In H.V. Hall (Ed.), *Lethal violence: A source book on fatal, domestic, acquaintance and stranger violence.* Boca Raton, FL: CRC Press.

Cannon, W.B. (1929). *Bodily changes in pain, hunger, fear and rage.* New York: Appleton-Century.

Caplan, G. (1961). *An approach to community mental health.* New York: Grune & Stratton.

Carkhuff, R.R. (1981). *The art of helping IV.* Amherst, MA: Human Resource Development Press.

Cissna, K.N.L., & Sieburg, E. (1981). Patterns of interaction confirmation and disconfirmation. In C. Wilder & J.H. Weakland (Eds.), *Rigor and imagination: Essays from the legacy of Gregory Bateson.* New York: Praeger.

Clark, R.A., & Delia, J.G. (1979). Topoi and rhetorical competence. *The Quarterly Journal of Speech, 65,* 187–206.

Cole, J. (2004). If America were Iraq, what would it be like? Retrieved December 15, 2006.

Combs, C.C. (1997). *Terrorism in the twenty-first century.* Upper Saddle River, NJ: Prentice Hall.

Cooper, H.H.A. (1981). *The hostage takers.* Boulder, CO: Paladin Press.

Costantino, C.A., & Merchant, C.S. (1996). *Designing conflict management systems*. San Francisco, CA: Jossey-Bass.

Craig, R.T. (1989). Communication as a practical discipline. In B. Dervin, L. Grossberg, B.J. O'Keefe, & E. Wartella (Eds.), *Rethinking communication: Volume 1 paradigm issues* (pp. 97–122). Thousand Oaks, CA: Sage.

Craig, R.T., & Tracy, K. (1995). Grounded practical theory: The case of intellectual discussion. *Communication Theory, 5*, 248–272.

Crisis Management Unit. (2006). *HOBAS statistical report of incidents*. Quantico, VA: Federal Bureau of Investigation.

Cupach, W.R., & Canary, D.J. (1997). *Competence in interpersonal conflict*. New York: McGraw-Hill.

Daly, J.A. (2002). Personality and interpersonal communication. In M.L. Knapp & J.A. Daly (Eds.), *Handbook of interpersonal communication* (3rd ed., pp. 133–180).

Daly, J.A., & Bippus, A. (1998). Personality and interpersonal communication. In J. C. McCroskey, J.A. Daly, M.M. Martin, & M.J. Beatty (Eds.), *Communication and personality: Trait perspectives* (pp. 1–40). Cresskill, NJ: Hampton.

Davidson, T.N. (2002). *To preserve life: Hostage-crisis management*. Indianapolis, IN: CIMACOM.

Delprino, R.P., & Bahn, C. (1988). National survey of the extent and nature of psychological services in police departments. *Professional Psychology: Research and Practice, 19*, 421–425.

Deutsch, M. (1973). Conflicts: Productive and destructive. In F.E. Jandt (Ed.), *Conflict resolution through communication*. New York: Harper & Row.

DiVasto, P., Lanceley, F.J., & Gruys, A. (1992). Critical issues in suicide intervention. *FBI Law Enforcement Bulletin, 61*, 13–26.

Docherty, J.S. (1998). *When the parties bring their Gods to the Table: Learning the lessons of Waco*. Fairfax, VA: George Mason University.

Donohue, W.A. (1998). Managing equivovality and relational paradox in the Oslo peace negotiations. *Journal of Language and Social Psychology, 17*, 72–96.

Donohue, W.A., & Kolt, R. (1992). *Managing interpersonal conflict*. Newbury Park, CA: Sage.

Donohue, W.A., Lyles, J., & Rogan, R.G. (1989). Issue development in divorce mediation. *Empirical Research in Divorce and Family Mediation, 24*, 19–28.

Donohue, W.A., Ramesh, C., & Borchgrevink, C. (1991). Crisis bargaining: Tracking relational paradox in hostage negotiation. *International Journal of Conflict Management, 2*, 257–274.

Donohue, W.A., & Roberto, A.J. (1993). Relational development in hostage negotiation. *Human Communication Research, 20*, 175–198.

Drake, L.E., & Donohue, W.A. (1996). Communication framing theory in conflict resolution. *Communication Research, 23*(3), 297–322.

Ekman, P., & Davidson, R.J. (Eds.). (1994). *The nature of emotion: Fundamental questions*. New York: Oxford University Press.

Elliott, R. (1985). Helpful and nonhelpful events in brief counseling interviews: An empirical taxonomy. *Journal of Counseling Psychology, 32*, 307–322.

FBI. (1996). FBI hostage/crisis negotiation in-service training program. Quantico, VA.

Feldmann, T.B. (2001). Characteristics of hostage and barricade incidents: Implications for negotiation strategies and training. *Journal of Police Crisis Negotiations, 1*(1), 3–33.

Feldmann, T.B., & Johnson, P.W. (1999). Aircraft hijackings in the United States. In H.V. Hall (Ed.), *Lethal violence: A sourcebook on fatal domestic, acquaintance, and stranger violence*. Boca Raton, FL: CRC Press.

Fellwock, H. (2004, October 2). Wife: He's not coming out alive. *Daily News: Bowling Green, Kentucky*.

Fink, S. (1986). *Crisis management: Planning for the inevitable*. New York: American Management Association.

Fisher, R., & Brown, S. (1988). *Getting together*. New York: Penguin.

Fisher, R., & Ury, W. (1991). *Getting to yes*. New York: Penguin.

Fisher, R.J. (1990). *The social psychology of intergroup and international conflict resolution*. New York: Springer-Verlag.

Folger, J.P., & Jones, T.S. (Eds.). (2004). *New directions in mediation: Communication research and perspectives*. Thousand Oaks, CA: Sage Publications.

Folger, J.P., Poole, M.S., & Stutman, R.K. (1997). *Working through conflict* (3rd ed.). New York: HarperCollins.

Folger, J.P., Poole, M.S., & Stutman, R.K. (2000). *Working through conflict* (4th ed.). New York: Addison-Wesley Educational Publishers.

Folger, J.P., Poole, M.S., & Stutman, R.K. (2005). *Working through conflict* (5th ed.). Boston, MA: Pearson.

Fuselier, G.D. (1981a). A practical overview of hostage negotiation: Part I. *FBI Law Enforcement Bulletin, 50*, 2–6.

Fuselier, G.D. (1981b). A practical overview of hostage negotiation: Part II. *FBI Law Enforcement Bulletin, 50*, 10–15.

Fuselier, G.D. (1986). What every negotiator would like his chief to know. *FBI Law Enforcement Bulletin, 55*, 1–4.

Fuselier, G.D. (1988). Hostage negotiation consultant: Emerging role for the clinical psychologist. *Professional Psychology: Research and Practice, 19*, 175–179.

Fuselier, G.D., & Noesner, G.W. (1990). Confronting the terrorist hostagetaker. *FBI Law Enforcement Bulletin, 59*, 6–11.

Geist, P. (1995). Negotiating whose order? Communicating to negotiate identities and revise organizational structures. In A.M. Nicotera (Ed.), *Conflict and organizations* (pp. 45–64). Albany: State University of New York.

Gettys, V.S. (1983). *National survey-negotiator selection and hostage negotiation activity*. Paper presented at the American Psychological Association Conference, Anaheim, CA.

Giebels, E. (1999). *A comparison of crisis negotiation across Europe*. Paper presented at the Proceedings of the first European conference on crisis negotiations, s-Gravenhage.

Giebels, E., & Noelanders, S. (2004). *Crisis negotiations: A multiparty perspective*. Veenendaal, the Netherlands: Universal Press.

Gilligan, J. (2001). *Preventing violence*. New York: Thames & Hudson.

Gladwin, R.N., & Kumar, R. (1987). The social psychology of crisis bargaining: Toward a contingency model. *Columbia Journal of World Business, 22,* 23–31.

Goffman, E. (1967). *Interaction ritual essays on face-to-face behavior*. Garden City, NY: Anchor Books, Doubleday & Company.

Goffman, E. (1974). *Frame analysis: An essay on the organization of experience*. New York: Harper & Row, Publishers.

Goldaber, I. (1979). A typology of hostage-takers. *The Police Chief,* 21–23.

Goleman, D. (1995). *Emotional intelligence*. New York: Bantam Books.

Gray, B. (2006). Mediation as framing and framing within mediation. In M.S. Herrman (Ed.), *Handbook of mediation* (pp. 193–216). Malden, MA: Blackwell Publishing.

Greenstone, J.L. (1995). Tactics and negotiating techniques (TNT): The way of the past and the way of the future. In M.I. Kurke & E.M. Scrivner (Eds.), *Police psychology into the 21st century*. Hillsdale, NJ: Lawrence Erlbaum.

Greenwell, M. (2006). Reservist due for Iraq is killed in standoff with police. *Washington Post,* p. B02.

Gregg, S.R. (1983, March 2). Inside a siege. *The Washington Post,* pp. 1, 8.

Guerrero, L.K., & La Valley, A.G. (2006). Conflict, emotion, and communication. In J.G. Oetzel & S. Ting-Toomey (Eds.), *The Sage handbook of conflict communication* (pp. 69–96). Thousand Oaks, CA: Sage Publications.

Gulliver, P.H. (1979). *Disputes and negotiations: A cross-cultural perspective*. New York: Academic Press.

Hacker, F.J. (1976). *Crusaders, criminals, crazies: Terror and terrorism in our time*. New York: Norton.

Hammer, M.R. (1997). Negotiating across the cultural divide: Intercultural dynamics in crisis incidents. In R.G. Rogan, M.R. Hammer, & C.R.V. Zandt (Eds.), *Dynamic processes of crisis negotiations: Theory, research and practice* (pp. 105–114). Westport, CT: Praeger Press.

Hammer, M.R. (1998, November 19–22). *Crisis Negotiation across the Cultural Divide.* Paper presented at the SIETAR International Conference, Tokyo, Japan.

Hammer, M.R. (1999, February 16–17). *Using the FIRE model in crisis situations.* Paper presented at the Baltimore Hostage Negotiation Conference, Baltimore, MD.

Hammer, M.R. (2001). Conflict negotiation under crisis conditions. In W.F. Eadie & P.E. Nelson (Eds.), *The language of conflict and resolution*. Thousand Oaks, CA: Sage.

Hammer, M.R. (2002a). World destruction: A cultural analysis of a threat communique. *FBI Law Enforcement Bulletin, 71*(9), 8–13.

Hammer, M.R. (2002b). The Intercultural Conflict Style (ICS) Inventory. Ocean Pines, MD: Hammer Consulting, LLC.

Hammer, M.R. (2002c). The Intercultural Conflict Style (ICS) Inventory: Interpretive Guide. Ocean Pines, MD: Hammer Consulting, LLC.

Hammer, M.R. (2003). The Intercultural Conflict Style (ICS) Inventory: Facilitator's Manual. Ocean Pines, MD: Hammer Consulting, LLC.

Hammer, M.R. (2005a). The Intercultural Conflict Style Inventory: A conceptual framework and measure of intercultural conflict approaches *International Journal of Intercultural Research, 29, 675–695.*

Hammer, M.R. (2005b). S.A.F.E. field guide. Ocean Pines, MD: Hammer Consulting, LLC.

Hammer, M.R. (2005c). S.A.F.E. assessment tools. Ocean Pines, MD: Hammer Consulting, LLC.

Hammer, M.R. (2005d). S.A.F.E. assessment tools tear-off sheets. Ocean City, MD: Hammer Consulting, LLC.

Hammer, M.R. (in press). The S.A.F.E. model for negotiating critical incidents. In R. G. Rogan and F. Lanceley (Eds.), *Contemporary theory, research, and practice of crisis/hostage megotiations* (under contract, Cresskill, NJ: Hampton Press).

Hammer, M.R., & Rogan, R.G. (1997). Negotiation models in crisis situations: The value of a communication based approach. In R.G. Rogan, M.R. Hammer, & C.R.V. Zandt (Eds.), *Dynamic processes of crisis negotiations: Theory, research and practice* (pp. 9–23). Westport, CT: Praeger Press.

Hammer, M.R., & Rogan, R.G. (1998, June 7–10). *Indochinese conflict negotiation patterns within the United States.* Paper presented at the International Association of Conflict Management annual conference, Washington, D.C.

Hammer, M.R., & Rogan, R.G. (2004). Threats, demands, and communication dynamics: Negotiating the 1991 Talladega prison siege. *Journal of Police Crisis Negotiations, 4*(1), 45–56.

Hammer, M.R., Van Zandt, C.R., & Rogan, R.G. (1994). Crisis/hostage negotiation team profile of demographic and functional characteristics. *FBI Law Enforcement Bulletin, 63,* 8–11.

Hammer, M.R., & Weaver, G. (1994). Cultural considerations in hostage negotiations. In G.R. Weaver (Ed.), *Culture, communication and conflict: Readings in intercultural relations* (2nd ed., pp. 518–527). Needham Heights, MA: Ginn Press.

Hammer, M.R., & Weaver, G. (1998). Cultural considerations in hostage negotiations. In G.R. Weaver (Ed.), *Culture, communication and conflict: Readings in intercultural relations.* (pp. 518–527). Needham Heights, MA: Simon & Schuster.

Hare, A. (2004). Personal communication.

Hassel, C. (1975). The hostage situation: Exploring motivation and cause. *Police Chief, 42,* 55–58.

Head, W.B. (1989). *The Hostage Response: An examination of US Law Enforcement Practices Concerning Hostage Incidents (United States).* Unpublished Doctoral Dissertation, The State University of New York at Albany.

Herman, C.F. (1963). Some consequences of crisis which limit the viability of organizations. *Administrative Science Quarterly, 8,* 61–82.

Heymann, P.B. (1993). *Lessons from Waco: proposed changes in federal enforcement.* Washington, DC: U.S. Department of Justice.

Hill, C.E., Helms, J.E., Tichenor, V., Spiegel, S.B., O'Grady, K.E., & Perry, S.E. (1988). Effects of therapist response mode in brief psychotherapy. *Journal of Counseling Psychology, 35*, 222–233.

Hocker, J.L., & Wilmot, W.W. (1995). *Interpersonal conflict* (4th ed.). Madison, WI: William C. Brown.

Hoff, L.A. (1989). *People in crisis: Understanding and helping*. Redwood City, CA: Addison-Wesley.

Holmes, M.E., & Fletcher-Bergland, T.S. (1995). Negotiations in crisis. In A.M. Nicotera (Ed.), *Conflict and organizations* (pp. 239–258). Albany: State University of New York Press.

Holmes, M.E., & Sykes, R.E. (1993). A test of the fit of Gulliver's phase model to hostage negotiations. *Communication Studies, 44*, 38–55.

Hovland, C., Janis, I., & Kelly, H. (1953). *Communication and persuasion*. New Haven, CT: Yale University Press.

Howell, W.S. (1982). *The empathic communicator*. Belmont, CA: Wadsworth.

Hunt, D.E. (1987). *Beginning with ourselves: In practice, theory and human affairs*. Cambridge, MA: Brookline Books.

Johnson, D.W. (1997). *Reaching out* (6th ed.). Boston, MA: Allyn and Bacon.

Jones, T.S. (1997). *Emotional communication in conflict: Essence and impact*. Paper presented at the National Communication Association Convention, Chicago, IL.

Jones, T.S. (2000). Emotional communication in conflict: Essence and Impact. In W. Eadie & P. Nelson (Eds.), *The language of conflict resolution* (pp. 81–104). Thousand Oaks, CA: Sage.

Jones, T.S. (2001). Emotional communication in conflict: Essence and Impact. In W. Eadie & P. Nelson (Eds.), *The language of conflict resolution* (pp. 81–104). Thousand Oaks, CA: Sage.

Jones, T.S. (2006). Emotion in mediation: Implications, applications, opportunities, and challenges. In M. S. Herrman (Ed.), *Handbook of mediation* (pp. 277–305). Malden, MA: Blackwell.

Jones, T.S., & Bodtker, A. (2001). Mediating with heart in mind: Addressing emotion in mediation practice. *Negotiation Journal*, 217–244.

Kelly, G. (1963). *A theory of personality: The psychology of personal constructs*. New York: Norton.

Kimmel, M., Pruitt, D.G., Magenau, J., Konar-Goldband, E., & Carnevale, P.J. (1980). The effects of trust, aspiration, and gender on negotiation tactics. *Journal of Personality and Social Psychology, 38*, 9–23.

Kohlrieser, G. (2006). *Hostage at the table*. San Francisco, CA: Jossey-Bass.

Krug, E.G. (2002). *World report on violence and health: summary*. Unpublished manuscript, Geneva: World Health Organization.

Lanceley, F.J. (1981). The antisocial personality as hostage-taker. *Journal of Police Science and Administration, 9*, 28–34.

Lanceley, F.J. (2003). *On-scene guide for crisis negotiations (2nd edition)*. Boca Raton, FL: CRC Press.

Lanceley, F.J., Ruple, S.W., & Moss, C.G. (1985). *Crisis and suicide intervention*. Unpublished manuscript, Quantico, VA.

Lawyer, J.W., & Katz, N.H. (1985). *Communication and conflict management skills*. Dubuque, IA: Kendall/Hunt.

Lazarus, R.S. (1984). Thoughts on the relation between emotion and cognition. In K.R. Scherer & P. Ekman (Eds.), *Approaches to emotion* (pp. 247–258). Hillsdale, NJ: Lawrence Erlbaum.

Lazarus, R.S. (1991). *Emotion and adaptation*. New York: Oxford University Press.

Lazarus, R.S. (1994). Universal antecedents of the emotions. In P. Ekman & R.J. Davidson (Eds.), *The nature of emotion: Fundamental questions* (pp. 163–171). New York: Oxford University Press.

Lewicki, R.J., Saunders, D.M., & Minton, J.W. (1999). *Negotation* (3rd ed.). New York: McGraw-Hill/Irwin.

Lewis, M. (1993). The emergence of human emotion. In M. Lewis & J.M. Haviland (Eds.), *Handbook of emotions*. New York: Guilford Press.

Lindskold, S., & Han, G. (1988). GRIT as a foundation for integrative bargaining. *Personality and Social Psychology Bulletin, 14*, 335–345.

Linnell, P., & Jonsson, L. (1991). Suspect stories: Perspective setting in an asymmetrical situation. In I. Markova & K. Foppa (Eds.), *Asymmetries in dialogue* (pp. 75–100). Hertfordshire, England: Wheatsheaf.

Littlejohn, S., & Domenici, K. (2006). A facework frame for mediation. In M.S. Herrman (Ed.), *Handbook of mediation* (pp. 228–246). Malden, MA: Blackwell Publishing.

MacWillson, A.C. (1992). *Hostage-taking terrorism: Incident-response strategy*. New York: St. Martin's Press.

Maher, G. (1977). *Hostages: A police approach to a contemporary crisis*. Springfield, IL: Charles C. Thomas.

Maksymchuk, A.F. (1982). Strategies for hostage-taking incidents. *Police Chief*, 58–65.

Manzo, J.F. (1993). Jurors' narratives of personal experience in deliberative talk. *Text, 13*, 267–290.

Maslow, A.H. (1954). *Motivation and personality*. New York: Harper & Row.

Maturana, H., & Varela, F. (1987). *The tree of knowledge: The biological roots of human understanding*. Boston: Shambhala.

McMains, M.J., & Mullins, W.C. (1996). *Crisis negotiations*. Cincinnati, OH: Anderson Publishing Company.

McMains, M.J., & Mullins, W.C. (2001). *Crisis negotiations: Managing critical incidents and hostage situations in law enforcement and corrections* (2nd ed.). Cincinnati, OH: Anderson.

McMains, M.J., & Mullins, W.C. (2006). *Crisis negotiations: Managing critical incidents and hostage situations in law enforcement and corrections* (3rd ed.) Cincinnati, OH: Anderson Publishing.

Middendorf, W. (1975). *New developments in the taking of hostages and kidnapping—A summary*. Washington DC: National Criminal Justice Reference Service Translation.

Miller, A.H. (1980). *Terrorism and hostage negotiations*. Boulder, CO: Westview Press.

Miller, R.S., & Leary, M.R. (1992). Social sources and interactive functions of emotion: The case of embarrassment. *Review of Personality and Social Psychology, 14,* 202–221.

Miron, M.S., & Goldstein, A.P. (1979). *Hostage*. New York: Pergamon.

Mischel, W. (1968). *Personality and assessment*. New York: John Wiley.

Mischel, W. (1999). Personality coherence and dispositions in a cognitive-affective personality system (CAPS) approach. In D. Cervone & Y. Shoda (Eds.), *The coherence of personality: Social-cognitive bases of consistency, variability, and organization* (pp. 37–60). New York: Guildford.

Murphy, G.R., & Wexler, C. (2004). *Managing a multijurisdictional case: Identifying the lessons learned from the sniper investigation*. Washington, DC: Police Executive Research Forum.

NCNA Guidelines. (2001). Unpublished document: Critical Incident Response Group, FBI, Quantico, VA: FBI Academy.

Negotiator, A.T.F. (2004). Personal communication on the Bowling Green, Kentucky incident.

Nicotera, A.M. (1995). Thinking about communication and conflict. In A.M. Nicotera (Ed.), *Conflict and organizations* (pp. 3–16). Albany: State University of New York Press.

Noesner, G.W. (1999). Negotiation concepts for commanders. *FBI Law Enforcement Bulletin, 68,* 6–14.

Noesner, G.W., & Dolan, J.T. (1992). First responder negotiation training. *FBI Law Enforcement Bulletin, 61,* 1–4.

Noesner, G.W., & Webster, M. (1997). Crisis intervention: Using active listening skills in negotiations. *FBI Law Enforcement Bulletin,* 66(August), 13–19.

Northrup, T.A. (1989). The dynamic of identity in personal and social conflict. In L. Kriesberg, T. Northrup, & S.J. Thorson (Eds.), *Intractable conflicts and their transformation* (pp. 55–82). Syracuse, NY: Syracuse University Press.

Oatley, K., & Johnson-Laird, P.N. (1987). Towards a cognitive theory of emotions. *Cognition and emotion, 1,* 29–50.

Ochberg, F.M., & Soskis, D.A. (Eds.). (1982). *Victims of terrorism*. Boulder, CO: Westview Press.

Office of Security. (1983). *Hostage negotiation: A matter of life and death*. Washington, DC: Department of State.

Penman, R. (1987). Discourse in courts: Cooperation, coercion, and coherence. *Discourse Processes, 10.*

Penman, R. (1991). Goals, games, and moral orders: A paradoxical case in court? In K. Tracy (Ed.), *Understanding face face-to-face interaction* (pp. 21–42). Hillsdale, NJ: Erlbaum.

Peterson, S. (2006, June 8, 2006). Kidnappings tear at Iraq's frayed social fabric. *Christian Science Monitor,* pp. 1–3.

Pittam, J., & Scherer, K.R. (1993). Vocal expression and communication of emotion. In M. Lewis & J.M. Haviland (Eds.), *Handbook of Emotions* (pp. 185–197). New York: Guilford Press.

Pruitt, D.G., & Carnevale, P.J. (1993). *Negotiation in social conflict*. Pacific Cove, CA: Brooks/Cole.

Putnam, L.L. (1994). Challenging the assumptions of traditional approaches to negotiation. *Negotiation Journal, 10*(4), 337–346.

Putnam, L.L. (2006). Definitions and approaches to conflict and communication. In J.G. Oetzel & S. Ting-Toomey (Eds.), *The Sage Handbook of Conflict Communication* (pp. 1–32). Thousand Oaks, CA: Sage Publications.

Putnam, L.L., & Holmer, M. (1992). Framing, reframing, and issue development. In L.L. Putnam & M.E. Roloff (Eds.), *Communication and negotiation* (pp. 128–155). Newbury Park, CA: Sage.

Putnam, L.L., & Roloff, M.E. (1992). Communication perspectives on negotiation. In L.L. Putnam & M.E. Roloff (Eds.), *Communication and negotiation* (pp. 1–17). Newbury Park, CA: Sage.

Rabon, D. (1994). *Investigative discourse analysis*. Durham, NC: Carolina Academic Press.

Retzinger, S.M. (1993). *Violent emotions: Shame and rage in marital quarrels*. Thousand Oaks, CA: Sage Publications.

Roberts, A.R. (1991). *Contemporary perspectives on crisis intervention and prevention*. Englewood Cliffs, NJ: Prentice Hall.

Roberts, A.R., & Dziegielewski, S.F. (1995). Foundational skills and applications of crisis intervention and cognitive therapy. In A.R. Roberts (Ed.), *Crisis intervention and time-limited cognitive treatment* (pp. 3–27). Thousand Oaks, CA: Sage.

Rogan, R.G. (1990). *An interaction analysis of negotiator and hostage-taker identity-goal, relational-goal, and language intensity message behavior within hostage negotiations: A descriptive investigation of three negotiations*. Michigan State University, East Lansing, MI.

Rogan, R.G. (1997). Emotion and emotional expression in crisis negotiation. In R.G. Rogan, M.R. Hammer, & C.R.V. Zandt (Eds.), *Dynamic processes of crisis negotiation: Theory, research, and practice* (pp. 25–44). Westport, CT: Praeger.

Rogan, R.G. (1999). F.I.R.E: A communication based approach for understanding crisis negotiation. In O. Adang & E. Giebels (Eds.), *To save lives* (pp. 29–45). Amsterdam: Elsevier.

Rogan, R.G., Donohue, W.A., & Lyles, J. (1990). Gaining and exercising control in hostage taking negotiations using empathetic perspective-taking. *International Journal of Group Tensions, 20*, 77–90.

Rogan, R.G., & Hammer, M.R. (1994). Crisis negotiations: A preliminary investigation of facework in naturalistic conflict. *Journal of Applied Communication Research, 22*, 216–231.

Rogan, R.G., & Hammer, M.R. (1995). Assessing message affect in crisis negotiations: An exploratory study. *Human Communication Research, 21*, 553–574.

Rogan, R.G., & Hammer, M.R. (2002). Crisis/Hostage negotiations: Conceptualization of a communication-based approach. In H. Giles (Ed.), *Law enforcement, communication, and community* (pp. 229–254). Amsterdam: John Benjamins Publishing.

Rogan, R.G., & Hammer, M.R. (2006). The emerging field of hostage/crisis negotiation: A communication based perspective. In S.T.-T.J. Oetzel (Ed.), *Handbook of conflict communication* (pp. 451–478). Thousand Oaks, CA: Sage.

Rogan, R.G., Hammer, M.R., & Van Zandt, C.R. (1994). Profiling crisis negotiation teams. *Police Chief, 61*, 14–18.

Rogan, R.G., Hammer, M.R., & Van Zandt, C. R. (1997). *Dynamic processes of crisis negotiation: Theory, research and practice*. Westport, CT: Praeger.

Rogan, R.G., & Lancelely, F. (Eds.), (forthcoming). *Contemporary theory, research, and practice of crisis/hostage megotiations* (under contract, Cresskill, NJ: Hampton Press).

Roloff, M.E. (1981). *Interpersonal communication: The Social exchange approach*. Beverly Hills, CA: Sage.

Roloff, M.E., & Jordan, J.M. (1992). Achieving negotiation goals: The "fruits and foibles" of planning ahead. In L.L. Putnam & M.E. Roloff (Eds.), *Communication and negotiation* (pp. 21–45). Newbury Park, CA: Sage.

Romano, S.J. (1997). Personal communication. Quantico, VA.

Romano, S.J. (1998). Third-party intermediaries and crisis negotiations. *FBI Law Enforcement Bulletin, 67*(10), 20–24.

Rousseau, D.M., Sitkin, S.B., Burt, R.S., & Camerer, C. (1988). Not so different after all: A cross-discipline view of trust. *Academy of Management Review, 23*, 393–404.

Rubin, J.Z., Pruitt, D.G., & Kim, S.H. (1994). *Social conflict*. New York: McGraw-Hill.

Ruesch, J., & Bateson, G. (1951). *Communication: The Social Matrix of Psychiatry*. New York: W.W. Norton.

Russel, H.E., & Beigel, A. (1979). *Understanding human behavior for effective police work*. New York: Basic Books.

Sandole, D.J.D. (1993). Paradigm, theories, and metaphors in conflict and conflict resolution: Coherence or confusion. In D.J.D. Sandole & H.V.D. Merwe (Eds.), *Conflict resolution theory and practice* (pp. 3–21). New York: Manchester University Press.

Scherer, K.R., & Wallbot, H.G. (1994). Evidence for universality and cultural variation of different emotion response patterning. *Journal of Personality and Social Psychology, 66*, 310–328.

Schlossberg, H. (1979). Police response to hostage situations. In J.T. O'Brien & M. Marcus (Eds.), *Crime and justice in America* (pp. 209–220). New York: Pergamon Press.

Scruggs, R., Zipperstein, S., Lyon, R., Gonzalez, V., Cousins, H., & Beverly, R. (1993). *Report to the Deputy Attorney General on the Events at Waco, Texas, February 28 to April 19, 1993*. Washington DC: U.S. Department of Justice.

Shaver, P.R., Schwartz, J., Kirson, D., & O'Connor, C. (1987). Emotional knowledge: Further explorations of a prototype approach. *Journal of Personality and Social Psychology, 52*, 1,061–1,086.

Slatkin, A. (1996). Enhancing negotiator training: Therapeutic communication. *FBI Law Enforcement Bulletin, 65*, 1–10.

Smith, C.A., & Pope, L.K. (1992). Appraisal and emotion: The interactional contributions of dispositional and situational factors. *Review of Personality and Social Psychology, 14,* 32–62.

Soskis, D.A., & Van Zandt, C.R. (1986). Hostage negotiation: Law enforcement's most effective nonlethal weapon. *The FBI Management Quarterly, 6,* 1–8.

Stratton, J.G. (1978). The terrorist act of hostage-taking: Considerations for law enforcement. *Journal of Police Science and Administration, 6,* 123–134.

Strentz, T. (1983). The inadequate personality as hostage taker. *Journal of Police Science and Administration, 11,* 363–368.

Strentz, T. (1985). *A statistical analysis of American hostage situations.* Unpublished manuscript, Quantico, VA: FBI Academy.

Strentz, T. (1995). The cyclic crisis negotiations time line. *Law and Order, 43*(3), 73.

Tajfel, H. (1978). Social categorization, social identity, and social comparisons. In H. Tajfel (Ed.), *Differentiation between social groups.* London: Academic Press.

Tajfel, H. (1981). Social stereotypes and social groups. In J. Turner & H. Giles (Eds.), *Intergroup behavior.* Chicago: University of Chicago Press.

Tannen, D. (1986). *That's not what I meant!: How conversational style makes or breaks your relationships with others.* New York: William Morrow and Company, Inc.

Tannen, D. (1993). What's in a frame?: Surface evidence for underlying expectations. In D. Tannen (Ed.), *Framing in discourse* (pp. 14–56). New York: Oxford University Press.

Tannen, D., & Wallat, C. (1993). Interactive frames and knowledge schemas in interaction: Examples from a medical examination/interview. In D. Tannen (Ed.), *Framing in discourse* (pp. 57–76). New York: Oxford University Press.

Thibaut, J., & Kelly, H.H. (1959). *The social psychology of groups.* New York: Wiley.

Ting-Toomey, S. (1988). Intercultural conflict styles: A face-negotiation theory. In Y.Y. Kim & W.B. Gudykunst (Eds.), *Theories in intercultural communication* (pp. 213–235). Newbury Park, CA: Sage.

Ting-Toomey, S., & Kurogi, A. (1998). Facework competence in intercultural conflict: An updated face-negotiation theory. *International Journal of Intercultural Relations, 22,* 187–225.

Ting-Toomey, S., & Takai, J. (2006). Explaining intercultural conflict: Promising approaches and future directions. In J.G. Oetzel & S. Ting-Toomey (Eds.), *The SAGE handbook of conflict communication* (pp. 691–724). Thousand Oaks, CA: SAGE Publications.

Tracy, K. (1989). *Conversational dilemmas and the naturalistic experiment* (Vol. 2 Paradigm exemplars). Newbury Park, CA: Sage.

Tracy, K. (1991). Discourse. In B. M. Montgomery & S. Duck (Eds.), *Studying interpersonal interaction* (pp. 179–196). New York: Guilford Press.

Tracy, K. (1995). Action-implicative discourse analysis. *Journal of Language and Social Psychology, 14*(1–2), 195–215.

Tracy, K. (1997a). *Colloquium: Dilemmas of academic discourse.* Norwood, NJ: Albex.

Tracy, K. (1997b). Interactional trouble in emergency service requests: A problem of frames. *Research on Language and Social Interaction, 30,* 315–343.

Tracy, K., & Baratz, S. (1993). Intellectual discussion in the academy as situated discourse. *Communication Monographs, 60,* 300–320.

Tracy, K., & Naughton, J. (1994). The identity work of questioning in intellectual discussion. *Communication monographs, 61,* 281–302.

Turner, A. (1995, October 20). Saldivar tapes show police negotiator's hard task. *Houston Chronicle.*

Turner, J.T. (1986). Is violence holding health care hostage? *Security Management,* 26–32.

Van de Vliert, E. (1997). *Complex interpersonal conflict behavior: Theoretical frontiers.* East Sussex, UK: Psychology Press.

Van Dijk, T.A. (Ed.). (1997). *Discourse as social interaction.* Thousand Oaks, CA: Sage Publications.

Van Zandt, C.R. (1993). Suicide by cop. *Police Chief, 60*(7), 24–27.

Van Zandt, C.R. (2006). *Facing down evil.* New York: G.P. Putnam's Sons.

Van Zandt, C.R., & Fuselier, G.D. (1989). Nine days of crisis negotiations: The Oakdale siege. *Corrections Today, 51,* 16–24.

Vasey, M.C. (1985). *Hostage negotiations: Policies, procedures and attitudes.* Unpublished Ph.D. Dissertation, University of Oregon, Eugene, OR.

Von Foerster, H. (1984). On constructing a reality. In P. Watzlawick (Ed.), *The invented reality: Contributions to constructivism* (pp. 41–61). New York: Norton.

Walter, J.L., & Peller, J.E. (1992). *Becoming solution-focused in brief therapy.* Levittown, PA: Brunner/Mazel.

Watzlawick, P., Bavelas, J.B., & Jackson, D.D. (1967). *Pragmatics of human communication: A study of interactional patterns, pathologies, and paradoxes.* New York: W.W. Norton & Company, Inc.

Weaver, G.R. (1997). Psychological and cultural dimensions of hostage negotiation. In R.G. Rogan, M.R. Hammer, & C.R. Van Zandt (Eds.), *Dynamic processes of crisis negotiation: Theory, research and practice* (pp. 115–128). Westport, CT: Praeger.

Weick, K.E. (1988). Enacted sensemaking in crisis situations. *Journal of Management Studies, 25,* 305–317.

Weiner, M., & Mehrabian, A. (1968). *Language within language.* New York: Appleton-Century-Croft.

Wethington, E. (1996). Crime and punishment. In U. Bronfenbrenner, P. McClelland, E. Wethington, P. Moen & S.J. Ceci (Eds.), *The State of Americans* (pp. 29–50). New York: The Free Press.

Wilson, S., & Putnam, L.L. (1990). Interaction goals in negotiation. In J. Anderson (Ed.), *Communication Yearbook* (Vol. 13, pp. 374–406). Newbury Park, CA: Sage.

Wilson, S.R., & Waltman, M.S. (1988). Assessing the Putnam-Wilson Organizational Conflict Management Instrument (OCCI). *Management Communication Quarterly, 1.*

INDEX

ABOUT THE AUTHOR

MITCHELL R. HAMMER, Ph.D., is President of Hammer Consulting, LLC, a conflict and crisis resolution organization, and Professor Emeritus of International Peace and Conflict Resolution at The American University, The School of International Service, International Peace and Conflict Resolution. He is co-editor with Randall G. Rogan and Clinton R. Van Zandt of *Dynamic Processes of Crisis Negotiation: Theory, Research, and Practice* (Praeger, 1997). Dr. Hammer frequently provides expert analysis for the media, including NBC News, CNN, *USA Today,* and the *Washington Post.*